NIMROD INTER

The Healing Arts

This issue is dedicated to
Richard A. Liebendorfer, M.D.
1927-2006
Devoted physician and former St. John
Medical Center chief of staff

ISBN: 0-9720993-7-9
Volume 49, Number 2

ISSN: 0029-053X
Spring/Summer 2006

THE UNIVERSITY OF TULSA
TULSA, OKLAHOMA

Nimrod International Journal IS INDEXED IN THE AMERICAN HUMANITIES INDEX

Acknowledgements

This issue of *Nimrod* is funded by donations, subscriptions, and sales. *Nimrod* and The University of Tulsa acknowledge with gratitude the many individuals and organizations that support *Nimrod*'s publication, annual prize, and outreach programs: *Nimrod*'s Advisory and Editorial Boards; and *Nimrod*'s Angels, Benefactors, Donors, and Patrons.

Angels	Ellen Adelson, Joan Flint, Mary Lhevine & George Schnetzer, Norma Lockwood, Susan & Robert Mase, John Ringold, Andrea Schlanger, The John Steele Zink Foundation
Benefactors	R. L. Hudson Company, Lisa Ransom, Ann Daniel Stone, Joy Whitman
Donors	John Barry, Margery Bird, Marvin Branham, Mary Cantrell, Ivy Dempsey, Susan & Eduard Douze, Marion & William Elson, Nancy & Ray Feldman, Patty Lou Floyd, Sherri Goodall, Helen Jo Hardwick, Mike Joffe, Inge Kahn, William Kellough, Linda & Bruce Kline, Marjorie Kroll, Lydia & Ted Kronfeld, Maria Lyda, Roberta & Dan Marder, Joe McGraw, Jim Morgan, Ruth K. Nelson, Donna O'Rourke & Thomas Twomey, Nancy Payne, Bobbye Potter, Kate Reeves, Patricia Rohleder, Joan Seay, Diane Seebass, Charlotte Stewart, Sarah Theobald-Hall, Frances & Bruce Tibbetts, Michael Tramontana, Melissa Weiss, Martin Wing, Jane Wiseman, Rachel Zebrowski
Patrons	M. E. Arnold, Ann Bartlett, Jan Blakely, Theresia Courcier, Elaine Dodson, Sally Donaldson, Linda Frazier, Susan Flynn, Carol Johnson, Geraldine McLoud, Kathleen Petrikin, Margaret Turano, Renata & Sven Treitel, Maynard Ungerman, Maralee Waidner, Marlene Wetzel, Masha & Yevgeny Yevtushenko, Ann Zoller

Editorial Board

Table of Contents

War: Bosnia, Iraq, Germany, the Pacific

Cancer

The Juggler: Stroke, Polio, Palsy, Tourette's

A Short History of Anatomy

Miraculous Voyage

Generations

Francine Ringold

Editor's Note

> It is not appropriate, in a household given to the Muses.
> No! Lamentation does not belong here.
>
> —*Sappho**

In this Healing Arts, Spring 2006 issue of *Nimrod*, the journal offers not only a non-sentimental, even tough, take on the cataclysmic events that are part of the human predicament but an experience in the many shapes and stages of healing. The subjects of the poems, stories, and essays included here range from flood, fire, whirlwind, and war, to the many diseases that afflict us: cancer, stroke, palsy, polio, mental retardation, herpes, trauma, Alzheimer's, Tourette's. The treatment, progress, human toll, of disease (dis-ease) and even its "design for living" fills most of these pages. Cancer, of all the diseases that have impelled the writings in this issue, leads the list. Perhaps it is because it affects so many; perhaps it is because so many now survive and live with this disease and even become "uncommonly alert . . . taking it all in . . . every molecule of light," as Sue Ellen Thompson describes in "Closing Up the Cottage."

Sound depressing? Amazingly, it is not. For here too is Yamamoto's cooling "ice cream" for the soul, Woessner's hawk that watches over us and keeps us safe—an unwinding of time and always—technique as discovery. Often, through image and overt statement, we are subtly reminded to pay attention, to *breathe*, to honor this miraculous voyage that makes us laugh and weep, pray and curse, as we journey through what Carolyn Miller calls "this realm of enduring sorrow and perfect rapture."

As we know, writing itself is an act of healing, largely because it too is process. Part of that process is the exercise of acquired knowledge and craft; part is a dedication to observation and empathy. That process not only enables the writer to move through the stages of grief, and through loss, disease, war, flood, but, especially when that writing is carefully honed, the writer moves, during the process of writing—to discovery. As we read,

---

*Sappho, "No Room for Grief," translated by Anne Finch, in *Lofty Dogmas: Poets on Poetics*, edited by Deborah Brown, Anne Finch, Maxine Kumin. University of Arkansas Press, 2005.

we re-enter that process, and often we are permitted access to our own experience as well as that of others.

I am not talking about diatribe or sermon, where the thesis is decided beforehand, but rather the complex, many-layered poem, story, or personal essay that, like life itself, reveals its meaning as it develops. It is such writing that *Nimrod* searches for and publishes. It is such writing that then serves as an illumination and a potential healing for the reader. Its effect, though seldom if ever measurable, is clearly felt and acknowledged. It is real.

When, in addition, the writer has another gift, actively participates in another discipline—medicine, law, history, science—he or she may also bring specialized details and information to enrich the writing further. From over 636 submissions to the Healing Arts issue of *Nimrod*, and from 93 carefully selected acceptances (at least two editors read every submission), 15 of those represented, over 40 pages included in this issue, were written by medical professionals: internists, surgeons, veterinarians, nurses. Avoiding jargon, yet honoring technical knowledge, we may come upon erythroblasts, the hospital nursery, the hospital room, the ER, and the hospice, as well as the garden, the kitchen and the battlefield.

It is on this battlefield, "no natural disaster," that over and over again, the poet, even this person of words, "cradling the child/ the body of the child/ in Mosul," is forced to ask, as Richard Schaaf does in his eloquent poems, "what on earth can [one] say?" and find even in that question a bit of solace.

In this Healing Arts issue of *Nimrod*, we experience the great "juggling act" of life, and, in part, are given a map of the interior, a geography of this miraculous voyage with grandmother's applesauce, Hamish Samey's Turnip Soup and harrowing experience, all in a polyphonic music that confirms the dark while it demonstrates how, as John Surowiecki writes, we "are made of light."

James Andrew Smith

Artist's Statement

From the earliest examples of written language, marks and shapes have been substituted for the ideas and objects they represent . . . . I have reduced my vocabulary to the circle because of its innate symbolic strength.

The circle is integral to the most basic biologic and atomic concepts. While the circular shape can be linked with representations of the female gender, it is nonetheless a neutral symbol of the unifying component of all life—a single cell. Similarly, the circular shape represents the reduction of everything to its most elemental component—the atom. . . .The evidence of circular imagery in ancient sciences, astronomical patterning and primal spiritual expressions is expansive. For centuries Chinese philosophers regarded the circle as divine in nature, and later in the Middle Ages it was symbolic of heaven. Circular paintings known as Tondi, from the Middle Ages, such as Michelangelo's "Holy Family" and Raphael's "Alba Madonna" carried twofold symbolism. Not only was the subject matter divine, but the circular canvases symbolized divine qualities. To this day, the circle is a symbol of divinity, strength, unity, eternity and completion and continues to beguile viewers with the possibility of communication through its iconographic power.

In the same symbolic manner, the paint has been systematically applied to emphasize the essential characteristics of pure and raw color. Colors have long been equated with emotional expression and I am fascinated with the multifaceted emotions generated by the color red. In all its shades, red confronts the viewer on a primal level. The instinctual emotional response will vary from viewer to viewer depending on his or her previous experience with the color red. Was the experience passionate or dangerous? Was it a Valentine or an injury? Even in our culture the color red has many meanings. It is used to remind us of our limitations and restricts our locomotion. Simply seeing red causes an immediate and decisive reaction. But red also reminds us of the limitless power of love. Even with the simplicity of a single color, the viewer must determine which emotion is at work in the painting.

The restricted vocabulary of these two symbols, the circle and the color red, provides ample opportunities for a conversation to develop between the work and the viewer.

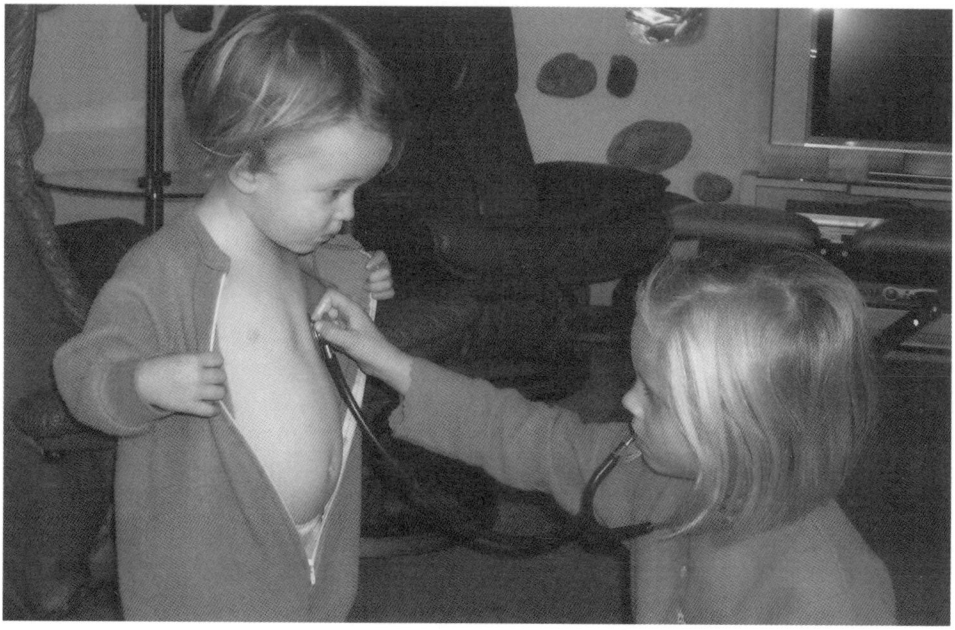

James S. Seebass, *First Patient,* photograph

Geri Rosenzweig

It Sings

Listen carefully,
You'll hear the incredible
song whispering
into the inlet, rippling
through the silted rooms
of small lives surviving
on the edge, and
if it's evening, brushing
the yellow legs
of the night heron
poised tense
as a comma against the shore.
You must be there, close
to the surge of salt
baptizing mollusk
and frog, snail
and slug, even the stone,
shorn of its algae,
glitters in the jubilant
swarm of the tide
ticking among reeds,
there, when the long,
whiskered heads sway like Cabalists
in the ecstatic swell.

Come with a Mild Countenance

Is it too much to ask
that you come with a mild
countenance, your voice
fine tuned to the tick
and rustle of childhood's
playhouse where I was bud
and leaf, was rain passing
through a branched roof, simple
as a bird shaking its wings.
Light as a dandelion
I'll be at home
on the far side of speech
with shards of tea cups,
foil scraps, plump
loaves molded from mud.
At ease with the dart
and scuttle of furred lives,
I'll lie down in the anonymity of roots,
a jewel deposited for now
in the lining of earth's coat.

LISA MECKEL

Media Harvest, Thanksgiving 2005

This year's dark harvest—such
a hard bringing in of the sheaves

a doomsday book of disasters,
natural and unnatural, so dreadful

the mind clamps its door, shuts
down on this awful contemplation.

Little is left for today but
to look at the wild sage, purple

against the blue of the sky,
caress the round orange

pumpkins humming in the field,
gaze at the one red tree

burning on the land, inhale
the breath of soup boiling

on the stove, bless
the eyes of children

in the sleek slant of sun
that gilds the agony

of this autumnal
day where for so many

everything's been swept

away

Charlotte Mandel

Front Page Photo (January 2005)

Instead of sand the shore ripples babies
          ringlets   rumps
and a woman who sits
          thin arms raised
sari and headscarf rough with grit
          shivering skin her mourning garment

Crawl the shattered temple steps
pick up like shells
the shards of buddhas and saints

A "natural" disaster—that is to say—
unlike
          bombs bursting body parts in air
          or machetes and scythes
          reaping villagers—
so-called "un-natural" deaths?

A father rode the massive wave his son in arms now his head now the child's above water until smacked against an edge the child
the man will reach for
          voice caroling papa abba
          aboriginal vowel—
the child torn from his rib
          pulsating phantom limb

What lunar hunger
uproots earth core from the deep?
Hell rises
into our common zone of daylight
not with fire
but its opposite

Bitter la mer el mar marah—salt
reclaims what came from it

These too are my children
cries the wave
and I want them back

Susan Varnot

Evening News: September 9, 2004

The television faces the field that unites
my yard and my neighbor's. All week,
the farmer has been cutting and baling hay,
leaning from his tractor seat
to inspect each row.

On the television, prisoners are taken from School
No. 1 in Beslan, children feeling their way
over gravel between fires blossoming
from burned-out cars. One girl
wears only underpants and an undershirt.
Through gunfire, a soldier
lifts her forearms, offering himself
like a dancer, but the girl stares straight ahead
as though memorizing thin curls of smoke
before they disappear.

The farmer's hay, the color of the girl's hair
floating up against the oiled barrel of the soldier's gun,
trembles in the sun. It is not that I expected
a woman lifted face-down on a gurney.
It is not that I expected the camouflage
or the huddling faces. But the soldier,
catching sight of the hair,
bends, his gun shifting out of its reach.

This evening, I will watch the sky
until the orange cannot be held by it
and the sun drains out of the valley.
I will hear the muffler of a truck choking
until it parks next to children
bouncing on a trampoline beside the woodpile.
I will not hear gunfire but daughters
laughing. I will see the farmer beyond the television
shaking hands with a friend as they meet on the highway,
then passing each other in their tractors. Finally,

I will see the lights of the grotto above us burning,
the virgin fixed in her plaster, leaning
away from the cliff. And I will want
to believe just enough to make out the white
face bending over the darkening fields.

M. Teresa Valero, from *The Levant: Lebanon and Syria Through Western Eyes*, photograph

Eve Jones

On Catastrophe

Once you could fend off the gods'
rage with bare hands sunk

in harvest, the sleep of prayer, your own
good heart better measure of turning

season than the sun, whose light diffused
to weakness, to nothing, or else

sucked the roots to thirst. Tolerance
as atmosphere, a blue willed only. Or so

it seemed. Still, the ice-slaked bridge waited
over the midnight ravine, the black seed

notched in a neighborhood girl's lung grew
quietly through, and even this forgiven, fact

of mortality, a grand scheme. The cold machine
of wisdom has no place here: a bullet arcing,

the black wall of a wave bobbing pastel
umbrellas, the woman in the cab's backseat

with a towel between her legs stunned
by failure. When it happens it happens

marvelously as fire. How else to explain the raw-
knuckled grappling, the well and the rope, how it's never

simply loss, a sky bringing itself relentlessly,
an open prairie through which the trains shriek.

JOHN NOLAND

Cosmology

Everyone's cosmology
is different, a do-it-yourself
kit, I suspect. Mine
was created at four. Even then
I'd seen big catfish
almost twice as long
as me with long, black stickers
around their huge mouths. I'd seen
their heads, hewn off, and nailed
to Osage-orange fence posts
by the river. I'd heard stories
about mudcats bigger
than a man. The day
my father and uncle went
catfishing and wouldn't take me,
they put three small bullheads
into a tin washtub and gave me
an old fishing pole and a couple
worms, then they hurried away.
Fishing, they said, was better
just before a storm. Clouds
darkened the sky as I fished
and thunder rumbled. I felt
the storm coming, felt
how it lifted me, made my hair
stand up on my arms. Suddenly,
I couldn't wait. I grabbed for a fish
just as lightning struck. The bullhead's
stickers burned my hand as the bright
flash of lightning blinded me. Thunder
crashed. I knew then everything
is connected—the sky, the river, the fish,
the thunder and the lightning.
All afternoon as my hand
throbbed, I pondered

on those fish that wouldn't bite
and what it meant
that there was darkness
inside the light.

Manly Johnson, photograph

Rebecca A. Spears

Last Things

(Dallas, Saturday, 23 November 1963)

The last wild green pear has fallen untended
onto a skirt of yellowed rotting fruit.
I squint from the car window into swerving sun.
A field between it and me: there's a distance I can't
estimate and barbed wire strung along the fence posts.

The season of cultivation is over.
East of town our car follows a disjunctive route
(it is Saturday after the assassination) and stops
under vaulted oak and pecan trees. Mother wants to
pocket a few pecans. They crust the road like

a disturbed cone of red ants. I can't help
but crunch them under my shoes.
Back home the television is all news and I would
rather be kicking in the leaves this rare crisp day.
We have watched enough (shamed, in silence):

Hyannisport. The children and father
roughhousing. Caroline under his desk.
Caroline all blonde bob and tailored clothes:
the image tags along with me all afternoon,
a younger sister.

Soon enough the caisson will carry the casket
toward the national cemetery and we will have
an unscheduled school holiday. The young widow
driven by grief will orchestrate a perfect funeral
and even eaten by sadness, she will shine.

I will ask my mother to drive again into
the countryside to hunt pecans while I look for
the one unbruised pear. It is all so unintended
and hard to know how long this will take.
Surely we haven't seen the last wild harvest.

The Neighbor's Story

1.
Always consider the netting. We were never quick enough at mending what our fingers tore through. In 1943, we ran out of quinine early in the season. It is not so different now.

Even with unchained dogs yipping and dive-bombing around us, even with fleas and mosquitoes, we continued our walks down to the spillway lulled by water pouring jade and pearl.

For a long moment, I left the netting off the baby. Something I'd read: *Unobstructed view develops the aesthetic eye.*

It was one of the few gorgeous things left. At night our neighbors were disappearing. In time, I assumed we all would.

In the humid dawns, the fine roses seemed unreal, their old roots we'd imported from Italy at a cost. *Rosa chinensis mutabilis.* 近义词
A hardy strain. Resists all the usual diseases.

On the porch the radio set dumped its screed: *Juden . . . ungeziefer . . . außrottend.* We ate black-market eggs in silence. What is there to do about deadly forces of historical proportions?

the inertia of our daily habits? Thomas and I brushed insects off our arms and ankles. *We need to know our past or we are doomed.*

2.
We lost the baby first, to the mosquitoes, or it could've been the milk. I carried the parasites in my blood—no more noticeable at first than a slight catch in the throat.

Maia's dark eyes brightened amber. Her skin chalked bisque. We inspected the stings. I asked for leeches, a declaration of war. None of us were immune; defeated, we drifted into bed

fell in and out of a gouged net of dreams. Imagined outcomes to questions we could hardly ask. The mattress recorded our impressions.

Thomas rose to beg cinchona from Jesuits in the next town. I lay in a small space trying to answer a heavy knocking, my hand slipping from the door, words flat in my mouth.

We found his body a month later, a bayonet holding it rigid. It could've been General R—'s troops or the Americans. Or perhaps our casual life-style gave us up.

And Maia's fate? our masterpiece? Had she only been spun in my sleep and never existed at all?

Take cover. Blacken the windows. I hid until it was over. Two years.

In 1945, a break from the madness. I returned to the bones of our house, and swear—Maia's imprint lay in the mattress, her smell in the sheets. I took this corpse to my flat

kept it intact for a year. Then burned it in the yard.

Carolyn Kreiter-Foronda

These Flecks of Summer

1.

Pink parasols everywhere:
mountain laurel releases
confetti at the feet of two
bickering cardinals. Snaps
one: *chip, chip. Cheer,*
cheer, the other, their red
robes slapping the thicket
in a pumped-up seed fight.
Slicing into view, a third
bandit: black-barred, blue,
the color of Caribbean sky.
Another, another, the feeders
flutter: a woodpecker
feathers the angry boys.
The birds disperse.
Their fits and starts linger:
soulful like a rain-flurry.

2.

A brooding sky pounds
the peninsula summer's
weather mutable: one
minute storms push
through, dismantle day's
labor, the next: a savory sun.
Bees leave the gazebo's
eaves, swarm toward
begonias, their jubilant
dance giddy. Like gusts
of milkweed, they swirl
through steamy air. Sticky
nectar sugars their tongues.
Honeycombs teem with

amber sweetness in harsh
July heat when river kicks up
soaked air and stirs the bees'
need to leave something
nourishing behind.

3.

All summer in woods
mountain laurel, hollies,
white oaks beg for rain.
Any amount will stop
their thirst, but ninety-
degree river heat bears
down for days. June slips
by, July creeps to August,
and then one day drops
fall steadily until trees
silver, light appearing
in the guise of drenching
rains—replenishing amid
the hum of all things natural.

4.

On loblolly-green, a frescoed
darkness falls, barely visible
in jacklight. Fireflies, lucent,
blink once, again. Split-second
later, mist showers wisteria,
catches moisture's unfurling
twirl, limbs braided into ladders.
The yodeling moon climbs,
piggish for a slice of time,
for an hour or two alone
in storied skies without
freewheeling storms soaking
to the bone. Moon pours
over stubs of zinnias, asters,
sunflowers that push through
lampblack soil, yielding

to night's fragrance,
to her gloss and shine.

5.

Bearded irises appear,
jouvence-blue, and expand
their supple wings: herons
in a beryl sky. Cut,
they spread throughout
the house in ornamental
porcelain. Regal
like guardians of dusk,
luminous lanterns, they light
the room. Blue and pink-
skirted tulips and phlox,
shrilled-voiced, trumpet
among leaves. On the table
by the stucco wall,
they step out, dazzling
like swift eddies of air.

6.

Late August, my garden over-
flows: food for butterflies
and hummingbirds, blurry
slivers whittled out of air
and shaped into stubby
wings racing. A hint
of ginger, nutmeg, sage,
and I'm nourished on
profusion, wonder which
spices heal as well as brisk
rain, saucy birdcall,
honey-cinnamon tea.
By herb pots, I stoop,
fill jars marked *parsley,*
rosemary, fennel. For winter
I select the densest tufts—
soft as bearded irises,

as I imagine the expansive
moon is to the touch.
I'll sprinkle them over
salads, meats, fish:
these curative dried flecks
of summer, marsh-aqua
and bird-foot mint.

Mark Weiss, photograph

Hurricane

Where was fairness the night
your buckling winds snapped
the still-green trees?

Where was fairness
when woodland squirrels
wailed like brash screech

owls and deer lay paralyzed
in the heartless dark?
Was it fair to dream

of porcelain air and fields
while deafening winds
pillaged the land?

Fair to suffer a hurricane
twice: first as a frightened
child and again in autumn's rill?

Fair to rebuke you, tumbling
on your unwieldy path,
pushing turgid waters inland?

Fair to mull over your anger:
the jungle of pines, remnants
of homes washed to sea?

Fair to name you *consagrada*
a Dios? I remember squirrels
scampering in a flurry, their hurl

through branches of surviving
oaks, the unexpected, dawn-struck
glory bowed to this thriving earth.

Amina Lolita Gautier

The Last Hurricane

Hurricanes that hit Puerto Rico have Americano names like Alice and even when they name one Hugo the weathermen don't pronounce it correctly. Hurricanes never have the names of your children or relatives. Names like Milagros or Rafael.

When they find out that another hurricane is coming your way, your relatives on the mainland—in New Haven, Hartford, Philadelphia, Newark, and New York—always call and ask if you are ready. If you need anything. They want to send you and the children things to help you cope.

But you know the truth.

They want to send you and the children things to ease the guilt that they feel as they sit in their safe condos and co-ops with central air and all the other amenities, as they put their feet up to watch the news for the weather report, smug that they are safe and warm while you are . . . not.

What will you need? they ask.

Clean water.

Hot water.

Ice.

Electricity.

None of which they can provide.

They want to send blankets, powdered milk, deodorant, Pampers. *This is not St. Croix*, you say. Besides, your children are too old for Pampers. Your relatives have watched one too many news reports.

The winds of the last hurricane that hit your town knocked out all the power lines for days and you had no light, no heat, no phone. It really wasn't that bad because you live in Carolina, near enough to San Juan and the *turistas* so that the problem was fixed *pronto*. But you heard that the people who lived farther out where the *turistas* hardly ever went had it real bad—no power for almost three weeks.

Imagine if you lived there.

* * *

The last hurricane knocked over the two coconut trees in front of your house and wiped out the crab and chicken pens in the backyard. You heard the chickens squawk as the winds carried them away as you sat in the dark with the wind hawking at your ears and your *hijo* Rafael crying because it was his job to bring the chickens in and he forgot. You tried to shush him by reminding him that he was your *jíbarito,* but Milagros was louder than you as she called him *tonto* and slapped at whatever parts of him she could find in the dark.

During the time of a hurricane, it is not good to be alone. Which is why you are glad you still have the hijos. Although it is dark and you cannot see their two faces, you cross from one end of the room to the other after you have sent them to bed, sitting by their sides and placing your palms on their foreheads. Your hijos smell sweet in the darkness; the scent of the tembleque they had for dessert lingers in their partly opened mouths. On a night like this, you don't bother them about brushing their teeth before bed.

Está bien, you say.

Calmase.

Estoy aquí.

You trace their worried cheeks. You pinch their noses for fun, to cheer them up, glad that you cannot see their eyes in the dark. You will sleep lightly tonight because your children cry in their sleep whenever the winds pick up and the rains fall heavily, fearing the coming of a hurricane or tropical storm. They have every right to be fretful. The last hurricane's winds reached a new high, hitting so hard that its name was retired. The *hijos* were too young to truly experience the last hurricane. All that your children remember is that it raged outside with their father in it. They remember that it took him away for good.

* * *

Tropical storms become hurricanes when the winds pick up. But the power of the storm, the strength of it, is represented by a central pressure reading instead of wind speed even though it is the winds that are terrible, deadly. The winds picked up and uprooted the banana tree that crushed your husband's limbs beneath its trunk and buried his face under its wet soggy leaves.

Hurricanes know who they want.

You could not get the last one to take you. You stood outside for hours, getting drenched. Raindrops fell with a forcefulness you could not describe. The storm within you was more frightening. It raged, picking up speed and swirling uncontrollably, pressing hard against your ribs, plummeting down to your stomach only to rise again and again. The beads of water slapped and pelted you, but the winds would not pick up around you and the stubborn trees clung to their muddy roots, uncooperative. When you finally dragged yourself back into the house, back to your *hijos*, you felt as if you had been in a fight and lost. So you decided to wait for the next hurricane. They come every five or six years, so by then the children would be old enough to take care of themselves.

The last hurricane knocked the power out of all the generators. With the children, you waited on line for over three hours for a block of ice. You carried your ice around the corner where the boys raised their guns to your head and took your block of ice away, the same as they had done to the people who had been in front of you, the same as they planned to do to the people coming after you. Nothing personal. Later—if you have the money—you can buy it back.

So when your relatives on the mainland—in New Haven, Hartford, Philadelphia, Newark, and New York—call to tell you that they have been watching the latest reports and say that the tropical storm is growing and it looks like it will be a big one and ask you how you are doing, you say, "*Estoy bien*."

This is the answer you give because they really don't care and they don't know anything about being a Puerto Rican in Puerto Rico anymore. When it is too cold on the mainland, they take paid vacations to fly over. They spend their money in the mall in Isla Verdes, buying clothing that is too tight for them, buying makeup that is now too dark for their wintry pale *Americano* faces. They ask you to go to the *cine* with them and you sit there in the theater in San Juan, watching movies in English with Spanish subtitles, wondering if the very irony of the situation escapes them, sure that it does. You and your *hijos* give up your beds to your relatives who sleep blissfully, full of the *pasteles*, *empanadas*, and *morcilla* they have begged you to prepare. They eat your mangoes and papayas as though they are going out of style, excusing themselves by reminding you that mangoes are so cheap here, that they often have to pay almost two dollars for one back at home (home is what they now call the mainland) that is half as sweet. The hurricanes and tropical storms can wipe the mangoes out for seasons at a time so that they become as rare as the *coquí* and there aren't any to be had by anyone except by the *turistas* and you sometimes have to pay much more than two dollars for one.

That is not what your relatives want to hear.

You have become a postcard to them. Beaches and good food, exotic fruit and salsa clubs; they are no better than the *turistas*. But you can't tell them so because they are *familia*.

* * *

When it is time for them to leave, you take them to the airport, proud that it is really in Carolina even though it is listed as being in San Juan. They don't allow family members inside or anyone who is not getting on the flight. You cannot walk your relatives to their gate. You drop them off at the curb. As you drive away, you catch your *hijos'* eyes in the rearview mirror. You hold their gazes and drop your voice to a whisper. You point at your relatives' retreating backs and warn your *hijos* not to ever become like them. You tell them that if they do, a hurricane will come and sweep them away and they will end up like their father.

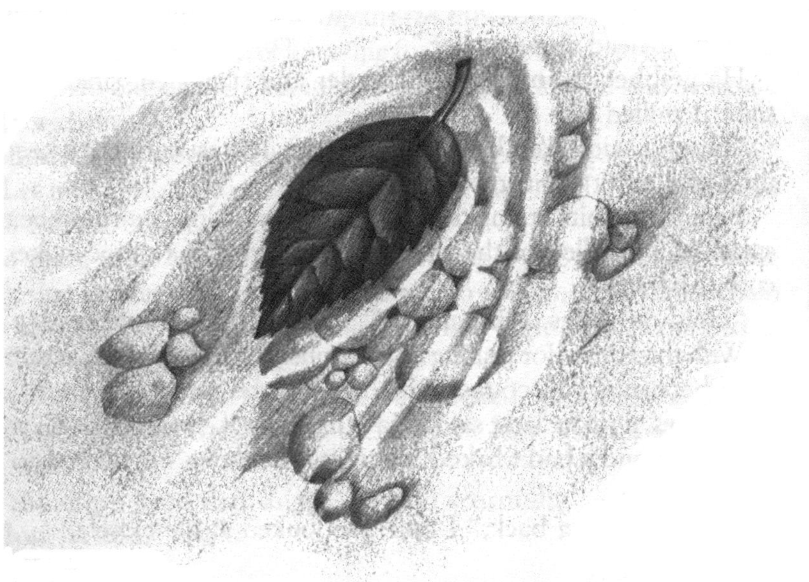

Judy Baker, pencil

Alison Townsend

Whirlwind

Stoughton, Wisconsin, August 15, 2005

Afterwards, the world lay so still it was hard to believe anything had happened, though everything
had changed. The rain stopped, as suddenly as it had begun. Four sandhill cranes, their white
feathers covered with mud, rose out of the marsh. The trees were very still, and there was even
a rainbow, its spectrum more distinct than any I'd ever seen, hung like a perverse stage drop
behind the places where the thing scoured the ground. We were a mile away, jogging
in the park, when the great, fat leg of it touched down, kicking its hob-nailed
boot at everything in its path. But all we felt in White Oak Woods was rain,
exhilarating as it needled our skin. I was happy, watching the shape of his
back, his long, wet legs taking the hill ahead. It was only driving home
we saw, branches across the road confusing, until they became trees,
tangles of downed power lines hissing and sparking around them like
nests of dangerous snakes, a whole neighborhood leveled, gone,
splintered by this temper tantrum of air. I looked for things
that were gone—The Tideman farm's red barn where dolls
had stared out a window, the field where a woman
grew gladiolus to sell at the side of the road,
a small wooden wheelbarrow packed pink
with petunias all summer. Weren't they
somewhere? the 10-minute drive nearly
an hour as we inched our way, not
sure our house would be there.
And how I prayed as I hadn't
prayed in years, words to the
23rd Psalm rising unbidden on
my tongue from some place
that remembered goodness
and mercy, as we rounded
the curve of our drive
and saw our house, whole
and untouched, burnished
by sunlight, the dog
and cats inside,
asleep in their
favorite places,
cloud-mountains
scudding overhead,
illuminated from
within like all
those childhood
pictures of
heaven.
And
it
was.

Medicine Poem for Holly

for Holly Prado Northup

All day, as the surgeon
opens your back to repair it—
adjusting each vertebra, unbending
the curvature of pain time
has slowly put there—
I keep a vigil on the couch
with the cats, bending
over my students' essays
the way you bent over my words
twenty years ago or more,
talking about the importance
of the spine that runs through it all,
so that ever since I have sought
that ladder of notched,
articulated bone, threading
the cord of words through holes
that in a deer's body
are shaped like hearts,
listening under the surface
of each poem for what connects things,
what backbone holds them up,
both our mothers
dead when we were girls,
what we have had to bend and carry
heavy, lonely, strange, though we
bent and carried anyway,
spine the center, spine the axis,
spine a kind of tree in the body,
column of light we call *spunk*
or *moxie* or *courage*, what I invoke
from half a continent away
as you lie there, being cut open
and then stitched together again,
so that you may stand,
straight and tall as any tree
you choose to call your mother.

My Father's City

(two days after 9/11)

"It's the musical equivalent of comfort food," the host says on NPR'S *Symphony at Six*. But tonight, as I drive home, it's Mozart's 40th Symphony in G, and I can't stop seeing my father in his tapestry wing chair, tapping his foot and conducting with one hand, his pipe cradled in the other. He'd sit there like that weekend evenings, happy, as if he had all the time in the world.

My father loved Beethoven most. *He's such a romantic*, he'd say, waving his hands in a way that meant, *Like me*. But the Mozart snagged him, its feeling measured with a careful hand, steady as his own on his lab notes, the ones some boss read and said, *You ought to be in advertising*. I never thought of him as anything but a scientist. I never understood he was anything else. And I always thought New York was his because he worked there, the World Trade Towers rising on the skyline like everyone's dream of the Emerald City.

It wasn't his, of course. Any more than it is anyone's who works there, the trains with their smoky yellow windows running out from it for miles . . . Yonkers, White Plains, Katonah, Croton Falls. He did it for years, over an hour each way, so that we could live in the country, his tan London Fog raincoat and tweed hat a kind of uniform he wore as he read the *New York Times*, wrote a novel in longhand, kept a diary where one entry read, "I hate my life."

I didn't read that till after his death. And in the diary the next day was better, as life almost always is. But tonight I can't stop hearing my father in the music, or forget how he gave me the City, taking us to the Met and the Museum of Natural History, poking for books in The Strand. I have every one he bought me those first months after my mother's death, lined up in the case where I keep poetry now. And beside them the copy for all his ad campaigns— Alka Seltzer, Tofranil, Stelazine, One-A-Day, their names once familiar as friends of the family, impersonal now as the gray faces of men on commuter trains.

But no matter what I do, I can't quite catch the poetry of that time. The way he knew to fold the *Times* in neat quarters. How easily he strode the avenues, one hand tucked firmly under my elbow. Those terrible frozen cream pies he'd haul all the way home from Pathmark, proud of his bargain. Or how safe I felt once, when I'd skipped out of school and hopped a train for a march against the war, to look up and see him across the circle from me in Grand Central, singing "We Shall Overcome," his "Give Peace a Chance" sticker shining on his briefcase in DayGlo blue and green.

My father smiled at me then across that suddenly small space lit only by candles, that was as brief as this music which ends just before I turn in my driveway, as if it is meant to stop there. While I think, for no reason, of the coat he bought me from a street rack nearly thirty autumns ago. It was white fur, splotched with tan and black, and smelled of dust and musk and some scent I couldn't name. It came from Afghanistan and I loved it. Like him, I thought I would have it forever.

Purvi Shah

Signs there is a hole in Manhattan

What outlasts all this business and craziness is poetry.
—Sunita Mehta

Die-hard New Yorkers gaze at the twin ends
of the island and cannot determine which path

leads downtown. The city immigrants are white sheets
garbed in Kodachrome and public telephone numbers. Call

any day, any time. People are unequivocally welcoming—
city strangers go to greet everyone, lingering.

The immigrants are outnumbered only by patriots
in their tricolored regalia. Old immigrants adopt

this new passport to safety. Lanky white women escort
groups of Muslim children to reach primary school.

Burkha-clad women refrain from public conversation,
skirt quickly through streets. Union Square

is the new civic center. Through the day,
through the night, the public carves the ground.

According to the sign taped to the cragged concrete,
the coffee-cart man is a block north

Every house glows with a TV buzz. Subway riders
over the Manhattan Bridge are pulled like moths

to the windows on the track to Canal St. Underground
transit is subject to detour. Some of the lines are reported missing—

Q diamond runs express. Q circle is local and becomes R.
W is N until Brooklyn when it's J or M or Z. Q=R; W=N—

Words with absent hearts: queer or when. So much is beyond delineation,

Beyond the circuits of language, like missing=bombs=smoked solace.

Diane K. Martin

Checking for Damage

San Francisco earthquake, November 1989

Now, as in France after Robespierre,
the terrifying exhilaration
of rules being broken. Drivers
turn and reverse, entering freeway exits
as cracks step down bricks,
flouting the caprice of the solid world.

Grandfather Morris, itinerant peddler,
found himself on the sidewalk
one April morning in 1906—in pajamas, barefoot,
with only his bear-tooth fobbed gold pocket watch,
inscribed with a profile of the Emperor Franz Josef—
and found shoes to go back
to the predictable grid and din of New York.
Strange that my peregrinations lead me here,
freeways crumbling into next generation's artifacts,
men in hard hats inspecting mortar, certifying
this building of 27 stories that twanged
like a bow-string is *Safe to enter*.

Pacific Guns

All morning soft pockmarks dent air floated east
from the Pacific Gun Club's volleys aimed above the tules
at projected arcs of clay pigeons, the sound almost comforting,
like the metallic tap of copper craft I hammered into bas-relief
as a girl. Here in the garden, fat bees squeeze into poppies
with furred hums, sparrows flit in the neighbor's untended apple.

Yanking weeds, scourging ivy, I think of an armless woman in Bosnia,
face bathed by her little sister. I read once that whole families came
to Bull Run, first battle of our Civil War, with picnic lunches.
They dressed up, tethered the horses, spread blankets, laid out
mustard, meat, bread, pickles—dandled their babies, listening to the guns.

M. Teresa Valero, from *The Levant: Lebanon and Syria Through Western Eyes*, photograph

Rebecca Givens

The Last City

Already in the morning, a dawn poem is written.
You wake and you are never early enough.

The windows barely hold the weight of sunlight
Coming down in tons on glass and hands.

You think of winters you were never warm,
How the cold stayed alive in all corners, all cracks.

Here the heat's so strong it won't admit of freezing,
Not even somewhere halfway around the world.

You sweat as if the sun were just bad news
That smiled and said how happy you should be:

No hint of any shadow to make you sad.
In the last city, all the men were tourists

And the women actors. The drinks had pieces
Of lemons cut from fruit the size of your hand.

Signs warned of workers and falling rocks:
"There are risks." "This is not a supervised locale."

(Here, all that seems gone, only a small house
Which you almost never have to leave.)

Intricacy

The trees move here the way a hand waves
After it's started thinking of somewhere else—

Of the old house, seen only through windows,
Hurried through and closed up like a man.

Then that house drops into a house of grief.

Now you are in a foreign country.
It's going well or terribly in that house:

You can't know. The trees are different there;
The language is not quite as clear to you

As this sky, this sea, closing like doors.

Touch and Go

what can you find here. ginger in the ashes.
a cooking pot. a hundred tinny pans.
when cooking a tinge of butter hurries
upward. wants to talk in butter language
about your past. go on tell us
if you have sins [the pot is heating]
tell us when the flame has just turned blue.
these are the wings of the family
making patterns. here the side flesh
of the peel is turning up. go on
tell us how you can be quiet
[these are the sorry stories you always
hear] the milk is fat. the sour cream's
made of roses. not really. of
roses and a hundred chives.

Nina Corwin

Memory of Fire

for the 123 young women and 23 men who died
in the Triangle Shirtwaist Factory, March 25, 1911

Saturday afternoon stretches thin as a thread
worn bare in its weave. Only minutes
to quitting time and at the ends
of the aisles, piles of fabric wait
to find their spark.
Many years later, the heat
of history still burns
in my face, neck hairs singed
with phantom recollections
of Lower East Side ancestry.
These girls who could have lived
to be my great-great aunts burning up
with youth and tenement
dreams of New World Symphonies
planting hope in their immigrant heads
till the fire at the Triangle factory
burns them all out,
thoughts of smoldering boys
from the corner grocery or across
the alley, seething
beneath stiff gabardine skirts,
flesh jumping over the clatter
of sewing machines stitching piece-
work twelve hours a day, their dreams
scripted in Yiddish, Russian
and Italian, dreams igniting
with a wealth they can scarcely imagine:
running water, every day
the finest cuts of meat
and shelves full of dry goods
from the merchants on Chambers
and Delancey streets, with chants
of solidarity and union victories,

the smoke filling the burning
shirtwaist factory, its doors chained
from the outside,
chained in by owners consuming
the dreams and the workers
who wouldn't jump
from an eighth-story window, couldn't
jump to save themselves
going up
in a thousand
tongues of
flame.

Marguerite Keil Flanders

Fire on Kingsbury Street

Lying in the backyard, I listen for what the house
has to say, to learn the password that will open
the red front door, before it is demolished,
before the soul of my parents' house rises
from a roiling bank of rubble, and is gone.

In March, the brutal wisdom of flame tore through
the shingles and beams, and smoke poured from
the gashes in the roof like an aria, measuring
the sky with soot. I want the house to tell me now,
while it still stands, what it knows about the living room,
where sunbeams hovered over the oriental rug
where the wood floors issued silent mantras, before
they were overcome by the drone of combustion.

I think the trees, swaying like kind aunts,
may have held this sour ending in their trunks
all along. Maybe I felt it as a girl, climbing the maple
and into the clustered hemlocks, now charred and dying.
If the house knew, it did not tell. But now, with the fear

that has made its home in my gut, I am listening,
recalling times when my love collapsed like a lung,
when one word from this house, cryptic
and in a foreign tongue, would have been enough.

I walk around to the front to say goodbye,
and I think of knives in the kitchen, cutting
the house free from earth, the explosion
of sassafras roots weaving the soil
under the spent garden, and song books
stirred by wind in the attic, their pages
flitting out the window like promises.

Then I do hear something. It is the sound of
everything I ever imagined and never expected
from life, igniting behind me as I skip
down the front walk, landing lightly
on the purple flagstones, seeing if I can make it
all the way to Kingsbury Street.

Prayer Rug

Let the beauty we love be what we do.
—*Rumi*

After the fire, I drag the rug, charred
and dripping, from my parents' house.
Long ago women gathered weeds, brewed
dyes as they'd been taught by artisans
of Mesopotamia. Their fingers loomed
what they loved: birds, trees, medallions, all
the green and dark red regions pointing east.

My great-grandmother must have walked
across these weavings on her way
to afternoon tea. Standing on the porch,
my mother tells me to take the rug home.
And somewhere in the furrows
of war is a descendant of the merchant
who sold this proof of survival.

In my looted sleep, I dream of rescue:
women with their fruits and rolled-up carpets,
in rooms of sooty damp, praying
for the windows to stop shattering.

I am hanging the rug like a wet flag,
waiting to be saved by its beauty.

JONATHAN GREENHAUSE

Nothing Is What It Seems

Today, nothing is what it seems:
Lightning bugs set the night ablaze,
and starlings clothe bare winter's tree.
Seagulls sever shoreline's surf
with beaks adorned with sequins, glass.
A small squirrel sows a row of pines,
and stray cats with their lovelorn chants
make domesticated felines pine.

Sunrays split the road in fire, shade,
and the sky is as blue as a flock jays.
Someone wails as if a thousand mothers died,
and clouds of dust confuse the heavens, earth.
Trapped angels sing from endless wells.
Wrapped rainbows dress the darkness, chase the night.
An ocean sleeps upon the tireless sand
as whales sing Homer's epics lost, now found.
The blind lead blind in orchestrated play;
today, the sun will burn another day.

Once Here

Ribs exposed gleam like ivory
licked clean by rains.

The skin has toughened, leather stretched
in a cross of bones.

Here was a child, an infant held
in her mother's arms.

Here was a beating heart and here
it burst at a touch.

The skull is cracked, concealed
by a layer of dirt

Look: Here were lips that cried; now outside
a jawbone lies.

Andrey Gritsman

Deer Accident in New Jersey

for B. W.

The story was on the news:
five high school seniors
died in a car crash
on the local highway in Maine.

My friend, who works at school,
made the videotapes from the archives
for the families: home economics,
school dance, field trips, as
the boys and the girls

were becoming shadows, reflections,
suspended in the hollow vastness,
somebody else's children
becoming genderless and shapeless.

The same morning you called me:
"Don't worry, Dad, it's just body-shop work,"
the road curve, three girls from school
laughing, dark shadow of a deer, grown from nowhere,
my mental tape: the undergrowth, trees running across
the windshield, resilient steel,
sky turning over, tires blown up,

you getting smaller in seconds,
thrown into my hands,
me, holding you as in the old childhood
photograph, you, being OK: "just the body work,"
me, talking to you on the phone,
rewinding my life, going to school
in the still frozen darkness,
sitting in my trigonometry class,
bored and horrified by the cold logic
of the absolute circumference on the blackboard,
already feeling your warm growth
inside my chest.

VA

My first job in the US
was at the VA Medical Center:
nights of the boxed breath
and the smell of stale piss,
chain-smokers, the collapsed lobes
overgrown by the relentless pink matter,
larynxless vets, talking in robot voices,
emaciated black guys in the men's room,
puffing through the tracheostomy tubes,
a burn unit survivor
hit by a Kamikaze
at the very end.

The young Jewish doctors
were rotating for a year or two,
running around with syringes,
dispensing chemotherapy, then
disappearing into the green sponge
of the suburban universe.

My way back to the new rented home
was graced by a sunset that touched
crosses on the descending lawn
by the Soldiers' Home, lit up
Rock Creek for a few minutes,
lingered pensively in the tree crowns
over the mansions at Connecticut Avenue,
then went underground somewhere
in Pennsylvania.

Around was the darkness
punctuated by a dialogue
between the towers on the flagships:
the Naval Hospital and the Mormon Temple,
guiding the large cargo planes,
gliding through the black milk
of the night breath toward
Andrews Air Force Base.

Berwyn Moore

Driving to Camp Lend-A-Hand

July 24, 2005

The day we picked our daughter up from camp,
goldenrod lined the road, towheaded scouts
bowing on both sides, the parting of macadam
as we drove, the fields dry, the sky lacy with clouds.
A farmer waved. A horse shrugged his haughty head.
We stopped for corn, just picked, and plums and kale,
sampled pies, still warm, and tarts and honeyed bread.
Sheets on a line ballooned out like a ship's sail.
Time stopped in those miles before we saw her.
For eight days we hadn't tucked her in or brushed
her hair or watched her grow, the week a busy blur
of grown-up bliss. It came anyway, that uprush
of fear—because somewhere a child was dead:
at a market, a subway, a school, in a lunatic's bed.

Interloper

Like a hand, insomnia covers her mouth.
She thinks of chores and spills and bills unsent,
of Gertrude's cough and fourteen weeks of drought.
The attic shakes. Her body bristles. The misspent
night she wills to light and fuss, to the chaos
of breakfast, laundry, kids with gifts of earth
between their toes, diversions from the loss
of sleep, the jangled nerves, the doubtful worth
of tangled dreams: A sprig of fire on a blue
lapel. The charm of wormwood in a cup of tea.
A tiger singing. Bones nestled in the dew.
A detached hand waving a skeleton key.
Love wears her out and lugs her to bed.
Love wakes her up, demanding to be fed.

Loren Kleinman

from *I Want No Paradise*

Paradise

Even so distant, I can taste the grief," writes Philip Larkin.* In its longest silence, trauma is even more present. It is the unsaid, the uncertain, that prolongs feelings of loss. How do we define this notion of presence and absence? What is the paradigm? Poet Li-Young Lee offers an analogy regarding presence and absence: he equates them to inhaling and exhaling breath. Our presence is marked by the inhalation. Oxygen spreads into our lungs and bloodstream, nourishing our bones, our cells, our skin. Breath is life. The exhalation manifests an absence or a silence, but still there is life. When we inhale speech terminates; communication is stunted. As we exhale speech is regained, but nutrients exit the body; the organs weaken; the lungs lessen in size. Lee describes this as "dying breath." When we speak we use dying breath. Meaning "grows in opposite ratio to presence and vitality." He suggests a kind of paradigm for life, especially in the case of trauma, in that as we die meaning is declared. The "less vitality we have the more the meaning of our lives gets disclosed."** That absence in our bodies translates as presence. Trauma narrative is born out of this relationship.

Thinking about trauma narrative, its types of witness and psychoanalytic process, I imagine my own trauma memory. It is often hard for me to separate myself from the research, and even harder to write about personal trauma in such an objective manner. My personal encounter with trauma began on May 28, 2004, when I was forced into an empty bathroom and raped by the doorman at a nightclub. I remember him following me around the dance floor. I couldn't get away. My friend had left me to go to another club, and I was alone. The days following the assault are something I can't begin to imagine how I survived. Like most victims of trauma I was living my life under silence, with the hope that someone would eventually hear me. For me, silence equated to a type of

---

*Philip Larkin, "Deceptions," *Collected Poems* (London: Faber and Faber, 2003, p. 67).

**Tina Chang, "The Totality of Causes: Interview with Li-Yung Lee," (*American Poet: The Journal of American Poets* v.26, Spring 2004: 16-21).

guilt: somehow I must have done something wrong to deserve this. Who would believe me if I spoke? Who would help me? This experience altered the way in which I lived my life, and for seven months I suffered from severe anxiety attacks, nightmares that replayed the rape, paranoia, i.e., the fear that it would happen again, health-related problems, flashbacks, and depression. I remember one repeated nightmare:

> I am waking up alone in the bathroom stall of the nightclub, and all I can see underneath the space between the stall door and the floor are his bare feet. He doesn't move, just waits for me to come out. My mother is at home, I call to her. My father is at home, and I call to him. My sister is at home, and I call to her. No one can hear. I sit on the toilet seat and wait for him to go away, but I just wait. I don't say anything. All I can see and hear, through a crack in the door, is my doctor's face. He is yelling at me and holding a vaginal clamp.

A large percentage of raped women I came into contact with during my recovery mentioned similar feelings: *I feel alone; I feel ashamed; no one cares; no one listens*. I remember trying to explain to my mother what had happened to me and her reply was: *You just have to move on. Get over it*. I didn't want to hear that, I wanted her to just listen, and not judge the progress or lack of progress I was making. I wanted her to hold my hand and tell me everything would be all right. I realized as the months went on that my only salvation was my art; that my art was the one place I could go; that if no one listened, the page would—it had no choice.

During my recovery, I also became obsessed with other people's trauma. Not only was I obsessed, but I became completely empathetic with their situations. It was depressing and sad, and I felt like my recovery was going backwards at times. My own trauma connected me so profoundly with the world around me that at times I felt I would break. I cared so deeply about every tragedy in the world, whether true or imagined, and it was cracking me in two. I empathized with their pain. I knew.

My recovery became a full-time job. It consumed me. Every day I thought: Why? Why does this world turn in on itself? I was really saying: why did this happen to me? I knew inside that it wasn't my fault; however, I still felt an overwhelming guilt. My writing became my coping mechanism. I have always had a passion for writing, but this was different. I felt compelled to tell my story, to continue to speak. Like Roland Barthes's discourse on love, this was my discourse too. The love I had for myself pushed me to understand my trauma, and forced me to break the silence. Even if no one cares to listen, you are remaking your place in the world; you are retaliating against the boundary your suffering has imposed on you.

*Death**

I cannot carry it
I cannot carry it,
if I could carry it,
I would carry it.

With mourning comes an unsayable pain.
Somewhere I am in a room,
a woman waiting to come back as a woman.

My own name is a stranger to me,
even my own death spread on
the narrow bed.

Where were You when I was alone
and wanted to turn my sadness
into a religion?

I cannot carry this head,
I cannot carry this all in my head,
if I could carry it, I would carry it
across the continent for the love of living, only

You only know, can only carry it,
listening there, next to the bleached
Broadway lights, watching
as the distance between us disappears.

---

*Lines from Yoruba poetry. Ulli Beier, *Yoruba Poetry: An Anthology of Traditonal Poems*. (NY: Harry N. Abrams).

The School With No Name

for the children of the North Ossetia school bombings

The survivors couldn't forget the feel
of the bodies beneath their bare feet as they escaped.
The children let inside offer money, but die thirsty.
Outside the mothers curse the teachers for leaving them.
The lucky ones were shot and killed. The ones left running
fall onto the meat of the ones who ran before them.
In a hallway a *shahidka* bursts like a balloon when she explodes.

In the gymnasium are three hundred small bodies.
The ones who used to walk to school
holding their mother's hand, the ones who argued
over the last rubber ball, kicking up the dirt behind them.
Now they hold parts of their skin together, negotiate their lives.

I can't even imagine the last thing children think of when they know
they are going to die. Maybe their mother, what they want to be
when they grow up, the life before today,
maybe nothing—the way certain things make them laugh
and they don't know why. The way, at certain moments,
they are scared of the dark. Or how in the beginning,
they were just the child, pulling the note from the lunch bag,
which began, "Dear Firefly—

Today

today this morning burns
pomegranate seeds burst
open like the rain
breaking into thousands of tongues
i will bring my mouth.

RICHARD SCHAAF

In Mosul

The Washington Post,
4 May 2005

Now this full-bleed
front-page photo
released by the U.S. Army
courtesy of Getty

This soldier
in battle fatigues
on his knees
in the sand
in Mosul

cradling the child
the body of the child
in Mosul

He appears to
whisper something
in the child's ear

but what on earth
can he say

Struck, Struck Again

No time to think
where they're going
what they're running to

We're running too
dropping everything

cell phones
eggs coffee
thoughts
work
the day's plans

the rest of our lives

running fast faster
than anyone can think

it's unthinkable
to think

just running
running

from no
natural disaster

Gertrude Halstead

fear knows no seasons

fear knows no seasons
what was it that scared you
when small scares you
now dreaming

left locked in the gardenshed
fog coming night incoming tide
the rush of roiling water rising
booted footsteps at the door
the shrill of sirens bombs dropping
silence
by night the sight of
rat's eyes to eyes
the deep piercing barbs of wire

Judith Arcana

Alternative Medicine

Can it be true about the shark
cartilage, that the shell
of that rapacious beast
(like cancer in its way),
may be of use if and when
our own simple parts
become tiny sharks,
attacking white cell divers
strapped in chemical cages,
submerged in lymph and blood?

Can reckless wild hope swim
inside a skin that rasps
like tiny teeth, sliding
long and gray as a living
bullet with blinkless eyes
and gills that never gasp
for breath as we do,
seeing the rigid fin coming,
slicing, opening the sea
like a fierce scalpel?

Judy Baker

Correspondence

The first cards had pictures:
Kodachrome, Vistaview
birds on mountains
flowers on walls
flying and climbing
in countries I'd never seen.

The early letters came
in clean blue envelopes
franked with bright stamps:
queens, castles
monuments with flags
rising, waving over graves.

Later a card said Honey
I've got to rush we're moving
but I thought you
would like this: scenery
lonely that way you love.
Gulls fly inland here for miles.

Later letters said Jesus
I can't believe what's happening
here. I mean: I don't
want to. You should believe
I'll come back, believe
so I will, like a fairy tale.

All cards stopped. Letters
came in thin brown sleeves
saying: How can I tell you
What can I say and When
will we understand how to
do this, how not to do this?

No letters. None. Long time.
Radio, tv, movies
magazines, newspapers.
I wrote: I was
answering carefully
what you might have sent.

MARGARET ROZGA

Imbalance

Cauliflower ears, size beyond sense
Spock ears pointing the way to heaven
Small ears flat against the skull like dried peach halves

A fleshy lobe, naked, inviting
Or pierced and studded, a challenge
To lick, taste, nibble

The ear—cartilage, skin, and flesh
An abalone shell without iridescence
A capital C; a question mark

Unanchored

An opening
A middle chamber subject to infection
Inner workings simple as a drum

And bones

To sift through sound for sense
Out there in our world
Thrown off-balance

Tympanic injury—ringing in the ears
War. Truck bombs. Explosions that send bodies
Flying, that blow out ear drums

Iraq, Israel, Palestine
Damaged ears and those undamaged
Who do not hear

The son returns home. Alive.

He sleeps in his childhood bed.
He does not have sand dreams.
In the morning, he descends the stairs
One at a time. She asks if
He is ready for pancakes.

At night, if he drinks, he does not
Drive. If he drives, he does not
See desert stretch out before him.
He understands speed limits, remembers
Rules of these roads, slows, yields.

Two-story buildings, walls grainy as sand,
Do not look like the Mosul Police Academy,
Flat-topped roof, exterior stairway where MPs
Can bound up stairs, two, three
At a time. There they do not think

About the way back down.

Here trucks dirty with sand speeding
Along boulevards carry only picnics,
Fishing rods. Their drivers look forward
To walleye, to old age and clean deaths.

As far as his mother knows
Spilling your guts is hyperbole, cliché.
He will not explode images in her life,
Will let her think she knows the whole
Gritty story, assume by some miracle

Even war-time deaths, if not quiet, are clean.

Debra Wierenga

Let Sleeping Boys Lie

Saturday morning, my living room's
wall-to-wall sleeping bags and bodies—
beautiful boys flung down in the ruins
of *Risk*'s plastic troops and cannons and countries.
Newly furred arms and legs at odd angles,
they lie where they fell among the black cords
of digital war machines in tangles
that trail like barbed wire across the floor.

Mothers at Troy, Antietam, Agincourt,
stepped just this way over still limbs
of silent young men, making sure
with wild glances each one was not *him*—
O God, let his wars be always in fun.
Let this soldier, my son, sleep fiercely on.

Fady Joudah

from *Pulse**

The Sky Is Yellow

The sky is yellow today,
because the dust also rises,
and holds your porous body
like a wounded tenderness waiting for rain.
Tonight will be so hot you won't sleep.
Tonight you will wake up the next day
to the same thing you never knew: it might
drizzle and the old man whose prostate
suffocates him might tell you a story
about clouds, before brother murdered brother
and called it god. It might drizzle
despite the burials, not always
six feet under. The coffin is a shroud.
Then comes sweet camphor bark and wood.
Then saplings and mud.
Then dry sand, if you can find it,
because I must tell you what you want
to hear: there is one race
killing another around here, it's
a girl-next-door kind of world.

**Pulse* is a sequence of poems relating to Dr. Joudah's experience in Darfur, 2005.

Christine Leche

Riding in a Humvee, the Sergeant Says:

Ma'am, I ain't kidding when I say that something like four hundred men was cleaned out of the dirt at a farm right up the hill. Bodies put in bags, stripped naked when they get over there in that low blue and white building we just now passing on the right. Laid them out on tables something like an assembly line. What I hear is that the UN pays a couple women good bucks for washing the clothes in outdoor pots, stirring with cut-off branches of trees. I can't help thinking it's sort of like a soup made out of shirts, pants, whatever. Couldn't get me near it, but they do a job I guess. Imagine all them clothes hanging in a room like a second-hand store. One lady found a brother by her own sewing on the inside cuffs of pants. In a war, the way it is, people leave home in a hurry. What they got is what they got. Maybe they take themselves some thread, a needle to fix things up. Even made underwear out of parachutes from food drops. Layers of duct tape across the bottoms of socks worked like shoes till it rained or snowed, which case the person's, excuse me for saying it, shit out of luck. Like my father always said, boy, he said, do what you have to. Ma'am, I got a CD player here under the dash, sort of a jackleg job but it works. Could either put on Reba or Loretta. Your choice.

Counting the Dead

All fall,
in this makeshift
Camp in Bosnia, I think
of you, and *you*. All fall
I think how death rhymes
with desire. I study
the lists of mass grave
sites—Kravick, Zvornik,
Nova Kasaba, bodies yanked
from a slit in the earth,
brought back to this endless
weeping fog with its one
rain song.

In Tuzla, again
I practice my pact with loss,
walk in a steady wash
of thin rain, sidewalks
pocked, water pooled
where mortar shells
struck, missing manhole
covers. Things once
fallen into we cannot
easily step out of,
life in fragments,
the dead seeming
to splash up over
my ankles in shreds.

Between mountains
of overripe trash, market
vendors sell bananas
and eggplants, fists
of garlic, peppers
bright and green
as lanterns. A man
unloads sides of beef
from a van, skins, hooves,
heads mixed up in a pile.

I follow a dead goat
wrapped like a baby
in pale cloth
cradled in a man's arms, loose head
bobbing over a wrist,
tongue like a new bruise
swollen with these words
I am trying to tell you.

How I wake
in the Bosnian night
to the ache of your absence,
the dream of your tongue
cool as water in my mouth,
you moving through the soil
of my body, coming and
coming like rain. How
I wake to loss without
possession, the failure
of hands, lips weeping.
I wake to impermanence,
this tent over me twisting,
lifting away from its
bones, the Camp collapsed
into pasture or cornfield,
green lines of trucks
waiting, humming you North.

Even so,
I chose to touch
you. To choose
to walk into you
is to choose death
in a foreign country
where words carry
no weight. Still
I tell you I wanted
to give you what I never
gave before—forest, honey,
breadfruit, a body unknown
to myself, a darkness

I taste in my mouth,
the winged bones
of my hips, only body,
only listening
to the language of rivers
flowing between us, waters
spilling out of our skins.

But I say
nothing.
This is a war zone,
downrange, deployment.
Nothing that happens here
happens. You know it.
Even these syllables
float from my mouth
like dandelion wisps
going nowhere.

Desire.
To want this
terrible wanting
is the way of the world,
an ache we ripen with.
In this gorgeous land
still lurching
from war, deep
in the hills' loins,
peasants crush plums
into wine for the lips,
for the mouth to open to,
one warmth filling
another, things
becoming other things,
tendril of vine rising
out of the heat.

Blood bearing the wildness
of our many, many, many breaths.

After Too Many Dining Hall Eggs

Bedrock Military Camp, Bosnia and Herzegovina, 1998

I like the feel of a hard
boiled egg still-warm in my hand.
I like undressing the egg,
the ritual crack of the shell
and the joy when the membrane
beneath holds tight and the egg
slips naked and clean in my palm.
I like the way the egg
will not lie still on the plate
but shimmies its way to the edge
as if to whisper an intimate word.

To love eggs is to bring one
day after day to my lips,
perched in the tips of my fingers,
to gently nibble the waxy
crown of white, long for the blue
haze hanging like fog on the yoke,
a vestige of madness, a sorrowful
bruise the egg breathes out at the last.

And then what's left?
The yellowy center of yellow,
the core and pith of the egg,
dense and lovely as pollen.
And the reason I keep coming
back to the egg, that powdery
taste always left on the tongue,
so like the dust this body is,
fine flour under the bread's shape,
or the shadow of loss after love.

Michael Kriesel

Early in the Plague

We were in the Outback
on this tiny Navy base
so far from anywhere that
stateside beer was 6 months old
by the time the barge arrived
some brands even added
formaldehyde as a preservative
we called it death in a can
our TV shows were last year's episodes
on tapes the Navy sent our cable station

I was the only newscaster there
in the middle of all that red sand
when people back home
started dying of AIDS
half a world away
the absolute sky
staring down at you
empty & blue every day
made it less real
still a few of us
had blood drawn
remembering
shore leave in the
Philippines & Tijuana
I sweated sand
waiting for my test results
to come back from Pearl Harbor
meanwhile
Live At Five each night
I read the latest death toll
to a captive audience

Feathers

We see it coming on TV
this possibility
birds carry

overseas
they're killing
chickens

more than
Colonel Sanders
ever did

there's a map
on TV
showing us

all the dark
migration routes
of geese

—

I hope it doesn't cross the ocean
I hope it doesn't jump
from birds to humans

a poet said once
hope has feathers

I hope it doesn't

—

I buy batteries
and pork & beans
in case we're quarantined

I'll crawl outside
if I think I'm dying
so I don't leave a mess

for whoever lives next
in this small green house
where ducks fly overhead

their silhouettes black
as enemy planes
in a war no one started

Manly Johnson, *That War*, photograph

Hedy Habra

Lost and Found

This could be an office, a temple or a church
Its thick crimson carpeted floor
muffles all sounds
as if we were walking over clouds
Here people wait in line for Lost and Found
drawn by an invisible cord
Objects with a will of their own, call names,
conjure up faces, find their way
on pre-labeled shelves,
uprooted lares and penates reappear,
faithful to their hosts . . .

Behind a counter, three matronly women
display heteroclite items:
a silver candle snuffer, a collection of thimbles, an enameled hand
mirror inlaid with semi-precious stones, a crystal chandelier,
brass engraved ashtrays and planters, an old gas Primus stove, a
miniature locket, a silver samovar, a powder case covered with petit-
point, an oval mahogany mantel clock, a jade Buddha, a copy of
a pink lacquered lampshade with pewter cupids my mother carved
when she was fifteen and even a deep-blue Sèvres porcelain
bonbonnière—a Bouchers pastoral painted on its lid—similar to the
one my father presented the day he proposed . . .

My mother and I have come regularly for years,
crossing oceans or land,
we never fail to meet at the threshold
of the crimson corridor
we still look the same as we did thirty years ago,
before the fighting started
Hand in hand, we wait in line,
talk as if we never parted, reviving
a once congealed image, a never-ending moment . . .

She hopes to recover her paintings,

or at least one, the Galleon or the Shepherdess
Perhaps this is what I'd like most to see,
her own work
"May evil come upon those who have them
on their walls," she says . . .

I'm afraid to go to someone's home in Lebanon
and see my life scattered all over,
fetishes sold at black markets
As if I owned a palace
As if it mattered
As if anything mattered
since our children left
untouched, unharmed.

M. Teresa Valero, from *The Levant: Lebanon and Syria Through Western Eyes*, photograph

Lee Sharkey

In Vigil

What I like best is standing tall together
in the driving rain at the corner of the
intersection my left foot planted behind
the pole anchoring one end of the banner
that the gusts belly that the rain bounces off
like silver seed observing the orderly
relentless movement of traffic the street lights
conducting each car's pause pace and sequence through
convergence the drivers glancing out through glass
through sheeting rain to see a line of women
most in black with colorful umbrellas still
in the moving weather holding banners their
hands holding out another way of seeing
what I like best is seeing motley multi-
colored America pass by this one spot
on which I and my sisters have planted our
selves and watching rainwater slide down the face
of old commercial buildings the cars stream by
without pausing but often often drivers
lean on the horn which I translate *you're standing*
there for me or inscrutable passengers
turn to stare their eyes move across the letters
of a new language and take what they need to
think about the girlfriends the children driven
from here to there a flicker an instant of
contact will one of them remember *when I*
was a child one day it was raining I saw
a long line of women standing on the street
standing there for peace I saw that could be done

Phyllis K. Collier

Peace in Our Day

She goes out among the madmen of noon,
Every intersection a sign of the cross,
Witnesses again the laws of nature: wind
Across burning grass, BMW through a red light.

Soon she will scan the day's massacres
Consoled in the part of her that would stay
An execution. She slips back on her loose linen,
Breathes deeply with the men who draft treaties,
Who pledge to ban weapons, tunes out
Voices of politicians who hold out a hand.

When the earthquake hits, she rides it
Alone under the kitchen table, watches her statues
Tumble from shelves. More than once, she has
Given her body to be burned. She knows
It is meant for her and the mountain to trespass
Against each other from time to time.

In the closeness of four a.m., she watches herself
Walk across the alley to her nameless neighbors,
Past the excessive purple of their flowers,
Break the glass of their kitchen door,
Enter and take what she wants. She understands
What comes next. She can wait.

Sarah Rossiter

Consider the Birds

for Susan

Consider the birds of the air, He said, and so
I did the end of May when six fledgling wrens
were coaxed from their nest by thimble-sized
parents, grubs gripped in their beaks, who
darted and danced through the green afternoon
as fledglings fell like feathered seeds to flutter
from fencing to lilac to hedge, straining for
nourishment not yet received though never more
than a wing-beat away. Until at last they reached
the swamp, deep in thorn thicket, hidden from
sight, and finally fed, or so I hoped, as well as
safely kept that night; though hope itself, I then
considered, a thing with feathers, someone said,
fragile as a child, dying,
buoyant as a bird in flight.

Jackson Wheeler

In Thomas Eakins' Painting, "The Gross Clinic"

for Hugo Leckey and John Prichard

In Thomas Eakins' painting, "The Gross Clinic,"
a surgeon turns from an incision
in the thigh of an etherized man.

The doctors do not wear
masks, gloves, nor gowns.
In this century before AIDS, the blood is safe.

I find some reassurance here,
the man on the table might still die;
of a staph infection, or gangrene.

But there is a better chance he recovered,
returned to an ordinary life. All that vivid red
exuberant in his veins.

Eleanor Berry

Like Anemones from the Blood of Adonis

Heal-all, *Prunella vulgaris*—common
on every continent, this cross of Eurasian
and North American subspecies—especially here
this year when a spring unseasonably cool and wet
followed a winter breaking records for warm and dry.
Now, in early summer, the brush is thick with purple bloom.

Heal-all, self-heal—always and everywhere
needed—ointment from the leaves
to dress torn flesh, tea from the whole plant
to drink for the heart. Greatly needed
now, when no continent is safe from harm.
But the recipes have been forgotten, if they ever worked.

Heal-all, common prunella—royal purple
for the common people—if not a salve or tonic,
then a purple sign of sorrow for the slaughtered
on every continent, so many handsome and young
as the bold hunter beloved of Venus.
Heal-all—springing up everywhere, as if from their blood.

Sue Ellen Thompson

Closing up the Cottage

Brightening at the prospect of an outing,
my mother let us gather her from where
she had been scattered by her illness.
Inch by inch she picked her way
across the lawn to where the car sat,
idling. My husband drove
while I stared hard at the undressed
landscape and my father made
the whooshing sound with which he'd filled
the rifts in conversation since
he gave up cigarettes. Once there,
we propped and cushioned her
in a wicker armchair, where she sat enthroned
like a child-queen, thin legs dangling
just above the floorboards.

As we went about the task of shutting out
a season we'd already brought indoors,
she seemed uncommonly alert
to her surroundings, as if she knew
this was the last she'd see of the world
beyond the room of her disease.
She took it all in—every molecule of light
that tumbled free when screens were lifted
from their hinges, every leaf that danced
in the heaped-up corners of the yard,
the gulping sound that water in the pipes made
on its final journey to the hard clay underground.
I like it here was all she said
that I remember—that, and how,
when we brought her home, we carried her
in a sedan-chair made of arms and elbows,
my father scurrying behind us
with his sweeping sound, closing
and then locking every door.

Mark Weiss, photograph

No Children, No Pets

I bring the cat's body home from the vet's
in a running-shoe box held shut
with elastic bands. Then I clean
the corners where she has eaten and
slept, scrubbing the hard bits of food
from the baseboard, dumping the litter
and blasting the pan with a hose. The plastic
dishes I hide in the basement, the pee-
soaked towel I put in the trash. I put
the catnip mouse in the box and I put
the box away, too, in a deep
dirt drawer in the earth.

When the death-energy leaves me,
I go to the room where my daughter slept
in nursery school, grammar school, high school,
I lie on her milky bedspread and think
of the day I left her at college, how nothing
could keep me from gouging the melted candle-wax
out from between her floorboards,
or taking a razor blade to the decal
that said to the firemen, *Break*
this window first. I close my eyes now
and enter a place that's clearly
expecting me, swaddled in loss
and then losing that, too, as I move
from room to bone-white room
in the house of the rest of my life.

April 1943

Why did they marry? We had heard
the story a hundred times: She was on spring
break; he was stationed in Texas, learning
how to fly a B-24. But things

got a little murky after that.
He met her at the train, having thought
of everything—a motel room, a ring—but in what
order? Indignation. A little sweet-talk.

The rector of St. Paul's-on-the-Plains made
an exception to his rule about marrying young
military couples. He liked the way
my father's hand on her neck kept the sun

off. Why did they marry? For love, of course.
Although back then they called it "the War."

April 1993

My parents were getting ready to celebrate
their fiftieth anniversary. "A family cruise,"
my brother suggested. "A compound at the lake"—
this from my sister. It was all a ruse,

the whole point being to invite us
on a free vacation. They let us talk.
Then my mother, her voice stripped by laryngitis
to its truest, most essential notes, locked

eyes with my father as she said, "It's all decided."
They booked the honeymoon suite on the Delta Queen
and watched, from their stateroom window, starboard side,
the West unfurl. I don't believe

they thought of us once, but only of the vast
country around them, in which they were alone at last.

Terminal Math

At the end of a lifetime
in which she'd done
nothing more to augment her looks
than pat down her face
with some powder,
my mother asked me if I
would tweeze her eyebrows.
Two months of chemo
had already claimed
her gray-blond frizz
and her lashes were gone
in what seemed like
a blink. What percentage lay
in deducting these last
few hairs from a body
already canceling itself?
She must have believed
that in ministering to what
remained, she could balance
the equation.

So I counted
the fine brown hairs
that traced her brow
and thought about what
I could do to improve
their distribution.
With her head in my lap
on the sunlit porch
and her gaze diluted
in blissful trust,
I braced my hand
against her skull
and started subtracting.

Colleen J. McElroy

Drawing a Line in the Sand

on chemo the brain
  flickers like a strobe. . .
follows a bouncing ball
  traveling along a song nobody

knows. . .you are always
  tired learning to sing
the song chemo demands. . .
  the brain restless zig. . .

zags in mental tachycardia. . .
  grows tired until zapped
onto the next stop. . .someone
  has salted your waterglass. . .

everything smells of mildew
  and all you know is out
of synch. . .you nap for the 3rd
  time in 1 day and 5 minutes

later you are tired of propping
  open your eyelids. . .3-5-6-8
how do you hallucinate. . .
  gray zone some subway terminal

where all trains switch tracks
  at a moment's notice. . .switch
back out of reason's reach. . .
  no wonder your hair falls out. . .

no wonder you can't recall
  if you pulled it by the roots
you can't remember your roots
  or what you'd give for a plate

of fried food and sweet pudding. . .
  you're tired of being careful
tired of trying to remember
  yesterday or five minutes ago. . .

or how much hair you've lost
  and what gets caught between
the skitter scatter of what
  passes for thought and what

you tell the doctor who looks
  younger than your daughter. . .
not that it matters when
  the lights go out. . . and at last

you sink into sweet fatigue. . .
  you'll see her again tomorrow
a week later or a month. . .
  you're on a slow running clock

and the doctor changes the dosage. . .
  drawing a line in the sand
and hoping it will stick. . .
  you let memory take you

  on the liquid highway past do not
enter past aimless circles
  the fine art of doing nothing
in a land of random thoughts. . .

someone's left a pot on the stove
  you smell it burning. . .now
your head is full of notes
  you'll never get to mail

J. I. Goodman

We're Useful

We're useful, until we're not
We're thoughtful, until we're not
We're verbal, until we're not
And then,
and then
"You gonna put me in the trash when I die?!"
The aide pushes the barrel down the corridor.
"You're not gonna die, Mary!"
She reaches a generous arm around the woman
in the chair, strong hug, warm shoulder,
shaking the weeping woman
"Don't worry, Mary, you're all right."
And Mary, in her pink sweater and blue print dress
rocks forward, back, in the lounge chair, muttering
muttering to herself, reassurances.
Attendant in green scrubs, on her way again,
and Mary shouts,
"I was so scared!"

Aren't we all. Scared. All.
Going to die. All.
Useful until we're not.
Helen sees me passing.
Waves, claps her hands, joyful
"Oh, oh!" Waving, she gestures, claps hands
"Oh, ab-ba, oh-oh!" . . . and I know
she is greeting me with knowing look
An old friend, I have never met.
She takes my hands, first the left,
touches the palms, then the back,
then the right, rubs the palm, pats the back
"Eees . . . un . . . bark!"
Again, touching the palm, the knuckles,
pushes them together, claps.
It takes me several repetitions to catch on
No, this isn't a clapping game

God! I am so slow—don't forget
she means something. She knows.
I begin to rub her hands, the right, the palm, the back, the left
Rubbing the arm, skin skidding, folds
under my fingers, pale and speckled brown,
"Helen" I read on her bracelet,
"Helen, does that feel good?"
"Yes!" she says, "Oh, that's good . . ."
And yes, I know you are in there

Mary mutters again, more worries
but now, at least, she is not trash.

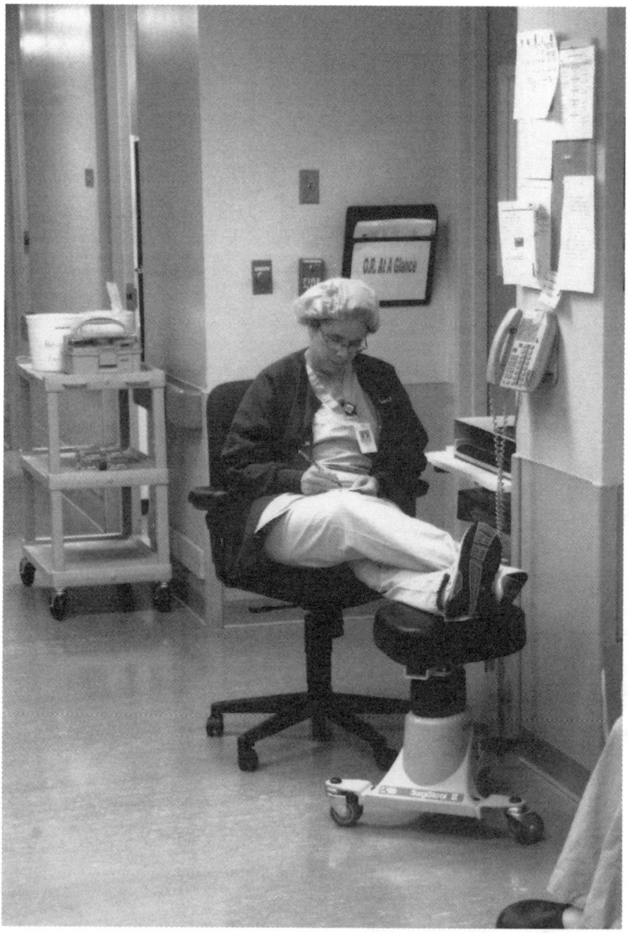

Mark Weiss, photograph

Jack Coulehan

Phantom Limb

I won it playing a game of cancer
on the ball of my thumb. The mole
was innocent until proven wrong.
The score teetered back and forth
like a devil's pact, until I won
my reward—an arm that isn't there,
the ghostly absence of symmetry.

The doctor says the arm is in my brain.
I feed it acetaminophen, codeine,
and Percodan at four and eight and noon.
It needs them to maintain a sense
of self worth. Without the pain, my limb
is nothing. But because it burns, it is.
I'm like a man who won a lottery–

one hundred thousand bucks a year
for twenty years. The next night he takes
a dive from the roof. Saved from death
by chance, he carries a load of nothing.
Nada. Zip. Don't you see what I mean?
I need this phantom arm to lean on,
to help me shoulder my good fortune.

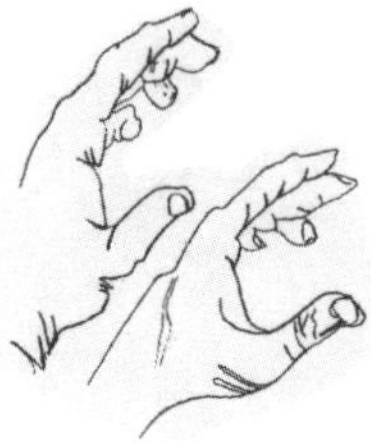

Gabrielle Parent

Pink Felt

The sound of pink felt blankets and snow gives me insomnia. They both seem to whisper all the time, just an octave lower than my hearing can pick up. It drives me crazy. I once had a big fat boyfriend from Israel with a wide-spreading chest covered in black lamb's wool, and a breathy accent that rolled from his throat like water over boiling rocks. He kept me awake too because he never snored. Not even when the alders bloomed and gave him bad allergies. I used to watch his lungs emptying and filling back up, efficient and soundless while I twisted myself to shreds in the blankets. He was so quiet he might as well have been dead.

When I was a little kid my mom explained my insomnia to me in terms of boats and beaches. She said my problem was that I missed the boats that sailed people over to *Sleep*, as if sleep was a place, because I was too busy exploring the beach. She explained that while everyone else floated away in a warm lazy heap I stayed behind tearing apart the stones, the rocks, and then the sand, until the beach was upside down and I had rubbed every speck hard between my long fingers. If I could just try to, she said, I could catch up. I just had to be very fast.

At bedtime I sizzled with fury at my mother's ability to sleep. She would tickle me for my forgiveness as we snuggled under the pink felt blanket that she loved so much, the same blanket Granddad had brought home for her from the paper mill that was just barely pink enough to prove it was her favorite color. But the very act of petting my hair and scratching secret stories into my seething back would shove her off across the water and I wouldn't see her again until morning when a smile would spread over her dewy lips and her eyes, bright and damp from rest, would open onto my face, raw and cracking with abandonment. It is long, that wait for sleeping people to come back.

I was born with hands that are long and curious like Jimmy H's or those people who repair cuckoo clocks with thin and precise screwdrivers. My mother the potter had hands like that too, hands like butterfly feet, gifted with a higher agenda. But nobody ever noticed what her hands could do except for old rich ladies whose upper lips twitched appreciatively at the potential of her vases and serving platters. My hands were made for gripping oars and pulling them into my bra strap, under my tiny boobs, over and over again until the water runs out and people applaud. I'll eventually be the best in the world at that.

I started rowing when I was twelve, right after my mom died. My granddad signed me up with the Kawartha Rowing Club to keep my mind occupied. For seven years now I have marched barefoot down frosted docks with a sculling boat on my head. Every day starts out cold, way before the fog on the Otanabee river has any inclination of budging. I warm up with the crews to the lift-bridge and back until all the farts and chilled yawns have been worked out of everyone's body. Then the coach boats start to rev around the eights and the fours, waking the smaller scullers and shooing the blue herons away in pissed-off swarms as they bark commands that make us want to churn up the bottom of the river. This is the part of the practice when they test us to see how young we are, and how far we have left to go before our potential becomes something we can no longer achieve. Someone comes over to me to monitor my strokes per minute, eyeing my balance and how well I drive down my legs when I am making my boat hurry up. When the crews are finally worn and malleable, and I've proved that I am willing to sweat, I am sent away to row alone down the twisting river; alone, with only the sound of the running bubbles underneath my scull and my blood rushing through every little part of my body. My toes and the curl at the tip of my eyelashes all throb red by the time I make my way back to the docks. My mom might have mistaken a neurosis-fuelled insomnia for a bubbly curiosity but she was right about the boats. They brought me exhaustion. They *took* me to sleep.

The Israeli arrived in my first varsity year, just as I had been ranked the number one lightweight sculler in the Kawarthas. It was the beginning of spring and my four-month separation from the river had finished with the first split in the ice. I had put my boat in the water the moment I saw the line of dark water melt its way through the white crust. Frigid drops of water that my oars flicked up were making my back snap into a variety of arches, but I hadn't slept since the snow had set in and I was anxious to dream. I was rowing slowly down the current, being careful of the waking river. And then there he was, waving, at a bend in the river.

With layers of t-shirts pulled tight over his massive chest and his ridiculously curly hair tied back into some sort of a ponytail, the Israeli tromped along the riverbank with poles and tools every morning, inspecting things. Sticking close to the shore, he weighed rocks with his palm and jotted down their numbers in his folded notebook. He was an ecologist, summoned here to restore the sides of the river because the river banks were falling to pieces.

The water from the Otanabee had hollowed out the mud from under the topsoil, leaving an outcrop of bottomless grass. Fences from the farms stood by useless as water seeped into the pastures. The tall cedars arced daringly towards the water, dangling their toes into the frothing current. It was so easy to see what was going to happen to these doomed trees, a death measurable in meters-to-go. Sometimes the tops of the trees reached so low to the water that I could brush my face against their soft needles as I rowed through the tunnel they made.

The Israeli took a lot of soil samples and sketched the angles of the trees with sharpened charcoal. Sometimes he chewed on the ends of his hair as he tapped on his notepad for solutions. He always waved and shouted a friendly good morning to me but I never took it personally since it was done out of his habit of being a nice guy.

One morning during a downpour I sat floating in my little boat, my oars resting in my lap, listening to muffled drops beat down hard on my cotton hood. My fingers were a surprising shade of purple and I was turning them over in fascination. The Israeli shouted out to me.

"Why on earth are you doing that for?" he asked, mimicking the gesture of pulling on an oar.

I just shrugged my shoulders and then asked him the same question. "Because there is no more ecology to be restored in Israel."

He was wearing a big green raincoat, water drops looping down his tightening tendrils. He was looking at me right in the face. I could swear his eyes were orange.

"How old are you?"

"Nineteen."

"You look like just a little kid," he laughed.

"Well, you look like you're fat," I had snapped back, miserable and freezing in my red sweatshirt.

"I'm not. I'm just big," he had answered without the slightest hint of offense. "I'm twenty-six."

I accepted his offer to go hiking sometime not because I was in love with him, or because I hated him enough to want to fuck with his head. I went because the girls who rowed crew were always talking about how good-looking he was and I wanted friends.

When my granddad stepped off the boat in Halifax from Ireland, he went directly to work for a paper mill in Southern Ontario. The mill produced all the paper used by the *New York Times* to stamp down the daily shocks and glees of the world. The pulp came from the forests of Northern Ontario and, once in a while, from the swampy woods out in Alberta. My mom used to tell me how Granddad's job was to take the smelly heaps of wood paste and spread them over gargantuan pink felt blankets. The blankets rippled softly and steadily, absorbing all the clumps and dribbles of innumerable chemicals until that wet gray mass became shimmering rolls of sturdy paper ready to be shipped off to the States. My granddad would always take the soft blankets home to my mom whenever new ones arrived. Tucking her in at night he would tell her she was sleeping under a tool of potential. Who knew what poetry and important stories would be written down on the paper her blanket had created?

The Israeli had skin like honey. But not just any honey. The kind made by the bees that pollinated the desert after a rain, running between flowers so concentrated with spontaneous color and aroma that the honey they produced looked like black gold. He also reminded me of honey because he was the first person who ever pointed out the difference between a hornet and a bee.

Like my granddad did to her, my mom spoiled me whenever she could. She made me an entire set of china for my dolls, complete with a gravy boat and ladle, and glazed it pearly pink. She painted each piece with lilac blossoms and even rimmed the spoons with tiny pink handles for the porcelain hands to grip. A few weeks before she died she sat at her wheel spinning a giant urn for us to put her ashes into. She almost made it as magnificent as an Egyptian urn but she got embarrassed of her own talent so she left out the fine details. Her urn remains gray and wet looking. My granddad keeps it in the solarium, beside the fountain and ivy. Sometimes when I'm trying to get to sleep I want to grab a sponge and polka-dot her urn neon pink just to make her louder.

The Israeli used to wait for me on the dock to finish my row. With a pastry and a newspaper, his big feet plopped in the water, he would patiently read about the world while I hammered out a few final practice starts. He never looked up at me, no matter how I grunted in effort, until he heard the clunk of the boat against the dock and the slide of my oars from the oarlocks. Then he would greet me with a massive crushing hug, kissing me all over my salty neck and face until I giggled and buried my hand into his wild hair. Picking up my boat and oar as if they were a handful of sticks, he would walk with me back up to the boathouse as we planned our day together.

I once teased him for being shy for never watching me while I rowed. "Why should I watch? You don't do it out of love. It is just something you are good at. I'll watch you when you have something that makes you smile."

"You're watching me now," I had said, staring up with a grin at his breath-stopping face. That made him blush.

None of the girls from crew liked me any more than they had before I got together with the Israeli. Actually, they ignored me more. But the men's crews all loved the Israeli, with his tales of his army service and the Bedouins, and the last legal place for the production of foie gras. We started being invited to bonfires up in the drumlins, and cottages for barbecues, and for midnight diving contests off the lift-bridge.

My favorite thing to do with the rowers was to swim out to one of the rocky islands in Stony Lake. We would each tie a bag to our waists, carrying beer and wine, cheese and cookies, candles, and matches. It was like being in the middle of a school of mermen and mermaids, bodies lithe from too much exercise. And the Israeli, naked and shamelessly doing the back crawl, would spout like a whale and sing us songs as we breast-stroked our way to the island through the warm summer water. The island was too far from the shore for the mosquitoes to bother with, so we could prance around in bikinis and towels, gathering up dried branches from under the skirts of the deformed island pine trees. The smoke from our bonfire would rise straight up and our laughter and squeals of delight would echo off the moon, answered by the coyotes nosing the crayfish along the good stinking shore.

On the swim back, while the rest of the rowers moaned through their drunken cramps, the Israeli would lay me across his chest and slowly scull us back to the beach, all the while telling me stories about the constellations he was seeing above my head, and about his favorite Arabian pastries with the almonds in the center. On those nights I used to try to stay awake, to remember them, but the sound of the water lapping at our bellies and the shrill of the ecstatic frogs easily overpowered my will. And I would sleep, my face pressed hard into the wet lamb's wool, sucking in water occasionally through my smiling, drooling mouth.

One day in the fall while I was helping him set the chicken wire along the river banks, I told the Israeli about maple toffee. I promised him that when it snowed we would make some. He told me he would be gone before winter but asked if I wouldn't mind sending him some in Haifa.

My mom's doctor had told Granddad and me the cancer was everywhere. Her blood and lungs and skin were stained with it. He had never seen such ravaged cells before. While he was treating her this doctor often asked my mom if she washed her fruit, if she had ever worked in a mine, if she was one of those people who liked to scorch her marshmallows black before she ate them. He was always searching for some clue. He still calls me up sometimes to ask about a makeup she might have used, if she ever had tree planted? I don't have the heart to tell the doctor about the blanket. Not while my granddad is still out watering the ivy and telling his daughter about my latest medal. He's a young doctor. He will learn about love, and the death it brings us.

The only time I can't row is when the snow arrives and plunks itself over the forests, freezing the river in its tracks, and covering up the islands so that everything looks the same, and sounds almost like nothing.

Judy Rowe Michaels

Recurrence Suite

1

After X-rays

I am in love with the lesion on my liver,
how its quick thickening
defines the dark.
Such lèse-majesté! I love how it flies a skull and crossbones
from the heart of the mother ship.
I'm in awe of its discontent.
How did it know me across a crowded room?
I love it with sleepless nights,
I love it on alternate days,
I love it incestuously.
My secret that defies the hot, bright shower of particles,
that eludes the fumbling knives.
How it clings to its bland, glandular host,
how it finds its way around my slippery defenses.
I am in love with its little suction-cup feet,
with its mysterious past, its hunger.
I could die for its grim dividings,
for its knowledge of hidden names.

2

Biopsy

The books call it a train you're on,
and each new test a station where you
might get off and watch the fear
pick up speed, new freight,
new distances. Metaphor
is a carrier—of disease, of terror.
Yesterday the technician,
a mere girl, curly and big-eyed,
missed my vein twice. The station

was 2, or maybe 3, announced
in a foreign tongue that you almost
understand from birth, but learn
to forget. Anyway,
it made my wiring flash
what if? The current locution
is *we don't have to go there*
yet. But mind has a mind of its own,
is already there—stage 3, 4, 5—of course
it knows people who went right
to the end of the line,
and in the name of self-control,
of be prepared, it's improvising
death. It remembers
the chemo nurse teaching my
mother to say *I'm buying*
some time, my mother
carrying everywhere the little green
plastic bowl to be sick in,
while her mind tried to shut up
about *quality of life*, and mine
went on celebrating in a terrible
secret refrain, *not me, not me,*
not me.

3

Waiting For News

When you wade the low tide
on a morning that is already singing
and your eyes wake more birds
high in the red-fleshed trees,
and you know for good and all
where the sure-footed, deep dance you
do with the slipping stones
comes from, how can you not
trust the dance in your cells—
kick, fire, split, die, kick.
If that is diseased, then so is
the quick-diving flow of the heron's neck,

and the breaking wave that receives him,
and the blue depth of sky
that colors my breath. These pierced
like a surgeon's needle
and found nothing but light.

4

Surgery Appointment

We're *all* terminally ill, my surgeon says,
his pony tail energizing the white room,
giving me numbers I was dumb enough
to ask for—*one* (shake) *to three* (shake) *years,*
three if you have the operation. No one but me
will hear this, loved ones believe in beating
the numbers. From wherever lost things go
I call back *irrationals* and *imaginary*
numbers. I used to love the words, their meanings
shadowy in the brightness of sound, chiaroscuro
of the can't win, beautiful as a luna moth
betrayed by hot lights, its wings beating out
green, luminous, shrivelling death. We know
in our crazed rhythms of loss and cling, oh how we
come to know, the irrational roots, how like
some shaky old jazz drummer we keep time
with all the imaginary numbers.

Daniel C. Bryant

The Return

Except for the bruise, the fine inch of incision, it looks the same. As before. As the other. The smooth downward slope, the beveling up to the edge of the areola. The nipple valentine-pink in natural light.

She turns further, into full profile, straightens her back as in the days of good posture. The geometry of the thing. Of her. But she does not admire. She does not wonder. She does not, in all her nakedness, grieve. For the moment, she is removed. She is someone she may have met once.

Champagne glass, Clark had said. He must have read it somewhere. Or could he have thought up such an image himself? But it was true: her breast would have just fit a champagne glass. Still might.

The bruise is tender when she touches it. Of course it would be. But there is nothing there now. Nothing palpable, as the doctor put it. *Palpable*. She presses into the breast with the pads of her fingers, kneading the hurt, defining it, daring it. No, there is nothing there at all now. Save the hurt.

She looks from the mirror directly into the window's glare.

* * *

Bun is sitting on the unmade bed, one back leg thrust mightily upward. He licks his black coat, extending his tongue, his neck, to reach the long hairs' very ends.

She watches him. Watches him work his coat to a luster.

She lifts the breast upward. She cannot reach it with her tongue. She cups it, simple as water, in her palm. She lets it down slowly until it hangs free. *This thing is hanging on me, Bun. It* is *me.*

There, under the bed, is Figi. Only a tail, but it's Figi: the puffiness, the grayness. It flicks once, twice, and is gone. Smoke.

Sanders and Macaroni are curled in the far corner of the living room. Hardly any furniture left, but they still obviously consider it their living room. Sunshine carpets the center of the hardwood floor. At her entrance, the cats look up as one. Sanders mimes a mew. *Tell me about it, Sanders. You tell me all about it.*

By the front window she looks out over the rooftops staggered down toward the harbor. A tanker, riding high, stately, disappears past the jamb, heading toward open sea. Its tugs pipe jauntily.

What about the cats? Yes, that's number one, the cats. She needs to deal with the disposition of the cats now, while she's able. She doesn't know seventeen people, is the problem. Nor would they all be willing, necessarily, to take a cat if she did. Some might take more than one cat, of course. Or at least until other arrangements could be made. If they knew her situation. People can surprise you, how they come forward in situations. She would. She knows she would be one of the first to come forward. But she's not going into detail with just anybody. Not yet, at least. She's not going to be pitiful.

Come to think of it, though, she does know seventeen people. More than seventeen. Not well, all of them, but well enough. *And there are shelters. Like yours, Fullbright, remember? There they don't put you down. They find you good homes. They keep you until they find you good homes. Really they do.*

The sun is warm on her bare breasts. But the glass, when she presses against it, sheer cold.

* * *

No. Carol, Mom. Your daughter?

Carol! Oh, my God! I lost your number. You've got to come out! I'll pay your ticket.

Come out? What's happening now?

This place, Carol. I can't stay here another week. You've got to come get me.

What about Todd? He's right there.

Just come out, will you? This call's costing you.

Let me call Todd first, Mom, okay? Okay? Mom?

The dial tone nags in her ear. She hangs up. It is dark in the bedroom except for the car lights swimming grotesquely across the walls and ceiling. Fullbright is a cloud of warmth in her lap, his purr increasingly exquisite between her legs. Abruptly she spills him onto the floor and drags the sheet up over her shoulders with both hands. It covers her completely, like a shroud. Like the tents her mother used to make to amuse her as a child on rainy days. But, close as she draws it around her, it is no sanctuary.

* * *

Moya, it's Carol.

Carol, how are you? Where you been keeping yourself?

Oh, I'm good, I'm good. How about you? Still painting, I hope.

Oh yeah. Well, yes and no. Been helping Roger with the books more. But, hey! I'm glad you called. We've got to get together sometime.

Sure. I'd like that. But listen, Moya, reason I'm calling is I might be needing a favor. Cat sort of favor, actually.

Oh?

Yeah. I've just been to the doctor. . . .

Uh oh.

Well, not too Uh oh. Allergies. He says I'm allergic to cats. Can you believe that? Me? Allergic to cats? After all this time? Anyway, bottom line, I may need to get rid of my cats and I was wondering, 'cause you always asked about them, if you'd consider taking one. Or two or. . . . They're no trouble, really. Fixed and everything.

Gosh, Carol. I don't know. If it was just me. . . . But Roger. . . .

No, that's all right, Moya. Really. It might not turn out that….

Yeah, Carol, I'm real sorry. You know I'd do anything. But give me a call—or I'll call you–after the Fourth. Been way too long.

I'll do that, Moya. Putting it on my calendar. Call Moya.

There you go. And good luck with those cats!

* * *

There isn't much on the shelves, but there is tuna fish. She makes tuna fish salad with the rest of an onion, and nibbles at it directly out of the aluminum bowl. Percy arrives first, rubbing his ear back and forth against the edge of the kitchen door, then against her bare ankle. In spite of his bad leg he springs up onto the table easily, landing without a sound. She feeds him individual particles of tuna. *Hey! Not so greedy!* She picks long orange hairs out of the salad, puts Percy on her lap and strokes him firmly enough to contain him. He licks her fingers systematically, one by one, the rough tongue tickling their undersides. *You're an evil, greedy cat, Perce. You know that? Evil, evil, evil.*

She's got to call Todd. She knows he's told their mother she must stay in the home, as she has herself every chance she gets. But obviously he needs to tell her more often, and face-to-face. It's just that, the way Todd asks questions, they'd get to the biopsy, and she's not ready yet.

Percy squeezes back up onto the table, compressing her breast as he does so. She touches the sore spot as she watches him devour the tuna fish. Three women she's known have died, horribly, lingeringly, from breast cancer. Or the treatment: you never know which. Others are just out there with that dread. Dread is permanent; it fills the crater left by joy, and stays. And from then on, every day, you wait.

She's not going to wait like the others. That much she does know. She'll keep her follow-up appointment, obviously. She'll listen to what Dr. O'Donnell has to say about the biopsy, ask the questions expected of her. But she's not going to spend what's left of her life waiting.

She stands and puts the empty bowl in the sink. Percy licks his lips, then the back of one paw. He begins working on his face and ear in circles of serious washing. *I'm not going to wait, Perce. You guys understand that? God damn it!*

* * *

Outside, she walks fast. Before she knows it, she's all the way down to Commercial, striding along the wharf side of the wide, dazzling street. Gulls are squealing like hinges overhead, engines rumble all around. Traffic is heavy: delivery trucks, dollies, vans, tour buses. Everyone is busy, even the tourists hurrying somewhere, as she is hurrying, somewhere. She knows none of these people and that is good: she doesn't want any reminders, any connections. From here on out, she has no past.

Excuse me. I have breast cancer.

She picks out passersby who have that look, that kindly look some strangers have. Of course, almost anyone would listen if she spoke up and drew them aside into a doorway. But what exactly would she say? What ultimately would she want of them? Without a past, where do you begin?

She is standing on the corner by the fish market, looking down the cobbled alley toward the harbor. Oil shimmers on the water. That would be one way, the harbor. After dark it would have to be. After the bars have closed, the cops gone back to Dunkin Donuts. She breathes in deeply the sea air, fresh as bleach. As her chest expands, she feels a tightness in her side, a jab of soreness. No one notices.

Of course I don't have breast cancer. I'm a normal person. How could a normal person have breast cancer? She is already down by the cargo dock, fingers laced through the chain link fence. A crane is hoisting crates, bright orange and big as 18-wheelers, onto the deck of a container ship. *My mother doesn't have breast cancer. I'm not on hormones. I've never been on hormones—the pill, but they said it was the weak one, and less than a year. No animal fat since Clark.*

On her way home, she stops at Rite Aid to buy two bottles of Tylenol Extra Strength Gelcaps.

* * *

She is not going back to work before her appointment. She has told them that at the office, but not about after, because she does not know herself about after. Working in the doctor's office is the last thing she would want to be doing right now. Plus, she would not be able to concentrate properly, and even though her job—filing—is sort of a no-brainer, you do need to have your wits about you.

She is quite sure about not working, but there is that whole thing about being around other people. So she's not a hundred percent with a plan. That's what makes telling the children hard. For that, she's got to be a hundred and ten percent. She will write a letter as a way to organize her thoughts, and then call. Not actually send letters to them—no one sends letters anymore and she's not an emailer—just call, scripted by what she's gotten down in black and white.

Cal is working on his paws again. Although Cal, or any of them for that matter, doesn't go outside, he always seems to be getting things between his toes. Probably because he's part Maine Coon, and got their extra toes. She can't stop watching the meticulous nibbling. When he's finished, she uses the plastic strainer to clear the litter boxes. There are three altogether—kitchen and family room downstairs, living room upstairs—and they need cleaning almost daily to keep the ammonia out of the house. She knows that even regular cleaning isn't completely effective, no matter how compulsive you are about it, and that her paranoia about cat smell is one of the reasons she hasn't had people in for years.

It's something she's not that aware of herself, even when she comes in from outside, but she knows the smell is there. From things Clark used to say, for one thing. She double-bags in plastic, drops the lumpy bundle in the barrel outside the kitchen door.

As she is filling the kitchen water bowl at the sink, she becomes aware of distant pounding. When she realizes it's a knocking, she follows the sound through to the front and, after struggling a moment with the deadbolt, jerks the heavy door partway open. A man is standing on the stoop in brilliant sunlight. Clark.

What are you doing here?

I was in the neighborhood, as they say. Thought I'd stop by.

Just like that.

Just like that.

What do you want of me, Clark?

How about, come in?

She drags the complaining door, so long unused, a few more degrees, and steps back to let him enter. His hair has gone shockingly white, but it's still thick, and he's still slender. Deeper creases angle down from the sides of his slightly bent nose. He's casually dressed, including scuffed running shoes, yet wears movie-star dark glasses with lenses the size of quarters. The dark glasses prove to be clip-ons, which he removes, finally letting her see the aquamarine of his eyes.

You moving?

Moving? No. Why would I be moving?

There's no furniture in here.

Oh, that. I sold some. Cats don't need much furniture.

He makes no comment about cats and furniture, which surprises her. As he wanders through the first floor, she follows him at the distance of a room. She feels like a Realtor showing a house to a stranger. But it's her house. Their house. After a few turns through the kitchen, a sort of inspection, it seems, he pulls out one of the two chairs and seats himself at the small table.

So, how's life treating you, Carol?

She stays on her feet, hands behind her, flat on the counter. *You must be selling something.*

Why do you say that?

You sound like people who call at dinnertime.

Well, it's not dinnertime. Is it? And, believe me, I've got nothing left to sell.

She watches him sitting there at her table, just like before, though he wouldn't have worn a tie-dyed T-shirt before. Wouldn't have spoken of Life. Fullbright pads in from the dining room and stops by the leg of Clark's chair. He gazes up for a while, squinting like someone searching for a word, then begins to tease one of Clark's shoelaces.

You don't want to know what I'm up to these days? I think you might approve.

I'm not giving him any answers, she tells herself. No purchase on my life.

Well, I'm a teacher. I teach high school English. Always liked English. Guess you never knew that about me, did you?

Clark, I don't know what this is all about, but after ten years it's way too strange. And to be perfectly frank, this is not a good time for me. Not that any time would be. I'm kind of busy upstairs. When I come back down I expect you to be gone.

Clark leans over and flicks his lace back and forth for Fullbright, who follows the movement intently, makes quick swipes, claws bared, at the curious, stringy prey. Carol walks past them smartly into the hall. She climbs the stairs.

* * *

It's dark. She can't tell which cats are on the bed. Some jump down and scamper off as she sits up. 9:37 on the clock radio. She is slightly hungry, or slightly nauseated. Before she can decide, she remembers. Cancer. Clark.

The first floor, thank God, is dark. The kitchen is empty; the chair he had sat in is pushed back under the table just the way it had been. She toasts a slice of bread and spreads the last of the honey on it. She feels better eating it. She drops the heel into the toaster slot, depresses the lever until it catches. She says out loud what she will write to the children:

Dear Newell. I am writing to tell you about some bad news, I'm afraid. I had a breast biopsy because of a question on my mammogram, and I have cancer. My reason for writing to you now, rather than calling . . .

She is not sure what the reason is. It has to do with wanting to be exact and objective. Wanting to be faithful, yet not beholden, to so many feelings. Wanting to give adequate expression to an overview of life that she wants her children to know, but that she hasn't yet quite formulated. As she munches on the chewy heel, she wishes she had butter. When she is finished, she licks the crystals from the smoothly threaded rim of the honey jar.

Back in the bedroom, she turns on the radio. The stations are offensive, even the classical one. Especially the classical one. How obscene to play pretentious music like that when there's so much suffering in the world! There should be no music allowed until suffering is resolved and everyone is free to listen. She's glad she sold her TV.

Clark is standing out in the hall. Because of the shadow from the door, she can't tell which way he's facing. If he's coming or going. Or, for that matter, if it's really Clark. Would that be so awful, Clark standing in the hall? Anyone standing in the hall?

She makes little clicking sounds with her tongue. No one comes. They know she has no food, so why should they bother? They may be cute as kittens and grow into the look and moves of care, but cat brains aren't wired for care. She's known that all along.

She sits at the card table looking at the note cards she's been trying to make. She can't imagine working on them now. She can't imagine how she ever worked on them, how Moya ever thought she could sell them. She's no Moya. She has no talent. And who gives a shit about note cards anyway? She picks up the iris one. She tears it in half. In half again. Again. But there's a limit: it's too hard to tear through eight layers of rag paper. Her fingertips burn from the effort.

Sanders startles her, springing onto the tabletop. She picks him up and carries him over to the bed. Lying on her back with him stretched prone on her stomach and chest, she strokes him. He begins to purr. He can't meow, but his purr more than makes up for it, and the vibration resonates within her as if they were a single beast.

Maybe, of all them, Sanders cares a little.

* * *

Clark is lying on his side behind her, snugged in close as a chair. His upper hand is on her shoulder, moving over it in leisurely circles, then down across the upper breast to the one she's lying on. She feels the nipple tense under his deepening massage, then a pinch on the side of the breast. What is he doing to her breast?

She hunches up on her elbow. Clark is not there. Nor is the pain, until she lets herself back down against the wadded corner of the pillow.

It's light out. She has cancer. She goes into the bathroom and, sitting on the toilet, smells coffee. A neighbor must be making morning coffee, she thinks, though she's never noticed it before. She's not even sure who rents on that side of her now.

Clark is working at the counter in the kitchen. Although her bare feet make no sound on the linoleum, he must somehow sense her presence because he turns at her approach. *Still take your coffee with cream and one sugar?*

How did you get in? Wasn't it locked? She pulls her robe around her more tightly.

Oh, I never left. Except to go to the store. You didn't have a damn thing to eat here, except cat food. You haven't turned into one of those people who eat cat food, have you?

I told you to leave, Clark. Last night. Didn't I?

Well, you weren't very welcoming, that's for sure. But I didn't really think you'd mind. I got eggs and bacon and some kind of special grain bread. And the OJ with the pulp you like. Have a seat.

Carol sits down in the chair he holds for her, though she doesn't like being offered a seat in her own house. She counts six cats around the kitchen, variously sitting, lying, grooming. Captain is following Clark's every move with his good eye. They never hung around Clark before, but then he never did food things before.

I'm going to pick up some sundries after breakfast. He sets a champagne glass of orange juice on the oilcloth in front of her. *Anything I can get you?*

What's with the glass?

They were still up on the top shelf. Sort of special, I thought.

She sips the juice. Its succulent pulp is delicious. The rim of the glass is so fine it is almost sharp against her lip.

And sundries, you say?

You know, toothbrush, deodorant, razor. Don't you call those sundries? I'm getting pretty whiskery. Look at me.

She can see, now that she allows herself to look, that he does have a slight growth of beard. Reddish, the color all his hair used to be. He would look very odd with white hair and red beard and those eyes. A man who didn't go together.

Don't you have a home, Clark? What about Lynn?

He breaks the eggs expertly, dropping each with a hiss into the hot, buttered skillet. *You were right about Lynn, Carol. And I dated some for a while, but that whole scene . . . Maybe you know. You going to . . . want strawberry, or how about this, what, ginger preserve I got?*

Strawberry's fine.

So, do you know?

Know what?

The dating scene—The Dating Scene.

No, she's not going to answer. Not going to let him know all the damage.

He turns the bacon with a fork, lining up the strips evenly in the pan. *Yeah, I'm more or less on my own now. Which is fine. And they raised the rent on me, so* . . . . The words morph into a shrug.

What about all the money, Clark? All your famous money?

He brings the plates with their breakfasts over to the table, picks Bun up off the other kitchen chair, puts him gently on the floor, and sits. *All my famous money. Well, somebody's pockets, I guess.*

And the buildings?

This one's all that's left. Not that it's actually left, seeing as it's yours. You ever get it paid off, by the way?

They prepare their toast, cut into their eggs, the yolks blooming golden on their plates. She pushes the bacon aside. Even if he asks, she's not explaining. About the bacon, the house, the furniture. Anything. She's better a mystery.

Way I figure, it's summer vacation, so what the hell? But how about you, Carol? Not a good time, I think you said. That caught my attention. Or was it just a brush-off?

You know how I feel, Clark. Which makes this all, like I think I said, extremely odd. Extremely.

Well, I know how you must have felt. But I have no idea how you feel. That's really what I came to find out. How you feel, after all this time. He's staring directly at her, his eyebrows arcing over the upper rims of his glasses.

She resumes eating. She's not hungry in the least, but eating beats talking. It serves a purpose. As if in agreement, Clark mops up the last of his yolk with a piece of toast and puts it in his mouth. More cats arrive, including the reclusive Figi. Carol doesn't know when she's ever seen Figi in the kitchen before.

I'm going upstairs now. Thanks for breakfast. But it won't work.

* * *

Slowly she blacks out the petals with her felt tip, then opens the note card. *Dear Lisa, I'm afraid I have bad news. I've just learned that I have breast cancer.*

She tears the card into ragged strips, the strips into ragged squares. What made her think she could write all she has to say on a note card? Calling's much better, only she should wait until after the appointment. She'll know more. Like her uncle, Lisa will keep pressing for specifics, and she knows nothing now. She really knows nothing about her body. She can't even remember the names the doctor used pointing at the X-rays. That will be important, because he said there are different types, but she's never been good with names. Her mother always said it wasn't a failure of memory so much as attention. That was one of her problems: she was inattentive, even as a child.

The house shudders: vacuum cleaner. She's never heard the roar of the vacuum cleaner from elsewhere in her house. Clark is vacuuming downstairs. Clark is out of his mind. Maybe he's on drugs, though he's not actually scary. Just not entirely Clark.

Cats are slinking into the bedroom. They've never liked the vacuum cleaner, and now, with this new perspective, she can understand why. Cal and Macaroni jump up onto the bed; peg-leg Percy jumps up onto the table. He circles in place a few times, then settles squarely on the little heap of torn-up cards and begins to lick the back of his bad paw. She strokes between the little panels of his shoulder blades. So soft. As if he's hardly in there at all.

The vacuum must be on the stairs, it has become so loud. The stairs act as a sounding board. He mustn't come upstairs, did she tell him that? Wouldn't a person know upstairs is off-limits? She closes the bedroom door without looking out.

She picks up the phone from the bedside table and pushes Speed Dial for Newell. The letter thing won't work for Newel—he's right brain like her. *It's me, but I'm out on my board, I hope, so... you know the drill.*

It's Mom, Newell, you there? Newell? Call me, will you? Nothing urgent but call me? Love you.

She pushes her mother's button. After one ring, she hangs up. It's not fair to tell people over the phone, especially your addled mother, that you're going to die. Thank God Newell wasn't there, though children do expect their parents to die, even if they don't know that they do. She takes the telephone book out from the drawer of the bedside table and leafs through the Yellow Pages to Delta Airlines.

There are many choices in the recorded menu. In spite of the closed door, the din of the vacuum makes it hard to concentrate and she loses her place in the numbers partway through. Maybe she really is inattentive. She hits Redial and works through the branching sequence all over again, arriving, finally, at hold music. Something New Age. Should airlines be New Age? As she listens, she watches Cal lick between his toes. Periodically a voice breaks into the music to say that her call is very important. She hangs up, frustration giving way to relief.

The vacuuming has stopped. The house is still. She has no reason to go downstairs, but resents the loss of that option. Outside her door the coast is clear. She walks across the hall into the living room. Big Guy is draped along the front windowsill. He's the only one in the house—other than Clark, perhaps—unfazed by vacuuming. She looks out the window. Two gulls are perched on the chimney with the cockeyed aerial directly across the street.

Why must some people assume the worst? She wasn't always that way, was she? That was an optimist who came east at twenty and married a Boston bartender. An optimist who moved to Maine pregnant, bought into the real estate venture thing. Had to have been.

I do not have cancer. I do not have cancer. I do not have cancer.

The gulls look all about, briskly cocking their sleek white heads against the immaculate blue. One looks down, right at her.

* * *

Clark is gone. That's a relief, though incomplete. In her situation, there is no such thing as complete relief.

He's not outside either, uphill or down. She walks in the direction of the office where she works, though she's not sure whether she's actually going to work or not, or whether it's even time to go to work. They can get along fine without her: a part-timer, just enough for benefits.

It feels good to walk. She speeds up, walking uphill, until she remembers she has forgotten about cancer. She stops. How can you forget such a thing? And how is it possible that the sky and the gulls and the traffic and the people passing on the sidewalk can all be so fucking ordinary when just beneath the film of her blouse, just beneath the film of her skin, something so horrific is going on? Cells loosed by the scalpel are bobbing along in the currents of her blood to distant parts of her body. Liver. Bone. Who knows, maybe brain. Brain already which is why she can't seem to get a handle on things. She looks down, desperate for some outward sign of all that is going on inside her, some confirmation of her new reality, but all she can make out through her tears is the blurry outline of a slight, familiar self.

Up Congress she hurries, past the shops, the restaurants, the people moving with such purpose. She hates these people on the move, and yet suddenly she adores them: they're all there for her, every one of them, set into motion on her behalf.

She walks past work. The parking lot is full, as usual. She can imagine the waiting room crowded with patients reading magazines, at least holding them. She can imagine the close, windowless chart room where she works filing away all those reports, reading them sometimes, though she's been told, and knows, she shouldn't. Across town, in her surgeon's office, some stranger is filing her report. But a word catches their eye and they're pausing to read it through, all the while knowing they shouldn't. It's the one thing that makes their work interesting. The one saving grace.

She sits down on a bench at the edge of the park just down from the office. It is better to be looking at the office from a safe distance than to be in the office. No way she could do her work properly if she went in. Every word she glimpsed or overheard would make frightful connections. And not just medical words, but every single word in the language of this new land. They would puzzle her as the foreign always does. Alarm her. Certainly distract her. She would misfile things. People would die as a result of her wanton carelessness.

She stands, eyes fixed on the distant office.

I don't want to die.

* * *

Clark is gone. Everything is tidy on the first floor, including the family room where he must have been sleeping on the couch. But when she reaches the doorway at the top of the stairs she can see him in the living room. Or it must be him, lying curled on his left side among the cats in the sunlit center of the floor. Not only Sanders and Macaroni are there, but lots of them, maybe all seventeen of them. With him curled like that. Fetal. Feline. Familiar.

She tiptoes into her bedroom. He has no right to make her tiptoe in her own house, even if it was his house once, even if he did work as hard as she, scrubbing and scraping and sanding and painting, back in the beginning. She is not going to tiptoe any more.

Clark! She's at the living room doorway again. A dozen ears prick up at her voice, but he makes no response. She goes over to him and repeats his name, loud enough this time that it echoes throughout the house.

He rolls onto his back and stretches, smiles up at her, upside down. Hungry?

Pissed.

He gets to his feet, walks over to the windowsill and picks up the small woven-reed tray they bought in Acapulco, and which she hasn't noticed perched there. *I made us veggie roll-ups. And V8. Good for what ails you.*

You have no idea what ails me. Not saying anything does.

No, I guess I don't. He sits down cross-legged in the middle of the floor, working his bare feet under his knees, and sets out the plates and glasses.

She kneels facing him. She's not going to tell him. Then she'd have nothing left.

He peels the wax paper back from the end of his rollup, and takes a bite. *I would like to, though. It would make my visit here worthwhile. More worthwhile I mean.* As he speaks, holding the rollup in both hands, flakes of shredded lettuce sprinkle onto his jeans. With one hand he picks them up individually and sets them in a neat row along the rim of his plate.

I thought you had left finally.

No. I've been in and out. You were almost out of cat litter, too, did you know that? And toilet paper. When you're that out . . . . He takes another bite and chews. Carol peels back her wax paper and begins to eat. The raw vegetables crunch loudly in her head. The dressing is spicy, but good.

So, what are your plans, Clark? You must be looking for a place.

Not really. I've got all summer.

You're not staying here all summer. You do know that, don't you?

I didn't say I was. He takes a long drink from his glass of V8, wipes his lips with the back of his hand. He licks his hand before he goes on. *What I've been thinking is, I could maybe help you.*

And how would that be? Vacuuming? Shopping? Or, oh, I know, you think I must be horny. Because you are. Can't find anybody else so why not give old Carol a try? An old times' sake thing, is that what this is?

No. This is thinking you might want someone to go to the doctor with you. I would. Want someone, I mean.

She sets her rollup down on her plate and stares at him.

It was on your calendar, Carol, in full view. Three appointments. Circled even. As if you wanted . . . .

You son of a bitch! Get out of my house!

She slams the bedroom door behind her.

* * *

He is touching her breast and licking her ear. Only, the pressure hurts her breast, and his tongue is so rough. It abrades more than arouses. Loving was never like this before. Never had this kind of an edge to it before.

Lorenzo yowls as she lurches up on the bed.

Everything all right? Clark sounds so close that he must still be on the second floor. She doesn't dare answer.

She has the phone book out on the bed. Or she could just dial 911. She has every right to call the police on an ex closing in like this.

Minutes pass and nothing happens. She will call Todd instead. It's midnight, but he's a night person at the edge of the time zone. She should have called him long before now. She will tell him she is coming out, spur of the moment. And then, once she's out there, she will tell him everything. They've never been that close, being eight years apart, even through their father's slow death and mother's scenes, but Todd is still her brother, her era. They have a certain history. He will have ins with Cleveland specialists, though he may want to do everything, the way he did with the feeding tube. And Carol isn't sure she wants to do everything. She isn't sure she wants to do anything. Maybe macrobiotics. Two hundred Tylenol. She does not want a feeding tube. Todd has got to understand that.

She paces in her room. She is as much a prisoner in her house as the cats, except they don't know it. You're not really a prisoner if you don't know it. But what's worse, she is a prisoner in her head. Her thoughts are bars she cannot get through: straight and hard and just close enough together. If only she could squeeze between them she could finally turn around and look back in on herself from a distance. Then she'd know what to do.

There is a knock at the door. *How about a little warm milk to help you sleep?*

Go away, Clark. Go away.

The door swings in slowly, silently, and Clark enters, carrying a glass in each hand. *I know it sounds corny, but they say this stuff really works.*

He holds out a glass of the white liquid. She takes it. It is smooth and warm in her hand. Breast-like. She sets it down on her bedside table and shifts over toward the wall, giving Clark room to sit on the edge of the bed. He tests his milk with the tip of his tongue. *Watch out. Still a little on the hot side.* He sets his glass down on the mat on the floor. *So what do you think about Newell's plans?*

Which plans would that be?

Coming back to Sugarloaf plans.

First I heard of it. 'Course his machine isn't all that talkative.

Probably wanted me to buy his plane ticket, is why he called.

He *called* you?

Clark doesn't answer. Maybe he didn't hear. Maybe—is it possible?—he doesn't want to hurt her by appearing to be the favorite of their son. She reaches for her glass and sips the milk, which tastes sweetened. *I'm going out west myself, soon.*

After your appointment.

I'm not keeping the appointment. It's not mine. It's somebody you don't know.

Oh, I think you should, Carol—keep it. We're getting to that age.

She lies back on the bed. Clark slips off his sneakers and lies back next to her, slowly, narrowly. It's only a single bed, yet he barely touches her side.

What do you think you're doing?

I'm harmless. He reaches up and turns off the bedside light. *Believe me, I've become quite harmless in my old age.*

In the darkness she can hear cat claws on hardwood floors. One of them jumps onto the bed, searches around among their limbs, then circles into the crevice between them. She can't tell who it is—maybe Big Guy from the size—but feels rhythmic pressure against the outside of her thigh as he licks himself. A motorcycle, loud as the vacuum, rumbles up the hill at top speed. Then all is quiet except for the familiar drone of Clark's snoring beside her.

* * *

She is alone in the house, except for the cats. She has checked every room and knows she is alone. She makes a bowl of cereal with yogurt and strawberries. Clark has left two boxes of strawberries from the farmers' market in the refrigerator. Farewells.

She will fly out to Ohio the day after the appointment. She will know what she needs to know, and can talk it all out with Todd. And then she'll be there to deal with her mother and can continue on out west to talk with Newell and Lisa face-to-face. One-on-one. That's the way you make decisions. And this whole Clark craziness will be ancient history by the time she comes back. If she comes back. Her only obligation now, as always, is to the cats.

As she's pouring more milk into her empty bowl, and setting it down on the floor, the kitchen door rattles.

Sleep well? Clark has a small white bakery box under his arm. He sets it on the table in front of her, breaks the string, and folds back the top to show her the contents.

Cinnamon doughnuts!

Cinnamon doughnuts. I'll make the coffee. As he gets out the coffee press and puts on the water, he tells her about the weather, which is cooler, he's glad to report; about his walk around the neighborhood. He seems quite animated and goes on about how he should have bought even more Munjoy Hill property back when they first got to Portland, and just held onto it. Ignored his greed—yes, she was right about that, too—and just held onto it. They'd be sitting pretty now, if only he had.

You'd *be sitting pretty.*

We *would, Carol, you must know that by now.*

She bites into her doughnut, which is crunchy on the outside, just the way she always liked it. She hasn't had a cinnamon doughnut in years. It's funny, but you don't just go out and buy a cinnamon doughnut for yourself. It's not the same. She licks the sweet granules carefully from her lips. *You need to be looking for a place to stay, if you really don't have one. But you'll have to get your own newspaper. For the classifieds. I stopped it a while back.*

Oh? He looks truly surprised, presumably about his having to look for a place to stay, not her giving up the paper. He seems unaware of the water boiling over on the stove.

Whatever it is you have in mind, Clark, won't work. You wouldn't want me now anyway.

He doesn't respond, which is a relief because she knew it could be trouble the moment she said it: the opening she had given him. Instead, he rises to pour the boiling water into the coffee press. He stirs, inserts the strainer, applies the cozy. *I'll house-sit and look after the cats for you. How's that sound?*

They can survive.

Yes. Yes. He sits back down at the table with the press and two cups. *All those how many lives among them?*

They sit in silence, watching Percy and Cal lick the last drops of milk from Carol's bowl on the floor. Captain jumps up onto the counter. Bun grooms. Fullbright tries to get something out from underneath the refrigerator with his paw. There is the sound of scratching from somewhere upstairs. When Clark finally pours the coffee, Carol picks up her cup and stands.

I'm going to take a shower. Sleeping in clothes makes you feel dirty.

* * *

The bruise is already turning green and yellow, the tenderness is less. No lump when she probes the spot, though in her mind's eye she can see what's growing in there, sending out its tentacles, its runners. Metastasizing, they write in their reports. She turns slowly, looking up and down her naked torso, and it's then that she realizes the phone is ringing. She peers out the bathroom door, dashes across the hall into her bedroom.

Hello?

Carol Fitzmorris?

Yes?

Just a minute, please, for Dr. O'Donnell.

The bedroom door is ajar. She moves to the limit of the cord, out of the line of sight from the hall.

Carol?

Yes?

Dr. O'Donnell here. Great news, Carol. No cancer.

The phrase hangs in the air before her: visible noise.

Thing we call a papilloma. Benign papilloma. Thought I'd call rather than make you wait until . . . .

She steps back toward the bedside table, the voice dwindling as she lowers the receiver. She inches toward the door, pauses, her hand on the knob, and is suddenly running across the hall and down the stairs two steps at a time, scattering cats as she shouts.

Clark! Clark! Honey!

At the bottom she pulls up short. The house is silent. She lets herself down on the first step. Drops of water slide down her face, down her chest between her breasts, leaving cool trails.

The house is silent. As silent as it was all those years ago when they entered for the first time, and looked about, and dared to imagine their lives taking hold in this strange new place and slowly, surely, filling up its emptiness.

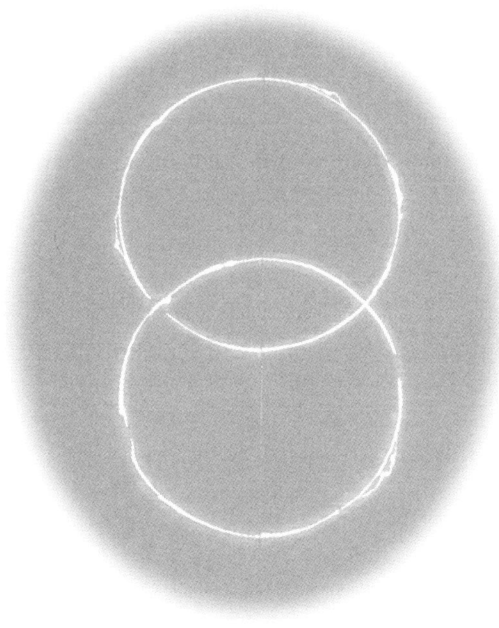

Tony Barnstone

from *The Gifts*

The Problem with Gifts Is that They Punish Us with Their Loss

Blessed is the bed in which they have sex.
Blessed the sheet on which she lies,
blessed her skin and blessed are her breasts,
blessed the body's lamps, her eyes
lighting the room, rolling in dream at night,
and blessed the darkness that descends
and carries them through sleep. Blessed the knot
of limbs entwined, a tangle without end
that only lack of love or death or time
can untie. Blessed moth that eats the wool
sweaters in the closet, blessed blind
earthworm that digs, the termite in the wall
that feeds on them like rot in fruit yet gives
them years alive with blessings in their lives.

Jeff D. Simpson

Hymn

The wrought-iron fence, decorative
metalwork intertwined with white roses,
is alive with the hum of summer bees.

Inside, Quaker pews face one another
like tapestries on opposite ends
of a home, and the hardwood floor,
heavy with the smell of varnish and pine,
shines in the light pouring through gothic
windows. No one speaks.

The idea, I'm told by the friend
who brought me here, is to observe
silence. It is so quiet I can hear
the slow breathing of the woman
sitting next to me who smells of lavender oil.

An hour into service a middle-aged man
stands up and begins talking
about his dead wife, her seven-year
battle with cancer, how he felt when he flung
her ashes into the Potomac on a gray afternoon
last February. There is no resolve
in his voice; he speaks from the gut.
No one replies—a few nod,
but most look out the windows
or carefully unwrap peppermints—
there is no sermon.

They say silence gives meaning to sound,
that if you're still long enough the world
becomes apparent, and you can hear
everything—cancer cells and worker bees,
river water and the sound of iron rods
being hammered and welded into something
beautiful for the climbing rose to cling to and die.

Carole Sineni

We Were Good at It

The first time I came after the news
and I asked "What can I do, honey?"
you said, "Just lie down with me, Mom."
We fell asleep, my arm across you.

Most of the time I wanted to just
scoop you up in a receiving blanket
and take you away with me to some
soft place.
You said, "People die you know, Mom."
I said, "Yes, but not now, honey."

I wanted to talk to you about God
and about all the things that no one
can imagine because this was a movie.
You looked away and opened your
beautiful lips to be fed.

But before things got that bad,
you could remember each turn
on the way to your appointments
while I drove those pretty Bucks County
roads.

You were dizzy and your face
was set as you walked holding on
to me down the corridor to the elevator.

That wig was a dead giveaway.

Tie Her Silk Ribbon

It is rose,
that filament, fine canyon of belief and apprehension,

that butterfly out of sight over the sea glass waves,
gray, and the butterfly dark, iridescent wing
as in a locket, or strange antique brooch.

That distance within nothing, as when hands
touch and their speech is palpable.

Magic as in faith.

The jubilant cosmos
is
no more
or less.

In these you are alive;
and listening as the quiet listens
to itself.

Hear, as though the sea seems to fan and rise,
seems to separate sound at its fragile middle

vibration.

***

Sometimes the stunning violence of disbelief
the incandescent opening of that brutal star
illuminating the space of the fragment

of where I am just then, just reaching for a book,
just looking in the mirror to pin back my hair,

just the melody intimating yearning over my shoulder
looking back, not daring to look.

Promise me you will not go no matter what.
Your soft hand.

Grief

It is in us to grieve.
Sorrow has its own seduction.
We may, like Job, beat our breast,
But the answer is always silence
And the same.
—In memory of Karen and John

We grieve

for lost little boys and drowned girls
whose innocence is offended by the shadows

in the lovely waving trees, the waves of sedge and sea.

We grieve for all beauty which goes away

sauntering the slope of the reclining beach and leaving
behind only sea foam

or one perfect whelk
on sand slicked by scalloped tide and shining.

And always the waves and the rosy clouds toss and toss
and the blue world is flung with dolphins and blue water.

The scarlet lightness of children's laughter
confounds us,
so ponderous and ponderous is the sea.

Richard M. Berlin

The Juggler

The juggler's drum
loud with my head's penny.
—*Paul Célan*

After he juggles three chainsaws and spins
twenty plates balanced on sticks, he moves
to the grand finale: ten bowler hats tossed
across the arena and stacked on the ringmaster's
head. He gets to nine and misses, and misses
the tenth three more times, cheers rising
to a roar with each failure, until the drum
rolls and the spotlight finds him for the final
throw when he nails the last hat on top
of the stack and the audience stomps their praise.

Next morning, when I straighten my hat
it hits me: the misses were part of the act,
the juggler knowing the crowd would admire
his skill, but would love him even more for
his imperfections. And when I arrive
at my office, where there are no stage lights,
drum rolls or applause, and the crowd
I work will only suffer more if I screw up,
I stand under my shingle juggling
the books and briefcase in my arms,
turn over the lock with a silver key,
and walk up the long flight of stairs,
my head bowed, rumpled hat in hand.

Last Concert of the Summer

The moon comes up like a melody
from a sad old love song. On stage,
the orchestra plays a Mozart concerto,
summer slowing down on the last weekend
before the world goes back to work.
This has been a season of sick friends—
heart attacks, Hodgkins, MS and cancer
all scraping their one-note symphonies.
Saddest of all has been the young man
I've known since birth, who sees conspiracy
in the stars and the moon's jaundiced eye,
the medicines of our trade and Mozart's
triumphant music too weak to cure him.
The white-robed conductor waves his wand
and sways like a dancer at the crescendo,
me in the back row picturing the way
I place a stethoscope in my ears and listen
to the heart when I've run out of things to say.

At the Chamber Music Concert

He aims his clarinet like a divining rod
pointed toward Brahms' body buried deep
in the clay, the notes shimmering through
the audience and pouring out the opened
windows, into the garden where the last lilac
blossoms glide to the ground and iris flags
stand tall and unfold their stellar blues.
The world has been so beautiful this spring
with rain falling in a random rhythm,
the tilled soil like cake in my hands,
days when high pressure built in and filled
the hills with cobalt afternoons and violet dusk,
high meadows and old trees fresh with green,
all the wildflowers shaking their heads
"yes, yes" in the wind. Now, at twilight
the night-blooming nicotiana filling the room
with its strong perfume, my friend Andre
next to me on a sofa, bald from his third round
of chemo, smiling as he nods his head
in time to the music, closing his eyes
when the clarinet caresses the last three notes.

Andrew Malan Milward

Forever Swimming

There is his brain, a hedge apple of noodly tissues, which without your knowledge has already begun to disappear. It's Sunday afternoon and you're strumming the guitar, working on a song you can never seem to finish as the hushed sounds of the television rumble below the bass line. Rain hits the concrete outside, sounding like thousands of jaws clacking shut one after the other. You put the guitar down and stare at the television as the dread of returning to work in the morning begins to set in, and you can feel yourself already stepping into your trousers, buttoning down your oxford.

It's not until you're in bed that night that the call comes from your stepsister, an inherently positive woman, but now her voice sounds strange, stuck in limbo between happy and sad. She's at the hospital and she's breaking a rule by using her cell phone, she tells you. "I can't talk long," she says. "It's Daddy." It will take several more minutes of confusion before you begin to understand that your stepfather has had a stroke.

It's all so ironic, you'll think, later. He and your mother in town, here in Missouri, visiting from New York, for only three days to celebrate Thanksgiving—a trip, barely long enough to contact old friends, that, for your stepfather, will end up lasting fifteen more days; two weeks of waiting at the hospital for clearance to leave, hoping those pieces of his brain, the shards of memory, return home like a wayward puppy.

The call ends cryptically with your stepsister saying, "I'm not allowed to use this here. They say I have to shut it off." It's the harrowing and selfless last communication of a spy before raising the vial of cyanide to lip as the enemy beats down the door, the ruse finally up. You're left standing there holding the phone, trying to understand what the hell has happened. Do you drive to the hospital? Should you try calling back your stepsister? Attempt to call your mom? There is no protocol for the situation, so you freeze.

You sleep on it, you tell yourself, *that's what you do*, and it's not until the next morning on your way to work that you stop at Boone County Hospital and get the whole story from the man you timidly classify as your stepbrother-in-law. He's your stepsister's husband. Your stepfather's son-in-law. Your mother's stepson-in-law—the nomenclature of divorce and remarriage is a thesaurus of familial synonyms, your connection not blood but the hyphen. Your stepbrother-in-law is himself a doctor, a mender of ears, noses, and throats. He's also your boss; you work for him at his practice downtown.

Some explanation is required, you tell people when the subject of your family comes up. There is your *brother*, the one with whom you share a mother, a tiptoe-walking, puzzle-solving poet. And there are your mother and father, sure, dueling professors on opposite coasts (he in California, she in New York), survivors of the sneak-divorce, now the practitioners of the post-lapsarian chilly phone call, committed to *doing what's best for our boys*. Your father was the first to remarry. So entered stepmother-one and your baby half-brother, whose earthworm fingers marveled you over a decade before when you first inspected him in the terminal at LAX after getting off the long plane ride to your father's; by that time you were already a seasoned traveler at nine years old and used to the *you-take-Christmas-I'll take-spring-break* shuffle between parents. Your father was also the first to get re-divorced and so followed stepmother-two several years later, and she came bearing gifts: two more boys, brothers, steps. And then there was this: after a decade of being single, your mom finally remarries, this time to a man 25 years older. He has one daughter and because of the age discrepancy your older brother, the poet, will drive you crazy by labeling her with the misnomer "aunt." But she's not our aunt, you say. She's our stepsister.

How to describe your stepfather:

He is a man, now retired, who owned an appliance store for forty years and knows the importance of washing off all plates before placing them in the dishwasher—he has seen a perfectly good Maytag with another five years of life ruined by a single defiant cantaloupe seed; a man who prided himself on "knowing every person in Columbia, Missouri," scanning passersby for a hearty handshake, a firm grasp of the shoulder, a winking off-color joke—he of the sickly smile, chicken-hawk sneeze, and infectious laugh track; he is a lover of the mounted electronic singing fish (which he will gladly play for anyone who indulges him), train songs from the '30s and '40s, and a closet devotee of hour-long teen-targeted television dramas; a man who, to his friends' and family's surprise, left Columbia and moved to Brooklyn with you, your brother, and your mother a decade before; a man who had returned to Missouri just days ago to visit his daughter's family for the holiday and who, after the turkey hangover and after you'd left to go back to your apartment, entered the guestroom of his daughter's house to take a nap and woke up repeating the same question over and over: *Where's Mary? Where's Mary?* (Mary, his wife. Mary, your mother.) And now he is the man who lies in the bed before you smiling, looking pleased as punch, completely unaware of the Armageddon going on inside his head.

For years you'll wonder about that moment, the moment he lay down to sleep and the stroke happened instead. What caused it? Some dreamlike terror or errant fancy in the throes of R.E.M., eyes aflutter like the wings of a frightened bird. (You think of dogs you've seen asleep, dreaming, and how they move their paws in front of them. They must be having a nightmare, you think. Someone is chasing them.) What was that final memory before they all began disappearing? It's the stuff of epic poems, the conundrums that cause you to stare off into space at work.

Here in the hospital your stepbrother-in-law dumbs it down for you as much as verbally possible and it's still a vocabulary you can't quite decipher. The how and the why remain mysteries, coded in physician's speak, but what's real and what you understand is that the person, this skinny old man, sitting up in the bed before you is not quite right.

He recognizes you, says hello, and then asks where your mother is. A further irony in this whole circus (or is it just a swift kick to the balls?—you tend to conflate the two) is that your mom has already returned to New York; she purchased an earlier return ticket than he did so that she could get back to teach by Monday and he, being retired, could stay with his daughter for an extra week here in Missouri. She must have arrived at Kennedy, you speculate, around the time he lay down for that last nap. At the moment nothing seems coincidental. When he asks where she is again five minutes later you understand the gist of what has happened: the stroke has left him with no short-term memory. She had to fly back to New York yesterday, you say, remember? "New York," he says, bewildered, like you're trying to trick him, like he doesn't know he's lived there the last ten years with your mom.

It's early in the morning before work. You'll return at lunch and then again after five to check on him, a pattern you'll come to live by and depend upon in the coming weeks, but at the moment you notice your stepbrother-in-law, your boss, glance down at his watch and you both know there are sick people already queuing up outside the locked door of his ENT practice like World Series ticket hopefuls, waiting to be prodded, poked, and cured. For you there are surgeries to schedule, insurance benefits to verify, and patients' charts you'll waste hours searching for. It is time to help people; you have to go to work.

* * *

At lunch you walk into his room and find your stepsister sitting at his bedside, eyes puffed up like portabellas from the combination of crying and sleeplessness. You're relieved by her presence, not ready to be alone with him yet. You think of stroke victims you've seen in movies and expect him to be paralyzed, comatose, or nonverbal, but he looks happy as a clam with his plate of cartoon food: formless and unicolor, served in gobs and dollops.

How are things going? you ask.

"Pretty good, right, Daddy," your stepsister says with a forced enthusiasm, looking at him and soldering a smile to her lips.

He doesn't answer and then looks at you and asks, "Is your mom down at the beach?"

Beach? You come to realize over the course of 45 minutes that he thinks he's in a hotel; your mom, he believes, is swimming.

"Daddy, you're in Boone County Hospital," your stepsister reminds him and then adds, "in Columbia, Missouri," when he looks at her confused. She is Sisyphean in her belief that if she says it enough it will start to register but he's always surprised to find out he's not on vacation at some seaside resort. Later, as a litmus test, she points to a banana and asks him what it is.

He chuckles like a boy-genius who's received a softie in the first round of a game show and says, "Applesauce."

It's more than just his memory that's impaired. A doctor informs you that this is normal for a stroke that affects this part of the brain. He analogizes the situation to the state of the universe after the Big Bang, saying that things have broken apart and are jumbled inside your stepfather's head, and, he affirms, there will be something of a reorientation period as, mentally, things start to realign—hopefully, that is. You stand there watching your stepfather, teething your chapped lips as the pulpy flakes of skin fall off onto your tongue. It's too much to take, watching him lying there completely unaware of what's happened to him, so you offer a quick goodbye and the promise of return. You leave the room to drive the long mile back to work, where despite yourself you'll break down between phone calls to patients who have scheduled surgeries with your stepbrother-in-law. People who have no money, high deductibles, and paralytic vocal folds, infectious tonsils, and mutant adenoids. Having worked there only a month, you haven't quite adjusted to your role as office hatchet man, collector of patient prepays. On the phone your voice quavers as the ball-less bearer of bad news: "I called to verify your insurance benefits and—good news—they will cover the surgery. So that's a good thing. Um, now you do have a $1000 deductible and none of that's been met. In accordance with office policy—that sheet you signed when you scheduled the procedure—we'll need that a week before the surgery." You labored over the writing of this spiel and have it taped to the plastic covering your keyboard, and yet somehow you can never manage to say it without sounding like a complete moron.

* * *

He's surrounded by family when you return after work that first day: his daughter, his grandson, his son-in-law, and now you appear, his stepson. It's the tableau of a morbid Christmas card. He's smiling and laughing. Everyone's smiling and laughing, playing the game where they pretend nothing is different. There is a basketball game on the television, the Tigers and Jayhawks are playing, and he looks at the game clock on the screen and says, "Twelve dollars and forty-one cents. How about that!"

You look at his grandson, your step-nephew, and wish he weren't seeing this happen to the man he idolizes. It's hard enough for you and your relationship with your stepfather has always been difficult. He came into your life as a seventy-three-year-old man, born and raised on a farm in rural Missouri in the '20s and '30s, at the time you were entering your misanthropic teenage years, used to being raised by a single mother. There were power issues and muted conflicts, which you both assuaged by becoming masters of passive aggression. A chortle here, a snicker there, an insincere *I-was-only-kidding* retraction. He recoiled more and more, comforted by the sermons of conservative talk radio and the impassioned belief that anyone under the age of thirty was culpable in driving the world headlong into the throes of hell, as did you, retiring each day after school to your bedroom universe to bang loudly on your guitar for hours on end. But there were those other times when, moments of compromise, listening to him tell an old war story or laughing at a dirty joke he'd overheard—going as a family to a romantic comedy in support of his secret idolatry of Julia Roberts—where things had been good, and while maybe not as your father, you saw him as a good man who loved and would do anything for your mother, and that, you figured, was just about as good as you could ask for.

You've got several years on his grandson (still a teenager) and seeing him over the past year in his pre-college wonder and infinite sense of possibility makes your life feel static.

Your life is this:

After four years of higher learning out west, you've recently moved back to Columbia, Missouri, the town where you were born, where much of your early youth was spent before moving to New York with your mother, brother, and stepfather ten years ago. And now you're taking some time off. Sowing your oats. Backpacking around your apartment. Taking a break. Decompressing. *You could use some rest, after all.* But what you're really trying to do, like so many philosophy majors before you, is to reconcile the practical and existential concerns of your existence; you're trying to figure out what the hell to do with your life. Right now that has something to do with making music, but it all feels so much less dignified and more desultory than your brother who's in New York City writing verse in the Masters program at Columbia—that *other* Columbia, academic and metropolitan, full of Ivy and subways. There is a salient difference between the two of you. Your brother is a *poet* and you're the poet laureate of mopy folk songs; he writes in syllabics and you in self-pity; he is a student of metrics and you of melancholy. You are the patron saint of the break-up song and a low fidelity impresario, tinkering on your analog 4-track long hours into the night after getting off work. You've graduated and this is your year off (either one of many or just one, you haven't decided), a year in which the only thing you've resolved to do is record an album that will surely be snatched up by an important indie label that will allow you to pay rent writing the same sad songs in different keys. A slight change in melody. A bridge here, an outro there.

That night, at the end of your stepfather's first full day in the hospital, you call your mom to break the news, to try to explain what's going on. You get hold of her just as she's entered the subway station and the reception on her cell phone begins to cut in and out. You expect her to crumble to the floor in shock but come to find your stepsister has already spoken to her. "Had a little stroke, bless his heart," she says with a tenderness usually reserved for infants failing their first steps. It runs contrary to the feeling you've felt all day, this confused stupor. You want her to feel it, too. In the background you can hear the slamming of train doors. "Does he seem okay?" she asks after a beat of static. You tell her that physically he seems the same, that most of the damage appears to be mental. "Oh, that's a relief," she says as another patch of static cuts between you and she adds, "What? Hello, are you there?" You have more you need to tell her. But it's like he's in another world, Mom, you say, starting to shout so she'll hear. You'll soon realize, however, that it's something you'll never be able to convey to someone who hasn't been there in the room with him. "I'm trying to get a flight back out, but it's almost finals week and having just gotten back here it's not easy to just turn around and..." she trails off. "I'll talk to the department chair tomorrow about my classes and get in touch with the airlines. See if they can get me back to Missouri. Tomorrow," she says. "I'm working on it. I promise." You can hear someone playing guitar in the subway for money and then a loud voice comes over a speaker, muffled so you can't make out the destination. She is cutting out. You can hardly hear her now. Mom, you say, where are you? Where are you going?

* * *

His second morning at the hospital he puts on his clothes, takes off his patches, wires and I.V., and walks out of his room, past the nurses' station, down the elevator, and out the sliding doors of the entrance. In a panic, with a fever that only potential lawsuits arouse, orderlies and nurses pull on their winter coats and throw their scarves over their shoulders like World War II bombardiers, descending on the surrounding neighborhoods to search for him. When they finally find him a few blocks away, he's blowing into his hands, wondering where he can get a hot cup of coffee. You get the story from your stepsister when you arrive a little later before work. The nurses are busy installing a door alarm that will beep any time someone enters or leaves the room. "Daddy went for a little walk this morning," your stepsister says. It's nowhere near that point at which the story enters the family mythology and becomes funny, something everyone can laugh about looking back. Your stepsister's shaking, with anger or fear you're not sure. You try to hug her, clumsily wrapping your arms around her, and looking over her shoulder you see him in his bed, hands clasped on his chest, blanket pulled up to his chin, and realize he's already forgotten about his little exodus.

* * *

The first time you're alone with him, watching him build little monuments in his mashed potatoes, the heart doctor comes in. He's a tall, strong-looking man who has a Tony Robbins-empowered goatee and *white, white* teeth that make you want to keep your mouth shut—the kind of man you can actually feel yourself shrinking next to, slowly disappearing. He has board-certified confidence and optimism from years of reasoning tragedy and disappointment. He is the kind of man who takes bedside manner as seriously as surgery, mussing your hair a little when you shake hands, like you're three years old. But for a few minutes the heart doctor slips, talking about your stepfather like he's not in the room—"he's going to need a pacemaker"—then finally looks at him, lowers his voice, and says, "I heard about the jailbreak this morning." Your stepfather just grins. It's a look you'll come to recognize. He'll do it often. It's a cover-up, this grinning smile, something that appears on his face whenever he doesn't want to admit he has no idea what you're talking about, like the nasal, soulless laughter at a joke you don't understand. Then the heart doctor's tone changes again. "We're gonna have to put you on that rat poison," he says, clapping his hands and rubbing them together. This must be how he deals with it, you think—adopting different characters to speak for him. His character now is some kind of southern pirate (part Black Beard, part Huey Long), who's adept in the no-frills communication of bad news. "Have to with the pacemaker," he drawls out. For a brief instant you'll consider using this technique when you return to the office that afternoon to make calls to patients who owe your stepbrother-in-law money, but you'll chicken out the second you hear breathing on the other end of the line.

"Rat poison? You mean Coumadin?" your stepfather says, perking up a little. Somehow he remembers this. Surely many of his friends are on it. "No, I don't need that."

"We're gonna have to. Gotta regulate that heartbeat so this doesn't happen again," the heart doctor smiles.

Your stepfather seems to like this man, seems to think this jokey report is fun, and laughing, puts up his hands and delivers a classic: "No way, man."

"You'll do fine— but you can't eat anything green," he says, still smiling.

Your stepfather just laughs. He's a health nut: king of Brussels sprouts, a champion of broccoli and antioxidants. God, you think, the times at the apartment in Brooklyn you'd walked into the kitchen, hit by the stale, flatulent smell of boiling broccoli. He's eaten it twice a day ever since you've known him. You worry this restriction will crush him, but for now he still thinks it's a joke.

The heart doctor, not wanting to be neglectful, turns and starts in on you, asking where you're from. I'm from New York, you say, then stammer, adding, and, well, Missouri. I grew up here in Columbia, but also New York, you clarify. We left when I was in middle school, when my mother got a job at a university in the city. The heart doctor whistles, long and slow, saying with appreciation, "The City." He nods his head. "Spent a little time there myself. What are you doing back here of all places?" The truth is that though you never admit this (you tell anyone who'll listen that you're a New Yorker through and through), Missouri has always felt like home. You don't say this now though. Instead you mutter something about your music, which elicits an eruption of spastic interrogation: *Music, huh; Folk songs, rock songs—like Dylan, you can do both; Change the world; Didn't he date Baez?; How about you—handsome guy like yourself?; Where's the little lady?; No ring, I see; But I guess you're a rock star; Girl in every port, right?* You want to tell him you haven't had a girlfriend in two years, sex in 5 months, and that you're still writing songs about girls who probably don't remember your name, but the man just prattles on and on until your stepfather looks up at him and, interrupting, says, "He's a musician, you know," pointing at you. It sounds odd coming from his mouth, distinguished almost. He leans forward, toward the heart doctor, and enunciating heavily, whispers, "He's going to give me the first listen of his compact disc." The heart doctor looks at you. You shrug and realize that after all those years living together in New York, no doubt having driven him crazy by turning up your amp too loud as you trundled through the various phases of your teens—punk, pop, grunge, blues, and garage rock—it's the first time he's ever acknowledged your music.

* * *

In the days that follow you notice that order becomes increasingly important to him. He rearranges his bedside table constantly, moving around his remote, ice water, orange, and blue-foiled yogurt a few inches every hour. He frequently reads the time and date off the wall facing him and announces it to you. Old friends from town, even former customers from his appliance days, come to smile, shake hands, tell a joke, deliver flowers, and leave. When he's nervous he picks at the skin of his fingertips or runs his palm over his bald head, tics you've never seen before.

One night after work you're watching the evening news with him when your stepsister arrives and takes a seat next to his bed. He can't follow narrative longer than a few minutes, and for this reason he enjoys watching commercials, but he seems to watch now to be polite. The main story is about the possibility of Iraq having nuclear weapons. You watch in silence and when it cuts to commercial your stepsister looks at him and asks, "Well, what do you think, Daddy? Does he have the nukes?"

He's looking down at his fingertips, picking at them, and without missing a beat assuredly confirms, "He's got twelve, but he's only going to use four."

The amazing thing to you is how utterly pleasant he is. All the negativity and pessimism that made him difficult to be around those years in New York seems to have vanished now that he's back in Missouri, now that he's had a stroke. The first time you and your stepsister eat lunch away from the hospital she confides, "This is how I remember my father. Kind, sweet, generous, funny." What she would never say, but nevertheless hovers in the air between the two of you, is that he didn't stop being all these things until he moved away from Columbia with you and your family. A slow-moving guilt settles into your stomach, nestling up to the burrito you've just inhaled after suffering though several days of the cafeteria's red Jell-O and three-bean salad. "Do you need anything else?" she asks, motioning toward your plate. I'm stuffed, you say, shaking your head and thinking that she's right. He is sweet and kind and funny, these characteristics he apparently always possessed, but they are hard won. He pays a price for them. For their return he must fight to maintain some control of his mind—to retrain it—by counting the stacked boxes of Kleenex in his room over and over, pointing and repeating aloud: One, two, three. One, two three.

* * *

After the surgery to put in his pacemaker, they move him to Intensive Care so they can monitor his heart better. It's the first time he's left his room since he snuck out and you're the only one there with him when they move him. He's flanked by two nurses and he smiles at all the people he passes, sometimes laughing and saying hello, as though seeing an old acquaintance. The nurses have their hands on his arms to steady him, but you see the restriction this puts on him. It's the image of an infirm Franklin Roosevelt, propped up by his security detail, unable to shake hands, struggling to maintain connections with people.

He lies down on his new bed and no sooner does he ask you where your mother is than the I.C.U. nurses come storming in and go to work, strapping him to machines and an I.V. They tape something to his index finger that glows red and will closely monitor his heartbeat. They are silent automatons, these nurses, and for some reason it's all done in the manner of extreme urgency. You're back against the wall and feel guilty, like a flat-footed bystander whose video camera happens to be rolling as a mugging occurs. You see, really for the first time, fear and uncertainty begin to prune his face, perhaps slowly becoming aware of the reality of the situation, that this is no hotel, that something bad has happened to him, and you start speaking, trying to explain what they are doing, that everything is okay. A minute later, when they are finished and leave the room, you see him look down in confusion at his glowing finger and shake it back and forth a few times. Then he folds his arms across his chest, looks at you, and smiles timidly. There are no words to exchange now, only looks, gestures. You can see he's still scared and that his smile is not an attempt to convince himself that things will be okay; it is meant for you.

* * *

The drugs they give him after the surgery make him slip in and out of sleep. He seems to dream the second he closes his eyes. In sleep his right hand reaches out before him. Initially you think it is the conjurer's pose, ready to bring something to fruition, but it comes to look more and more like what it is: a hand reaching for something always a little out of grasp.

* * *

Columbia is the exact halfway point between Kansas City and St. Louis. It sits in the middle of the state, lonely as a tennis net, the forgotten and sullen middle child. At times you crave the speed and activity of New York, but you've warmed to this town again, the place where you grew up so long ago. You haven't played a song since it happened. Most nights after you return from the hospital the guitar sits quietly in the corner of the room as voices from the apartments surrounding you on all sides filter through the vents and walls. You feel as though you're suffocating and begin going for long walks downtown in the evening. You stroll past the closed and lighted shop windows of stores that line 9th Street and stop before the tall windows of the building that used to house your stepfather's appliance store. Today it is a cigar shop. You stare into the window and try to imagine him inside selling fridges to customers, but the waning light is tricky and when you pull back all you catch is the outline of your form in the dirty, print-smudged glass.

Afterwards you stop at the cheap bar for a dollar pint and smoke, watching whichever Missouri team is playing on the television, then leave, again walking, offering cigarettes in lieu of change to the last of the transients, who will soon clear out of the downtown for winter only to reappear in spring like dogwoods in bloom. You walk and walk until the backs of your knees begin to smart and usually end up near the university, catching the last bit of sun sinking between the twin stacks of the power plant before disappearing altogether.

* * *

He's less lucid now, but you're still there with your stepsister's family, listening to him sleep. You want to be there for the moments he's awake, having begun to jot down in your notebook all the strange things he says—to turn them into song lyrics, or just to remember, maybe. Each night you call your mom to update her about the situation and to find out when she'll be coming. You want to ask her why she hasn't arrived yet, thinking that it shouldn't be taking this long, but she tells you horror stories of wrangling with the airlines and trying to find people to fill in for her at the university. "It's not just teaching," she says, "there are committees, meetings, conferences, doctoral defenses, writing the final exams...obligations, you know...." You tell her you know, scrolling over your youth for testaments of her devotion to the academy: missed dinners and gigs, postponed birthdays and holidays. Some nights she sounds terribly sad and others strangely happy. You wonder what being away from all of this must be doing to her. At the end of the nightly conversations, when the pauses grow longer and more awkward, you tell her something funny that your stepfather said that day and she chuckles wearily.

One afternoon early in the second week his eyes open suddenly and he begins reciting his favorite joke. It's about the time he was running an air base in China during World War II. Air raids from Japanese planes would send the men running for cover into the slit trenches. On this night a young private was late in making it to the trenches and when he jumped in he landed on top of the base chaplain. "Oh shit, Father," the private says, "I'm sorry." But the chaplain's so deep in prayer that he doesn't respond. The air strikes are crashing all around them and the private starts to get nervous, crying. He hasn't been in too many of these situations, so he begs the chaplain, shaking him, to send up a prayer on his behalf. This finally breaks the chaplain's concentration and he turns to the whimpering private and says, "Pray for your own Goddamn soul!" You've all heard it a hundred times, and it makes you happy to hear him say it now. No one else could get a laugh with this story, but it's hilarious the way he tells it, and your stepfather is wise enough to know it succeeds because it's true. You like this joke and, having the sense of humor of a pet rock, you try to learn from it. Six months from now, long after he's returned to New York with your mother, you will attempt to make your first and only joke. The joke goes something like this:

So there's this old man who's had a stroke and has never fully recovered. Physically he's fine, but mentally he's a little spotty. Mostly it's memory and time perception problems. He has to take a lot of medications and this makes him very tired. He spends most of his day in the same spot on the couch before the running ticker of the market, looking at stocks he's long since lost money on and sold, falling in and out of sleep the entire day, and when he wakes it's in a fog of dream and memory. He asks strange questions. *What farm are we at? Did you make the call? How long have we lived here?* His wife's 25 years younger and is a professor, but manages to fix her schedule so that she can be with him most of the time with the exception of one night class a week. On this night she asks her son, who happens to be a poet, to come over and spend the evening with him and make sure he eats and takes his medicine. So one night the son comes over and, with his noisy arrival through the entryway, wakes up the old guy, his stepfather. The old guy is slow to come out of the fog and the first thing he says is, "Why's he looking at me?" It's just the two of them, so the stepson says, "Who?" and the old guy says, "That black guy," pointing towards the wall at an African tribal mask his wife traded for years ago when she was in the Peace Corps. "It's just a mask," the stepson says, but the old guy is so disoriented that he doesn't believe him. It is night and the house is dark, so the old guy gets up with a flashlight and inspects the mask, shining the light directly on it. "I'll be damned," he says, running his fingers over the wooden carving.

It's funny to you and you'll tell it a few times, but the reception will be lukewarm, a polite half-smile, a light snort of the nostrils or perfunctory chuckle—no deep belly laughter. The set-up takes too long or is missing something, so you'll decide to stop telling it.

* * *

It becomes a waiting game. He is waiting to pass a test that says he's safe to fly and you're waiting for your mother to arrive and take him home. She's gotten other professors to cover her final exams and has even finagled the airline into moving his initial return ticket, now lapsed, to a future date. She's a little tickled when she calls from the apartment in Brooklyn. "Now we don't have to eat that ticket," she says. She sounds relieved, either for not having lost money on the ticket or because she'll finally be able to see her husband, you're not sure. She has to stay to teach a couple more classes, but just two more days, she says. There is a pause as you try to figure out what to say, wanting to tell her she should have been here sooner. "The city is beautiful," she says, stretching out the words. "They're decorating the buildings and trees for Christmas. They'll turn the lights on soon. Remember the lights?"

* * *

The frustration begins to show. Periodically he'll start to take off the wires and get up from his bed, saying, "Well, I think I'm going to go home now. When Mary gets back from the beach, tell her I'm in the car." And when you or your stepsister tell him no, that he has to stay, he says, "I do?" in disbelief, and then leans back down and gloomily concedes, "Okay." His arms are all bruises from blown I.V. lines and injections. Sometimes he'll lift up his arms and turn them underneath the overhead light, saying, "What the hell happened to me?"

* * *

You take the Saturday night shift so that your stepsister can have her first evening alone with her husband. You were going to catch a band at the Blue Note, but it's okay, you have come to actually like the whole roiling cosmos of the hospital—its regularity, the cycles of pills, meals, and tests, the abject grace you see daily in the broken bodies of the sick and dying. Mostly you like being in the room with him, listening to him talk or watch television. Tonight you're in luck; one of the networks is showing *It's a Wonderful Life*. The two of you watch in the dark and periodically he laughs whenever someone says, *I wish I had a million dollars—hotdog!* And later, as Jimmy Stewart runs through the streets of Bedford Falls screaming *Merry Christmas*, trying to make it home *to his wife, Mary*, you begin to cry, like you always do. It's one of the few films that does this to you and you're not sure why. You look at him and he seems to be asleep, but a few minutes later, as the credits roll, he says, "That's a great show." He looks over at you and sees you're wet-cheeked in the dark corner beside his bed. He leans forward a little to look at you. "Do you need some fire?" he says, pointing to the lamp beside him. "I've got some over here. Would you like some?" You say, no thanks, and he looks back at the TV and becomes transfixed by the singing elves of a holiday commercial.

Your mother is asleep in Brooklyn and in the morning she will board a plane for St. Louis, where she'll rent a car and drive the two hours to Columbia. You picture her alone in her bed and it makes you think back to the afternoon your stepfather lay down for that last nap before the stroke. The questions still fester. You wish somehow you'd been inside his head so you could see what he'd been dreaming in the moments before it happened. You take out your notebook and flip through the pages of notes you've taken down over the past two weeks, scanning his drugged and infantile dictation for clues. You haven't touched the guitar in two weeks and you know you'll never be able to write a song about it. You wish your brother had been here to see this and write about it. It's the job of the poet, you think. You want to understand and, as you once heard some writer say, to write *is* to understand. But still, it seems the kind of poem one could spend a lifetime trying to write and never finish, because to do so would be to square all proofs, to bridge the disconnect between word and thing, to complete the epic. It would mean putting yourself in someone else's head and erasing entire years of conversations, whole transcripts of daytime radio, ten years of memories that made them afraid to leave the house, loathing the world. To understand would mean believing you're always somewhere other than you actually are and that your wife, locked in the grasp of a treacherous undertow, drifting away in the ocean like one of your own feathered memories, is forever swimming.

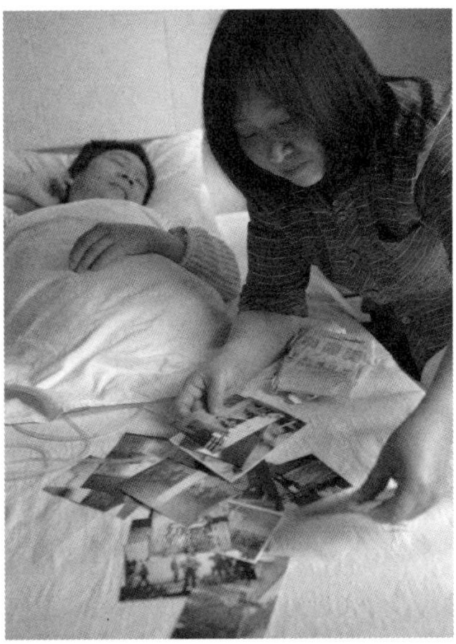

Jia Yuchuan, *Half-Body Man: Peng Shuilin's Story*, photograph.

Rafael Campo

Absolution

The moon rises over the willow tree
like an aspirin in the sky,
bright white pill for all the world's ailments
remember Nonna at age eighty-three

refusing to take all her medicine.
She said she'd rather be read to in bed,
an old-fashioned love story, or instead
an article from *Reader's Digest*. When

my uncle found her one morning, her face
in halves, one peaceful and the other slack,
the doctor said she'd had a major stroke.
Two white pills sat there on a china plate,

just like the ones you bring me now. The night
is like this headache I can't shake, so full
of shapeless troubles: brave young soldiers killed,
the rising price of crude, gay marriage rights,

and worst of all, my fear of losing you.
"Doctors make the worst patients," you declare,
which sounds like something she would say before
she lost her words. Like her, I want a few

good moments rooting for my hero to
return, I want a happy ending. "No,"
I say, and push the pills away. You go,
the moon outside our window bathing you

in what seems, briefly, the absence of pain.

John Surowiecki

from *American Stroke*

1
America Wakes up in a Hospital Room

America believes he's talking to his brother Stanley
who drowned ten years ago in the summer of 1956.
Gienka, America's devoted wife, and I, his only son
[freshly re-minted by our state university], are there
as well, only less radiant. He tries to speak,
but his words slide *glissando*-like in and out of meaning.
He says something about Stanley being a fish out
of water, a *Pan Ryba*, a Mr. Fish, the indifferent hero
and purple-hearted warrior who refused to march
in parades or drink the drinks a grateful nation
wanted to buy for him. Gienka says that Stanley
was by far the handsomest of the three brothers:
She says: *He looked a little bit like Franchot Tone.*

2
America Develops a Taste for Jell-O

America never ate Jell-O at home which makes
Gienka wonder if she'd been making it wrong
all these years. *You just add hot water, no?* The nurses
say that maybe she didn't cover it with Saran Wrap
which keeps the hard film from forming or that
maybe she'd kept it in the fridge for so long

it took on the smells of whatever else was in there,

e.g., carp and pig's feet. She could've done this for him,
dazzled him with orange, cherry, strawberry, lemon,
added pieces of apple, even bits of marshmallow.
The nurses bring him the Jell-O no one else wants.
He can't get enough of it and tells Gienka the secret
to good-tasting Jell-O must be serving it in cubes.

3
Mr. Szmykleszczwladeczeryniecki

America finds himself in a small semiprivate room
with Mr. Szmykleszczwladeczeryniecki who once worked
in a foundry and speaks little English. He says it saddens
him to learn. His head is large and severely triangular.

It looks like a Vicks cough drop. Gienka likes him
because he's sweet and has European manners.
He says something bad is living inside him,
but none of us understands what he means.

Is it a virus? a germ? a tapeworm? We ask:
Jak to sie nazywa po angielsku?—What do you call it
in English? He puts his hand to his stomach and says:
Oh, cancer.

6
Two Old Women

America manages to talk about a day
In January when he and Gienka
went walking along the beach,
deserted except for them and two
old women who wore lacy black hats
and stood on frail birdlike legs.

America showed them conch shells
filled with living ice, greenish and aspic-
speckled. Using their walking sticks
they wrote their initials in the sand
and smiled to each other when the Sound

erased what they had written. Like gulls,
they were slow to sidestep the spreading
fans of waves: they barked at each other
and engaged in short irritated tangos
that brought them within inches
of where each dance began.

10
The Angel of Life

Mr. Szmykleszczwladeczeryniecki says
every hospital is a hotel for *anioly smierci*,
angels of death. They live in unoccupied
rooms and if the hospital is full they live
in the basement near the furnace.

He sees them every day, human-shaped
globs of plasma, speckled with dust,
gliding in and out of doorways, writing
and erasing names in their watery books.

Gienka, he says, is the angel of life.
Just the sight of her in her mustard coat
and black beret adds another day to his life.
All he sees of her body are her hands and face
and these, he insists, are made of light.

Terry Blackhawk

Missing the Caves

—in the south of France

At the hospital in Sarlat, we found him
struggling with what Roethke might have called
a loosening into the dark.

My mother wanted him to slough off the vision
he'd set underway, but he insisted on incense
and candles, a cantor's song—and even,
or perhaps, some priestess—chanting.

My father dreamed for years
of epiphanies he'd find beneath the hills
of the Dordogne. I guess he'd meant to turn
his "Homage to a Cromagnon Stone Carver"
into pilgrimage, but now there would be

no door opening in the side
of a hill, no torch-lit walls covered with lions,
mammoths or black hairy rhinos.
No ancient hands signaling from stone.

Instead, inner flickerings: a wild-eyed
woman with dangling breasts
and stretched wide mouth staring
him down through his dream.

As he swore she hovered,
luminous and laughing—*there!*—in a corner
of the air, I recalled his fling with artwire
sculpture—nudes, torsos, twisted
sinuous strands.
I was thirteen. His crucifix
showing Christ's penis stunned me, then.

Less startling, the mask
with flaming hair. Flimsy as it was,
I took it to my room, tacked it,
for the shadows it cast, upon my wall.

It Is

It is not down on any map.
True places never are.
—Herman Melville

. . . mid September, days of dry
silent sky, and now this humid haze,
a fog my father shares as he sits
on the deck barely one week home
home from the hospital, babbling less
but searching, more often staring
up at the maples and through them
to the school on the other side.

It is early yet,
weeks before he will be able to explain:
Blasted. I was blasted, he'll say.
And later: *A great hand went through*
and swept everything away.
Within a year, he will have tried
and given up, tried and given up
and finally declined cards or books
on tape or any more well-meaning notions
of change.
But this is the day when
the prompt is *egg* and he writes *shirred*—
amazing, we agree, so much language
still intact, but how laborious to un-
cover, how hit-or-miss to probe.
An hour and he's still at work
on twelve short items, the slow
pen laboring over the speech
therapist's worksheet, the Palmer hand
with its discipline and rhythm
but the elegant slant is shaky now,
so frail and lacy anything might slip
through—*cloud puff, sign bubble* . . .

Coffeestone! he proclaimed,
when the intake nurse with her clip-

board form asked him for his name.
Call me . . .
In his eyes at the time
I saw Lear on the heath—or was it Ahab,
his internet bridge handle, password
to the game?

Today that bridge stands empty,
all decks cleared, the virtual
waves he loved to travel
have ebbed, hissing from his shore—
and what's his memory now but sea
wrack, beach glass, spindrift
bits of legend dissolved
from ink and paper
into air—
like his long ago
annotations in those shoeboxes
filled with index cards: his own hand-
made concordance to the metaphors
in *Moby Dick*.

Then he'd been the
eager grad student, awash in the symbolic
ropes and lines, light, dark and all
the watery wild—
and what shall we call him now—
Ahab or Ishmael? wanderer or scribe?

His hand wavers
off any map we know. I hope he is
finding some true place
but for now he must write *the first
word that comes to mind*. It is . . .

Paula Weld-Cary

Polio

When my father came down with polio
he blamed it on the dirty barn he had helped
tear down hours before fever sent him tumbling
into fiery dreams where like a bewildered soldier
he joined frontlines filled with children
who only days before had played at dusk
in summertime yards, hopping like insects through
tall grass, never knowing their games would soon
be over, never guessing they would wake without wings,
their legs strangely withered.

His fever gone, my father woke under cover not far
from where the old barn had been. Luckier than most,
he climbed up out of the wreckage, his only scars
a weakness in one leg and a bothersome limp,
which he would forever try to conquer, bringing me as a
child up hundreds of mountain paths that meandered
through dreamy forests, wound slowly up onto
bald-faced summits where the wind whipped at our faces,
and the word "polio" was not once spoken.

Roy Jacobstein

Palsy

I could try to dodge the rain
of blows when the bullies struck
or flee should I see them first,

but what could he do, strapped
to his chair, except sit there aslant
that rubberized, yolk-yellow padding

as he was wheeled into Science
each morning, his head tracking
its slow, repetitive, delinquent path.

How good it felt to be a part
of the pack, anonymous, to pierce
the carapace of somebody else.

Post-Op Panopticon

In a kind of semi-carnal,
semi-maternal incarnation
Nurse Nell eased her needle

into his left flank, too thin
by a third. The crude narcotic,
elixir of pseudo-poppy, Siren

of no known note, hypnotic
harpy, clawed & gnawed all
ham & hock away. O optic

antics, & the too cruel crawl
to the intractable sciatic altar . . .
twisting his sheet, a crewless yawl

listing in stagnant backwater
(brackish, scummed, foamy),
he trawls flotsam for the buzzer,

the bell, the spent *he* he used to be,
or, far better yet, for *her,* fair Nell,
Great Mother of Nurses, eternally

knowing, unknowable Nell
but the shift has gone: knell
for Nell—& for him as well.

Kenneth Lee

Emptying the Room

A plethora of basins; their immutable pungency,
plastic, stainless steel,
a receptacle for each orifice, its ample effluent.
The wobbly nightstand next,
support for his whole universe
as darkness closed.

The hardest leavings are attached
to the parts of dying he actually seemed to enjoy:
a fine enameled delftware bowl for baths;
equestrian St George, the dragon undulates the rim,
a pitcher to match, tandem saint and beast
eternally confront each other.

The TV too,
so as not to squander consciousness,
when books became too hard.
His handbell by the intercom
I try its mild tinkle—shatter
ill-constructed dams,
loose long-sequestered tears.
The table lamp from Sears,
its cream-white bulbous base,
you only have to touch to turn it off.

I Examine a Biopsy from a Patient with Jaundice

I climb in the cockpit, grab throttle and stick;
reconnaissance across familiar skies.
Beneath me the liver, my mission: find the prick
that got inside; ravished and terrorized
the honest hepatocyte; transformed
its finely speckled cytoplasmic stuff
to glabrous globs and vacuoles, then wormed
into the nucleus, got really rough—
and seized the ship's controls; a pirate raid
that drove it onto shoals—fragmented gel.
The rest it forced to swell—and masquerade;
sardonic mimes that mock the mother cell.
My radar shows a blip: The bastard's framed.
I call coordinates. The missile's aimed.

Jen-Mark Sens

Bruised Heart

> I never yet did hear
> that the bruised heart was pierced through the ear.
> —*Othello* I, iii 22-23

Lean curves of a ribbed cage
so ample and empty now
it once housed breath
where a fist-size heart would resonate,
muscle pumping blood.
All human softness gone
a skeleton leans to cold perfection
the earth holds still till it seeps its imprints—
marrow first crusting into dust, bones porous and sallow
all liniments web a blank shadow
next rain will erase quick with lime like chalk.

How final, abstract, and so external
a body looks devoid of the garb of life.
Othello, black Othello, ultimately
whitened his bones out of his own marrow.
So late and futile
to call of passions vain
when changed into bare bones
we will still beg for the beat,
plangent of the heart piercing through the ear.

Michelle Bitting

Leaving the Therapeutic School

After four long years
shuffling him through hospital doors
to a room dressed for the ordinary:
Lego bins, a rainbow rug,
tempera prints of glitter-dusted hands,
the alphabet strung
around four white walls.
Only here
we huddled each week
behind a two-way mirror
and cried with the other worried parents.
Here we watched
our children struggle—every task
like nails on a chalkboard:
tossed chairs, flung boxes,
the spitting, hitting
when pressed to share a toy.

After that,
you'd think we'd erase
every scrap of time spent,
never conjure again such terrible scenes.
Thing is,
they loved our boy
and never let him down—
his teachers, interns,
Ernie the guard
who met him each morning
with a grand high five—
all that got him, some days,
to his seat, to graduation,
got him wings, eventually,
across the city to a place called normal—
got us
the education in love
we didn't know we needed
and never asked for.

Alex Grant

Hamish Samey's Turnip Soup

My Grandfather's neck would bulge
with veins thick as a horse's cock
when he swung the axe to the wood,
the thunk of metal on rings
cracking the morning air.
Wood flung on the fire,
flames swept upward
in the huge fart of the leather bellows,
screaming sparks crackling
up the black chimney.

Dark days, indeed, made bearable
only by the thick turnip soup
my Grandmother cauldron-boiled
over the wet peat heaved
from sullen bogs. Fat shards of pepper
would float like frog-spawn
in the turgid brew, daring
the faint-hearted to slurp down
the lung-sticking potage.
No stranger to daring myself,
I gobbled the turnip innards
like a starving goat in a midden.

Red and purple-veined
vegetable, I stand before you now,
in this suburban supermarket,
consider your heft and proportions,
shiny, bulbous and stippled, waxy,
like my Grandmother's skin, purple
as my Grandfather's nose.

The Curse Of Tourette

Enfer foutu!
—Gilles de la Tourette

In Arles, Domaine de la Tourette,
Gauguin painted "Self-portrait
dedicated to Vincent Van Gogh,"

who held a straight razor
to his throat, then reeking
of absinthe and remorse,

sliced off his ear because he
"didn't need to hear the paint."
Ten years later, in the asylum

at Lausanne, Gilles de la Tourette,
the man cursed by the affliction
named for him, died in obscurity.

They met, briefly, in eighteen-
eighty-four, *Meneer* Van Gogh
and *Monsieur* de la Tourette, each

touched by the flickering light
of near-recognition, each naïve
to the impending flux—each

oblivious to the connections
being forged and the black
crows circling overhead.

Marjorie Roberts

A Handstitched Bridge on her Back

> A pair of deer
> groom each other hair by hair
> with increasing care
> —*Basho*

The hospice elevator slams shut,
two attendants push the gurney swiftly
bearing a man with advanced metastatic
lung cancer, a woman runs alongside,
she wears a handstitched bridge on her back.

Husband and wife are miffed at one another,
he because she insisted he consult a specialist,
she because he canceled the appointment,
both gasp for their next breath.

Doctors and nurses convene in calm haste,
the man hooked up to a morphine drip, when
pain subsides he sleeps, the woman's anger
melts, she hovers, caresses his shrunken
face, traces the burrowing in his cheeks, prepares
herself for the coming trek, the grappling and auscultations.

With tender cunning she keeps him alive almost two weeks.

I'll bring your favorite soup tomorrow...
We'll celebrate your birthday in three days...
Next week's our wedding anniversary...

They weave a span of dignified suffering
to halt the pummeling of destined departure.

How she monitors his every hell-bent wheeze
and gurgle, his eyes pivot to her early morning arrival
with home-made ambrosias, she re-arranges
the farewell sheets, squeezes an eyedrop
of water on the slit that was his lips.

Shepherds his barely-thereness with fragrant
generosity, staves off the unmooring and homelessness,
this is what their lives have become.

He cries "mama" when she hums a lullaby,
cradles his bamboo limbs shriveling as sun betrays day,
steps beyond her unarticulated weariness.

Our nephew is coming in a few days. . .
The man in harmony with his wife's request.

He notices she is girding herself with fortitude,
taking charge of the unforeseeable, cleaving
but steadfast.

She observes his tranquility and compliance,
emptied of anguish and the fractured past.

One day she tells him,
You go on ahead,
I'll catch up.

When she arrives with violets and broth
her greeting flies out to him like a sonnet,
her attempts to feed him fail,
the end song a soft sibilation.

She has carried him to this place, waited with him,
both bore the daily sorrowing,
bowed to the simplest persuasion
the way summer honors autumn rust.

Field of Black Poppies

for George Klawitter,
Alzheimer's patient 1994-2005

People shuffle by, I have nothing
to offer them, I am a hint
of someone, barely able to find
my way, the day I came
to this place I knew
I was lost.

Others arrange me, button and zip
my shirt and pants, brush my teeth,
slide a razor across my chin,
Trim my hair and nails.

I am bathed and fed.
I am here, l am not here.

Keep it in perspective, someone told me.
Keep what in perspective?

What I once understood no longer exists.
What survives, instinct and vigilance,
despair and grief, occasionally I recognize
a familiar voice, scent of skin
and breath, feel a force like wind
pushing me around and around
in an empty house.

Words I once possessed no longer on my teeth
and tongue, my mind cannot browse or hang on
to a fresh thought, I lack insight, ability
to reason or be reasonable, a famine
of mind, body, soul.

Someone cries out down the hall, yet I go
to a man sobbing, wipe his stye eyes
and runny nose, he thanks me by standing

directly in my path, pats my back, we study
one another's faces, have a fool's leaden lines
across our foreheads, shoulders made heavy
by the weight of the heart.

My current occupation is to pace the long tunnel
passage to exit signs at both ends. I get down
on my knees, inspect each door from every position
and angle, rub my hands across the cool metal
and steel surfaces. If only I could devise
a strategy of release, discover the logic
of hinge to knob.

Walk upright from this field of black poppies.

Juan Franco, photograph

Jane Ellen Glasser

In Extremis

> . . .the taste of it is so full of memories
> it encompasses the whole history of losses.
> —*Stanley Kunitz*

Imagine a well
of ill fortune
deep as your history.
Start the winch turning;
bucket begets bucket.
The scream, say,
of a metal grill
wedding itself
to a tree
brings up
your father's belt
slapping like a beached
eel in a trawl.
In the no order
of remembering,
your five-year-old fingers
caught in a car door
might succeed
the jellyfish
of your mother's
lopped-off breast
or your sister's
sin of silence.
There's no
associative ring
to the sequence.
A hangnail
might snag
a dead dog;
a simple lyric,
love's bankruptcy.
As if present and past

weren't enough,
whatever dread thing
hasn't happened
imagination fills in.

Isabel, September 2003

I was afraid for the trees
already shaky from weeks
of ground-pooling rain.

Wind whipped in from the sea.
By noon it was twilight,
harpies racketing
in the branches,
their black skirts
screaming downstream.

At high tide, my yard
was a lake of wading pines
bent low as if caught up
in a baptismal fever.

And still it rained
leaves and limbs.

Some groaned,
reclining in slow motion.
Others toppled like dominoes.
Even the huge,
army-fatigued sycamores
threw up their arms.

There was something obscene
in the afterward.
Crushed vehicles.
Invaded houses. Neighbors
out in the streets, chatty
as if on holiday.

And the exposed butt-ends
of so many trees,
snaky with roots.
And the gaping holes,
raw and deep as graves.

John Milisenda, photograph

Martina Nicholson

I Am the Way

Trying to drive without eyes
In the deepest fog,
With just the moan of the trees,
The wind in the branches,
And the sound of the creek for nearness,
I feel my way
Through the ruts and potholes.

Here I could fall into the ravine,
Here I could break my neck
On the low-lying branches

Here I smell the jasmine,
Here is the driveway;
I creep up the broken road,
Past the roses with thorns,
Past the lavender and blackberry vines,
The road widens and straightens.

Keep my feet on the safe paths, Lord,
Redeem me, and give me strength,
I am listening with my heart, Lord,
Guide me home.

The Girl Who Didn't Have Herpes

> You must live the questions themselves, like seeds.
> Someday the answers will rise out of you like gardens
> —*Rilke*

The girl who didn't have herpes
Has a mom who is dying of cancer.
All pain is relative;
There is peace sometimes in the worst day,
The day the bomb fell and caused your life to be a crater of moonscape.
The day you felt even breathing caused the most exquisite pain.
The girl on the phone is gasping and crying,
And saying that she just couldn't face having herpes.
As if one diagnosis made the other impossible.
Lightning is not supposed to strike twice.
The words feel like cold oatmeal in your dry mouth.
You don't have herpes.
I am so sorry about your mom.

Praying with Both Hands

The baby's heartbeat slowed to a dull thud.
The meconium was thick as mud—
Thick and sticky as the mud the Israelites
Used to build bricks for making the pyramids,
When they were slaves in Egypt.

The parents' faces were tired and scared.
And so I prayed with both hands,
Slipped the forceps in, to lift the baby—
Lift the head, hugging the cheekbones,
With a mighty effort,
Like bringing the children out of Egypt,
Like Miriam,
Lifting Moses from the muddy wadi.
Praise to you, Lord God of Hosts.
The pink baby
With the glorious cry
Of clean lungs,
Singing out loud to her parents and to you—
Blessed be You,
Lord God of All Creation!

M. Frost

Erythroblast

Originally, any nucleated erythrocyte, but now more generally used to designate the nucleated precursor from which an erythrocyte develops.

—Baillière's Comprehensive Veterinary Dictionary

A

"The poets must give us
imagination of peace, to oust the intense, familiar
imagination of disaster. Peace, not only
the absence of war."

—Denise Levertov, from Making Peace

I'm tracking it, bloodhound down this urban artery . . .
the van before me dirty with a red cross.
I follow blood, imagine the van full of it:
thousands of labeled units in refrigerated storage.
Cars have become weapons. The van slams
on its brakes, and I imagine the road covered
in slick clotless pools, all the waste—
the highway shut down—the cost, the waste.

On the radio, an ambulance bearing
a red crescent explodes as Ramadan commences.
The announcer uses words like
humanitarian and *neutral*.

Blood is not quite neutral,
a pH between 7.35 and 7.45,
maintaining a base so that its first property,
buffer, can be retained, so that acid does not rise within us
on long marches, lactates building within muscles,
carbon dioxide hydrogenated in several states.

Buffers do not exist in war.
Blood no longer spills but shatters, explodes,
incinerates, turns entirely unrecognizable.

We hang bags and bags of it, units flowing
through foreign filters. The noise we hear on the radio,
filtered. Still, it keeps flowing.

B
Origin of the word from
Old English *blot*—guttural, like the
German *blut* I learned in Amish country,
cutting capillaries, wading through great clotting pools of it,
feeling the visceral thrill of a uterine artery
as it fed the fetus at my fingertips.

I remember its warm iron scent,
the burn of my muscles as I shoveled mounds of it
like manure, repeating the word as prayer:
blut,
der kuh, sie blut.

O
I am the little *i* without the ability to produce
antigen, reduced to O-negative,
most-desired blood type because it reacts
least, lacks dominance altogether.

i is the most common allele in the human
condition, crossing racial boundaries,
crossing borders, crossing creed and faith.
Blood reduces us to this ancestry:

ii the O, its blank staring roundness.

AB
" . . . yet see you but our hands,
And this the bleeding business they have done"
—*William Shakespeare, from* Julius Caesar

What a strange vampire I have become,
collecting blood not for the taste of it,
not to roll over the tongue like fine wine.
I collect it instead because it has a price,

deliver it in plastic veins, stimulate it with erythropoetin
(anemia's cure), reduce it to states fluid and formed;
each corpuscle under the microscope—erythro-*sight*—
each cell painted pale with mauve, stained themselves which stain.

The four-crossed hemoglobin remains the only component
after the nucleus is cast out, the cell reduced to working membrane,
eliminating carbon dioxide and delivering oxygen.

To deliver oxygen, the purpose of CPR.
We call them our ABC's:
airway which means oxygen which means blood,
which is not the B, but C for circulation,
vascular highways which must be primed by that pump
which has nothing to do with love. I slam my fist
down on the chest—it *has* to move, the heart
has to pump—sans life, blood still flows:
a false thread on the artery, a false glow to the lips,
a twitch to deadened muscle—but ultimately, blood pools,
the heart bruises under each constant thrust,
the corpuscles diminish into blue.

Cow Poetry

A Dadaist poet printed words
onto the ribbed sides of cows.
He released them from their barn;
they scattered along the whims of pasture
layout, entropy, wind, and social rank—
he collected enough organic lines
to fill four books and a NY show.

I am no such artist, but
I once passed a Guernsey
with a perfect star on her face.

In a stall at the county fair,
I saw an enterprising Jersey,
the brown manure on her rump
dried into a precise map of America.

My favorite remains Number 1357, marked
in her left ear, a prime purebred Holstein.
She pushed out twin heifers, red and white.

Two months into her milking,
her stomach twisted like a Q.

I painted her brown with iodine,
sliced a thin red line down her flank
then notched a smaller hole below it,
repairing her stomach to a U.

She healed with a scar.
Everything she did that summer
bore an exclamation point.

Jennifer Perrine

Ex Ovo Omnia

A newborn dubbed "The Monster of Ravenna" was
starved to death by order of Pope Julius II in 1512.

And what of the mother of the monster,
    the Pandora's box of her womb? What crack

in the world did she peer through to impress
    this upon her child: eagle's foot and horned

head, serpents dripping from its waist, bat wings
    folded over a superfluous eye?

What can we say for the mother except
    from the egg, all—newt and rodent, human

and worm? What could she know of genetics:
    cistrons that pump out seven hearts, twin mouths,

or a form more common, more humble? What
    could she do but watch while her infant starved?

What could she do but what we all do—hold
    our faults close, their names like stones on our tongues?

Leslie Adrienne Miller

Parous in Paris

Grief whittles away at the last of my maternal
fat as I cross the Seine in feeble autumn light
to present myself for rendezvous
with Monsieur Director, *Institut d'Anatomie*.
Only to wait the requisite four French hours
for him to show: my thinned skin zinging
with each squeal of the secretary who rifles
invoices (for God knows what) and flirts
with a man lolling about in scrubs,
his knuckles blue and chapped from his work
in the fridge. But it's this man who later reads
my grief as the small thing it will one day be
when we join him in the cadaver room
where he sings and slings cold heads
from bin to shelf for dental students
to unclench. I've left my only child
home in another country for this walk
into a history of the body of woman
in labor, so all four hours I kill
waiting in the unforgiving chair,
the coppery scent of formaldehyde
sticking in my throat, I fight down
the unthinkable news delivered
at dawn via e-mail: someone else
is in my marriage bed, her broad thighs
loading up on genes, the very same
that give my son his dazzle and dash,
his own sweet power to sunder.

Map of the Interior

a mostly found poem

Vesalius has failed to give his name
to any anatomical part. In this
he differs from intrepid others
who found it de rigueur to map
with pen and paper after they'd applied
the knife. Hence we have the airway
of Eustachius, the tube of Fallopius,
the duct of Botallus, the circle
of Willis, the lobe of Spigelius,
the fissure of Sylvius, the glands
of Bartholin, the island of Reil,
the ganglion of Gasser, the cartilage
of Arantius, the sinus of Valsalva,
the tubercle of Lower, the valves
of Morgagni, the torcular of Herophilus,
the veins of Galen, and the alleged
spot of Grafenberg.

The penultimate ten lines of this poem are taken verbatim from Charles Singer's *A Short History of Anatomy From the Greeks to Harvey*, 1925 (page 115).

Torso of a Woman Gone with Child, 1774

Why Jan van Rymsdyck made two versions
of his drawing for Hunter's *Anatomy
of the human gravid uterus*, we can only guess.
The female torso has her dress
peeled upward like her skin, to reveal
the giant egg-shaped uterus
in its nest of shining entrails,
below which a smattering of pubic hair
smudges the upper thighs, and the tops
of her ungartered stockings sag
as if she had just wandered out
of any one of Lautrec's dance hall scenes
and keeled on the spot. More curious still
is the fact that one of Rymsdyck's
drawings has an open book between the thighs,
the slim entrance to the world of this woman's
gravid uterus curtained with a gilt-edged spine,
as if her nether parts were deep in study
of some esoteric subject, as if her reading eyes
were there where her desire once lived.

Marianne Taylor

Christmas Gift from John

The suicidal amaryllis finally did it. She plunged
from refrigerator top, decisively breaking
her elegant neck on its cold, black edge.

Truth is, she'd shown signs.
Swollen with beauty, her head grew larger
than she could bear. A week ago I thought

to hold back her water, stunt
her steady surge (an inch a day, says my son)
as if I could. No, straight as an unsheathed sword

she shot her stalk till it measured 42 inches
and burst into summer's full bloom, east and west
together, then north and south. She lasted

less than a day. Then threw herself down
and hung there. Above one son's penguins
another's self-portraits, a spelling list,

photos of shorebirds and children
squinty-eyed, throwing ecstatic
fistfuls of bread toward the sun.

Of course I could have saved her.
Tied her to a stake, watched her wither and brown
feel the life force slow in her stem. But no.

I have taken her head, four-faced corolla,
lipstick red striating to pale chartreuse
in the funnel to her now shallow core,

and placed it in a vase of clear crackled glass.
This holiday present from a very good friend
measures a mere foot now. But her six

amber-tipped stamen, a sex-furcated tongue,
thrusts toward me like a trombone slide
while the curling pistil invites me inside

to drink through her torn stem, consume
her truth for a day or two. And I think of you,
my friend, and hope you are well.

Winter is long, our beauty is gone,
and apart we must measure
with incremental knowledge the trail to spring.

Juan Franco, photograph

Barbara Crooker

After Rotator Cuff Surgery

And if your right hand causes you to sin, cut it off
and throw it away; it is better to lose one of your
members than that your whole body go to hell.
—*Matthew* 5:30

The weather of my shoulder:
a sunset of bruises,
occluding the skin, forming
storm clouds, a formidable line
of squalls. Royal purple.
Blue black. My arm, my hockey-
playing right wing, hangs limply
at my side, a dumb sausage,
or swings at right angles
in its canvas sling.
The starboard side
has listed to port.

I can not:
line my eyes with carbon brown,
buckle my sandals, or clasp
my watch. Can't drive stick
shift, cut up steak; dead-
head roses, swipe the cool
ball of deodorant under
my arms. Lift a kettle
of water to boil for sweet corn.
I'm a wreck on the recto side.
But at least I've never voted
for a right-winger, and I do
know my right hand from my left,
and my hat from my glove.

I go back to cataloguing
bruises: swirls of magenta
and burgundy blooming

into hideous roses.
I sink back in the recliner,
hugging the ice bag, high
on Percocet, rocking
in the waters
of the sweet black night.

DOROTHY WALL

Passing

> Who says I am obliged to be what you think I am? Or what I think you think I am? Or even what I think I am but sincerely wish I weren't?
>
> —*Brooke Kroeger*

No, not that kind. I'm not secretly gay or black or Jewish, my fair skin and aquiline nose giving me a stab at what everyone wants—opportunity, freedom from judgment—despite the chance alignment of my DNA. The kind of passing I did is, I suspect, more widespread and less discussed, more ordinary but no less wearing. The day-to-day effort at dissembling is an exercise in ingenuity, dogged determination and fear, no matter its particular permutation. Ill with chronic fatigue syndrome since 1980, an invisible illness, I know passing to be a peculiar, liberating and punishing art.

Its beginning, for me, was insidious, as these things often are. In a repeated scenario from the early 80s, when I was stumbling through life in a fugue, I see myself collapsed on my maroon overstuffed living room couch with its saggy springs, the room vibrating with my exhaustion. I didn't understand this virus that had hit me with a primitive vengeance and never receded. Somehow I was managing to shepherd my daughter to third grade—bow-tie barrettes, peanut butter sandwich and all—and drag myself off to a pastiche of part-time jobs teaching writing at Bay Area colleges. But an hour and a half in front of my class left my throat raw, my chest burning. As soon as I pulled into the driveway, delirious with fatigue, I'd make a dive for that couch.

Maybe I need to exercise, I'd think, struggling to understand my enervation. Maybe I need fresh air. I'd haul myself up for a walk around the block. After ten yards that iron dragging weariness would press me to the ground, my head in a billowing cloud. I'd sit on a low concrete wall one block from my house, overtaken with the strangest sensation of a wavering lightness and heaviness at the same time, unable to go on, my neighbor's bulbous rhododendron a blur.

I became intimately familiar with the scuffed linoleum of the ubiquitous medical cubicle at my HMO, as a parade of doctors peered into my ears and mouth, appropriated my blood and urine and nodded their heads at the results. "You're fine." I'd leave in a daze, struggling to work out a fuzzy inner dissonance: I had a recurring virus and there was nothing wrong with me.

I once had a heated spat with a good friend because I was, again, too fatigued to go on the hike we had planned. David, a public defender, paced the wooden floors of my flat in exasperation. "It's not normal to be sick all the time. I deal with murderers and crazy judges all day and I don't get sick. There's something wrong with you."

"There's nothing wrong with me," I snapped back. "I'm just run-down. My blood tests are fine. You don't know what it's like to be a single mother, commuting all over, trying to make ends meet." I was furious, misunderstood, in odd collusion with my ignorant doctors.

* * *

How strange that my induction into the grueling practice of "true" passing was the result of a victory of truth over ignorance. Sometime in 1988 my friend Susan H. handed me a short clipping from the *San Francisco Chronicle*. I have only a vague memory of standing in my yellow-painted entry hall—she must have just stopped by—as she fished in her purse, waves of russet-blond hair curtaining her face, then handed me the newsprint as if she'd almost forgotten. Her words I remember clearly: "I'll bet this is what you've had."

I unfolded the column of print and held it to the light. In matter-of-fact prose, the article described an illness newly recognized by the Centers for Disease Control, "chronic fatigue syndrome."

My attention was instantly focused, as if someone had grabbed me by the shoulders. I read the piece several times, the words coagulating until a frisson of comprehension slid down the back of my neck. Chronic fatigue syndrome. It was one of those light-bulb moments, those rare revelatory instants that happen only a few times in life, when disparate, scattered particles in your brain fly together. I stared at the newsprint, a zing of energy racing along my nerves. A name for that beast. Validation. Medical recognition.

"Huh," I said.

Satisfying and juicy as this moment was, it didn't shake my world. By the end of the 80s my health had significantly improved, and aside from the initial jolt that settled quickly into "of course," this new knowledge was filed away in that place for things I didn't have time to focus on. I was chauffeuring my fifteen-year-old daughter—picture braces and purple eye-shadow—to the Roxie II movie theater on Shattuck Avenue, following her adamant instructions to drop her off a block away so the boy she was meeting wouldn't see me. And as if adolescent idioms were contagious, I found myself caught up in romance myself. I was busy teaching fiction writing and meeting privately with writing clients, delving into the intricacies of fictive worlds, then hurrying back home for barbecued ribs with my new love, Bill, where I was quite satisfied with the corporal and real. Love and fiction, enough distraction. That name, CFS, floated as a shadowy, curious headline to a life in the past, one, thank goodness, I seemed to be leaving behind. I didn't yet understand the persistence of this bug, nor its terrible capacity to revive. I didn't yet know I could become more ill than I'd been.

* * *

February of 1992 found me, my health worsening, in the office of a doctor outside my HMO who had a large practice treating CFS patients. In a few short years I'd gone from being well most of the time, if still worn out, to being sick ten and a half months a year. Where I'd been able to walk three miles I now could walk only one; instead of seeing ten writing clients a week I could barely manage two. I was determined to get to the bottom of things.

The doctor had ordered a complete work-up, blood, stool, urine. On this day he scanned the computer print-out of results as if perusing a menu, the tip of his nose following in an invisible line his pointed finger. Tall, Shakespearean, with dark-haired good looks, he had a tone of high command. He was my age; he'd once briefly dated a friend of mine.

"Hm, hmm." He flipped through pages. Everything, inside and out, completely normal, except—at this his eyes lit with a proprietary interest and his finger tapped the paper—I had no IgG (a class of antibodies), something he often saw in CFS patients. This meant little to me. But something else he said meant a lot.

He leaned his back against the wall, hands clasping the rolled-up print-out behind him like a bat. I peppered him with questions about the body that were really questions about the soul, and finally asked about my chances of recovery.

"You'll always have this illness." His words slapped me like a plunge into icy water, one that leaves you numb and tingling and shocked long after. How could he say something like that so definitively? I had always been sure I would get better, sure my years of illness would be limited: "Those years in the 80s when I had that virus."

I'd dismissed the doctors I'd seen throughout the 80s, knowing their observations about illness were wrong. This doctor with his disturbing pronouncement that I was indeed ill, permanently ill, I also dismissed, unable, unwilling to believe he could be right. I left the doctor's office rattled and angered by his cavalier words. I didn't go back. Some years later I learned he'd dismantled his practice and gone to acting school.

It had been more than a decade since I had crossed the line into chronic illness and encountered physician disbelief and ignorance, biomedical limitations and biases. Now I was crossing another border, entering another new world, one that would require a changing self-image and a wrestling with meaning, a confrontation with cultural attitudes and interpretations of illness, with stigma and otherness. I wasn't yet ready for this crossing.

I wanted that exhausted self behind me. I rebelled at the thought that she could once again take up residence, become a part of me. On a downhill slide, I faced the difficult, convoluted challenge. Who am I now? Do I continue the story I'd so fervently believed—I'm just rundown, I'll get better—now that I knew I'd invented it all along, albeit out of ignorance? This belief in ordinariness, so avidly held against the complaints of the body, how could I now give it up? Especially since my illness allowed me to appear to function normally, why should I relinquish the privileges of anonymity?

For someone with a lifelong antipathy to acknowledging or talking about weakness, a ramrod-straight Protestant ethic of self-reliance, the idea of "coming out" as a seriously ill person went against my grain. All evidence to the contrary, I believed I could get better, believed I could soldier on with only small, private adjustments. The truth about my body I held at arm's length, like a disturbing object I could neither let go nor accept. That "rundown" story, ruse that I now knew it to be, allowed me to cling to what I had. I stuck with it.

* * *

I went on with what I was doing, focused on other things, the things that mattered. I met my writing students, showed up for brunches and parties, heading for a comfortable couch to ease my aching muscles, sitting mutely if I was too exhausted to talk. One hostess thought I was rude because I didn't offer to clean up. Other people who didn't know me well simply concluded I was the quiet type. The misconceptions grated, but they seemed better than the alternative. Passing, to all except those closest to me, enabled me to pull a protective cloak around something vital in myself, some key element of identity. As long as I had an invisible illness, people met me as simply the person I was, writing consultant, teacher, neighbor, not as an ill person.

Throughout that spring of 1992, in the airy, familiar rooms of Dwinelle Hall on the U.C. Berkeley campus, my fiction students and I debated the uses of the unreliable narrator and interior monologue, a breeze carrying in the monasterial noontime bell of the campanile. But the washed-out undercurrent of my illness was there. I'd stopped teaching evening classes, stopped teaching anywhere except U.C. Berkeley, a mile from my home, and scheduled just one class a semester. Even so, only one week that term did I feel well enough to teach. The other nine weeks I went through the motions as if underwater, dredging up thoughts through resistance, my voice launched against the weight pressing my breastbone.

When I browsed through my student evaluations at the end of the semester I came across one that sent a hot singe through my chest: "She seems low energy." Instead of mailing it in with the others to my administrator, I threw it away, something I never did, even when I got a bad write-up from that occasional grumpy student who rated my class slightly above spoiled fish. That comment—she's low energy—was a crack in my story, a tear in a screen. I didn't want it seen. I would rather have someone disparage my teaching than disclose my secret self. It pains me now to think how unspeakable those words were to me, how hard I worked to prevent their utterance. Those words stung not only because they exposed my illness. They revealed that all my efforts, all my performances, my willingness to continually hurl my ill self into the world, all that was not enough. This illness was becoming stronger than all my impersonations, all my willpower.

How is resistance expressed when the body is ill? By controlling the narrative, what one chooses to reveal. By insuring that other people's view conforms to the one you want to be true. By investing in them the normalcy story, making them the carriers of the picture of reality you can no longer maintain within yourself. If they don't see the truth, you can feel saved. The liberation achieved when others don't see is a false liberation, but it can buy time. It can act as a buffer as you sort through those gnawing, difficult inner schisms.

I remember the jarring moment a friend referred to me as disabled, probably in 1993. Sprawled around my living room, a group of woman friends and I were trading mid-life hormone horror stories. Marcy, who has a disabling back injury, was lying on her back on the carpet in an old baseball jacket and mentioned something about being disabled, then waved her hand vaguely in my direction. "Oh, Dorothy's disabled, too." Her words shook me. I'd never thought of myself as disabled, never would have attached that word to myself. Was I? Ill, yes. Exhausted, yes. But disabled? I slid the word around in my head for months after that, knowing on some level it fit. In some ways, in some contexts, I was.

My friend Myrna, a lesbian, said to me gently one day as I expressed to her my angst about "coming out," "It's always best to be fully who you are." But when I asked Marcy how she handled the situation of working with a disability, she said she told people of her limits or special needs on a need-to-know basis. To come out as a lesbian is an issue of identity and pride. You want to value and embrace who you are, so that others can as well. But do I want to embrace an identity as an ill person? What does it mean to incorporate into one's identity physical limits, pain and incapacity? What alchemy could transform the body's shifting, unseeable complaints into a positive sense of who I am? I had a deep ambivalence about identifying with this part of myself, about letting it define me.

With an invisible illness—and in my case one gradually worsening—you can remain for years in a borderland of confused identity. When things are not black and white, but marbled and shifting, how and when do you come out as an ill person? Where is that clear-cut point of delineation, a line you cross, a specific moment you say, there's a new me here I have to acknowledge? Was it last month? This week?

* * *

One day in the summer of 1993 I dialed the number of a CFS support group, an act that in itself was a capitulation. I'm not sure what impelled me, whether it was a voyeuristic curiosity or some inner instinct that I was descending to a place where help and connection would be vital. Did I really want to hear others lament their brain fog and fatigue? Did I want that mirror lifted up to me—this is what you are, this is where you fit in? I was holding myself apart with that snobbery of the able-bodied, even though most of the time I could no longer place myself in their company.

A woman from the group gave me directions and explained the elaborate carpool arrangements they had devised to make travel easier. "I drive to the BART station and meet Charles, then I lie down in the back seat while he drives over to Linda's. Then Linda drives the rest of the way there so Charles and I can rest."

She offered to hook me into their driving loop. "I can drive myself," I said tersely.

We met in a young man's sparse, depressing apartment, one of those square, cinder-block places students call home. This felt increasingly like a wrong-headed venture, going backward in time. A circle of hard, mismatched chairs. Cracked, random tea cups. All nice people. Very nice. A bearded young man unable to work who lived with his mother. Huddled under an afghan, a pony-tailed newly married woman—the one I'd spoken to on the phone—disabled by a flea-fogger her husband set off two days after the wedding. A petite, curly-haired speech therapist with all the appropriate therapeutic language, how we need to open a space for healing. And on the futon couch a feverish man slick with sweat, half-lying, half-sitting as if just pulled from a river, a shiny leather jacket tugged around him. He was profoundly depressed and suicidal.

My bones ached in the hard-backed chair. Exhaustion poured through me. I needed to leave.

"I don't think I can go on." His voice wavered up from some deep pool of despair.

The pony-tailed woman reached her afghan over him. The speech therapist went into high gear about healing spaces.

How do you excuse yourself when a group of people you've just met are trying to talk someone out of suicide? Well, good luck, I have to go now. What I'd hoped would be an experience of patient empowerment was fast becoming a sinkhole. The disabled trying to save the drowning.

Guilt-ridden, I stayed longer than I should have. I didn't go back.

* * *

Passing is something you do when you're alone with an inner world, and it's something that makes you more alone. Yet it's an attempt to be less alone, to blend in, to fit a public notion of what the self should be, what is valued and rewarded. In my own stumbling way in the early 90s—going to a doctor, a support group—I was trying to be less alone, to find support and understanding, others to lean against, someone to spread an afghan over my tired limbs. But to be truly less alone you have to loosen your grip on the determination to blend in. You have to face what it is that marks you as different.

"Spoiled identities" is what sociologist Erving Goffman called it: the identity that doesn't conform to a society's ideal, that carries stigma, otherness, shame. "An individual who might have been received easily in ordinary social intercourse possesses a trait that can obtrude itself upon attention and turn those of us whom he meets away from him, breaking the claim that his other attributes have on us." These words strike me with a sharp clarity. Just as often as an ill person is met with compassion, she is met with judgment. Something about the state of being ill—its frailty, proof of weakness of character or vulnerability—invites opinion and inference, or at least wariness.

The stigma of illness carries a particular tinge, reminding us of our bodily failings, from which—unlike race/ethnicity or sexual orientation, other stigmatized identities—no one is immune. It's this pervasive fear of the body's frailty that creates the palpable stigma of illness. Particularly in a society like ours that places high value on productivity and effort, the weakened body is deeply suspect, and feared. The weakened body that doesn't recover is even more suspicious. You must not want to heal. You must have given up hope. People leap in with antidotes and suggestions. I'm referred to the Center for Attitudinal Healing, or offered Caroline Myss's book, *Why People Don't Heal*, offers loaded with presumptions.

Like Philoctetes, Sophocles' character who has a wound that will not heal, the chronically ill become the "other," stigmatized and isolated because of their unreasonable bodies. Philoctetes' tale, one of Sophocles' late plays, is fired with bitterness and vengeance. I read it with a fascination born of identification and repulsion: Philoctetes is an awfully self-pitying fellow, ravaged by suffering, swinging wildly between anguish and lust for revenge. Bitten by a snake on the island of Chryse on the way to Troy, he has a wound so odious and putrid that his fellow Greeks cannot bear to be around him. They abandon him on the deserted island of Lemnos for ten years and come back for him only when they need his magic bow to win the Trojan War.

Here he is as he rages and laments his betrayal by his fellow Greeks: "This is where they abandoned me, alone with my wound. . . . Can you imagine what it was like for me, waking up here after they'd gone? Getting up that day? Imagine the tears, the cries of anguish. Picture me, seeing the ships I had traveled with all gone and not a soul here: no one to help me; no one to ease the weariness of my affliction."

The flawed, wounded body in this story is deeply anti-social, a constant, undeniable sign of otherness that is repugnant and repelling. It makes Philoctetes an outcast, confined on an uninhabited island and left to survive on his own wits. It exiles him to his own territory, where the polluting effect of his wound cannot contaminate others, much as lepers inhabited their "cities of the damned" or the insane their asylums, which originally meant sanctuary. Sanctuaries become prisons.

Philoctetes suffers from his wound; he suffers more deeply from isolation. Aristotle's definition of what it is to be human is based on social connection: a being who is part of a social structure, a *polis*. This, he said, is what separates man from beast. Those who are disabled will say—and I know what they mean—that it is not the disability (wound, flaw, illness) that is the greatest burden and source of grief. It is the reaction of others that is most devastating, the barriers erected through stigma, misunderstanding, rejection. Behind my fear of identification with the ill is the ultimate fear: that like Philoctetes I will be left behind. Left to a small, circumscribed world. Deprived of the company of the healthy who will sail away.

I sometimes think of that drowning, suicidal man at the support group, hugging his arms around his leather jacket, his face slack with despair, and wonder what happened to him. Did he get better? Worse? Is he still sweating through his sickness?

He seemed almost unreachable in his island of misery. And I had backed away, fast, to save myself from a similar drowning.

* * *

Although today there is a growing disability pride movement, it hasn't permeated the culture or changed public attitudes in the way the gay pride movement has. There is still an enormous stigma attached to the wayward, uncontrollable, sometimes offensive, imperfect body. And there are hierarchies of stigma; some conditions carry greater disgrace than others. Someone who has no control of his movements or who drools is more of an outcast than an otherwise healthy paraplegic. These hierarchies are internalized even by those who are ill.

Poet J. D. McClatchy offers a revealing comment about his good friend, poet James Merrill. Everyone knew Merrill was gay and knew, as his health declined in the 90s, that he was ill. But he kept secret the knowledge that he had AIDS. Says McClatchy: "For once, he had difficulty speaking about something; his lifelong frankness about his homosexuality never yielded to an ability to talk about the still more volatile subject of his AIDS. It was the only situation in which I've found him literally speechless. . . . But it's in the nature of this disease that the accounts of its onset are shrouded in repression, lies, half-truths, forgotten circumstances, etc."

Like a stain, the taint of AIDS—its unsavory implication of sexual transgression and licentiousness, of bodily fluids and orifices—adheres to its victims. Those with CFS are also defiled. Our taint is less egregious, less reviled, but still condemned. Our transgression is fatigue, with its implications of weakness of will, moral lassitude, self-indulgence, social uselessness. And because our fatigue is supposedly unexplainable, we're sullied by a sickness that is irrational, raising the specter of malingering, emotional instability, even hysteria.

"Why didn't you tell me what was going on?" a colleague and friend, Susan P., asked me years later. She was miffed that I'd kept from her the facts, that I hadn't let her help. I flailed about for an answer. To tell someone who knows me I'm ill is to deliver a punch-line, a surprise, eliciting a radical transformation of their perception of who I am and requiring they go through, in a small way, the same process of revisioning I have. There'd been times, out to dinner or at a meeting with other writers, my head fat with exhaustion, when I'd formed the words in my mind, ready to spill them. Something always held me back. It's amazing how strong is the grasp, as to a lifeboat, on that old self.

Was my silence akin to the denial of the alcoholic, or the resoluteness of the person who doesn't want to face impending decline? Was it projecting a fictitious self, or keeping an old self from leaving me? Was it independence—bred in me by my Protestant, "where-there's-a-will-there's-a-way" parents—taken to the level of folly? Or shame, that skulking partner of weakness? Or optimism bleeding into denial? Or avoidance of the projections and misconceptions of others, always close on the heels of the ill, especially with an illness so little understood, so open to misinterpretation as CFS?

I could paint it many ways. I only know that I was packing my body each day into sweaters and bright scarves—a crucial accessory for the pale-faced ill—the way a teenager crams herself into pants one size too small out of an intense need to have them fit. It was what I needed to do. As long as I could get away with it, I would.

Sometimes I want to cry for that person struggling incognito, for every day she went to work when her body ached for rest. Other times I want to berate her for not insisting on her truth, not demanding that she be seen for who she is. In the end it was my body that spoke, no longer able to keep up my double life. It was my body that brought the end of my time of passing. In September of 1995, after an ill-advised trip to New York, I arrived home in a wheelchair. I was bedridden for three months, my brain a swollen, sodden sponge, my body aflame with aches, as if I'd been beaten head to toe with a rubber hose. It would be nine months before I could walk to the corner and back, a year and a half before I could walk four blocks. I had become invisible to the world, cloistered at home, my public presence gone. In my disappearance, I had become fully seen.

Endnote: Also called chronic fatigue and immune dysfunction syndrome (CFIDS) and myalgic encephalomyelitis (ME), CFS is a serious, debilitating illness affecting an estimated 800,000 adults in the U.S., twice as many as have multiple sclerosis. CFS is characterized by unrelenting exhaustion, muscle pain, sore throat, cognitive disorders including "brain fog," difficulty concentrating, light and sound sensitivity, and a myriad of other symptoms. Some patients are bedridden, some housebound, some able to work part-time or even full-time, though they then do little else except rest. Research is being conducted on many fronts, including immunology, endocrinology and neurology, but a cause remains unknown.

Gay Baines

Let Me Rail, Just for One Day

against the rule of open air,
let me relish the white
lockup of winter, balm
to my restless, lazy nature.

Let me be prickly too,
like the thistle burrs on my spring jacket
that strayed from jacket to sweater,
from sweater to sandwich, from sandwich
to finger & thumb, to the round brass cup
on the bookshelf.

Let me wander in the burr's domain,
outside, where spring remains hidden
or barely visible—the golden aura of willows,
the blood in thin maple branches
pinking the sky.

Let me wallow in spring's exhaustion,
the awful realization every year
since I was fourteen that the pain
felt on Monday means fever on Tuesday,
syncope on Wednesday, only to realize
it's the fear of Last Time, a disease
I caught early & relive every April.

Midsummer's two months away.
Let me smooth over by June,
my original month, with its heat and perfume.
Today, let me resist, then welcome
that sweet giving in, that letting go
in the darkness.

Jenny Noller

The Power of Sugar

The day I came home from business on the East coast, I discovered what makes me powerful. I'd met this man on the plane on his way to Bali. His name was Bob and after three champagnes he took a white gauze scarf with golden threads out of his bag and wrapped it around his head. "You know," he told me, "I did an article on artificial sweeteners for a magazine. Seventy-five percent of all the complaints the FDA gets are from people complaining about sweeteners. Stomachaches, headaches, ulcers, blindness, cancer."

"Is that right," I say.

"And people still drink it," he says and points to my Diet Coke.

"I'd believe it. People will do just about anything for a rush."

"That they will. Sugar to shooting, they'll get the heart rate jacked so the breaths come deeper. Living and love, living and love—know what I mean?"

He stares at me so long I realize that he wants me to answer, so I tell him about this lawyer I went out with, this short tennis player who wore round glasses and rubbed his lips a lot when he was thinking. This lawyer worked on the team with the people who kept Nutra-Sweet on the market.

"Is that right," Bob says. "That's scary stuff."

"You better believe it is. He said not a one of them drinks diet drinks anymore."

"I don't drink diet drinks," he says. "I only drink alcohol when I fly." And Bob lifts his glass of champagne to toast.

"Why?"

"Why only when I fly?"

"Yes."

"Because it relaxes me," he says like he's about to sing a mellow jazz song. "And, because I hate the smell of airplanes."

I tell him how I hate it too. How I hate the stale coldness that smells like new clothes, new leather mixed with spearmint. "Too many people chew spearmint gum on airlines."

"Hear, hear," he says and motions to the stewardess for another bottle. He tightens his turban and sticks a finger in his champagne. "You know, I fell in love with this Balinese weightlifter last summer. I don't even know his last name." Bob licks his finger and drinks half the glass.

I like this man, I think. I usually hate it when the person next to me on a plane starts to talk to me. I've got the head tilt away, the engrossed reading down pat. Maybe I don't give people enough of a chance. Maybe all that's needed is the full second, a full breath, anything that reminds you that you're alive, that all possibility blooms only out of realized and seized opportunity.

"I have pictures," he says and roots through his army knapsack. Lord, I think, I do *not* want to look at these. But I force myself to be open because it seems to me that relationships are built on little offerings such as these. He pulls them out, five of them. They are bad pictures, bad composition, and developed on cheap grainy film. In one there's a woman with bright fruit piled high on her head and her eyes closed in a blink. "That's a festival where the whole village takes offerings to the temple," Bob says. "Umi took that one."

"The weightlifter?"

"His sister," Bob says. In another photo, one Bob took, a fisherman stands in the surf casting, but the picture has no good movement, the line from the rod already sunk in the water. "That was on the north side of the island. See the black sand?" I nod. Only one picture really catches my eye, this one where the weightlifter holds a wispy little girl. The weightlifter is rather slight by American standards, but his skin glows like warm bronze. He and the girl sit on a log with a bright blue sea behind them, black sand underfoot, a banged-up dinghy in the background. The little girl holds a basket of woodcarvings and she's offering one to the weightlifter. "That one's nice, isn't it?" Bob says and takes the picture from me. He smears a thumb across the weightlifter's face. "I even like his gap teeth." He hits his own front teeth. "Sexy, don't you think?"

"Not really."

"You don't think?"

"No." Bob's half-drunk so I don't feel too badly about being somewhat rude. Then I do start to feel a little guilty so I ask, "What's it like in Bali?"

"The whole country smells of jasmine," he says and leans his temple on the airline seat. "And it's really cheap. I could live there for months. I'm a writer."

"That sounds exotic."

"What do you do?" he asks.

"Me? Nothing important. I sit at a desk. I travel, a lot."

"So you must be important. If you travel so much."

"There is nothing more pathetic than the anonymous traveler," I say and hit the button for the stewardess.

"And nothing more empowering than the traveling soul consciously maintaining anonymity."

I was going to ask why he would say that, but the stewardess comes and I ask her to get me another Diet Coke. Bob looks at me, then at my glass, and raises his eyebrows. "I know," I tell him. "I know."

"The pleasures of the present never outweigh the future."

"Save it," I tell him and take the last drink. I open my magazine and read about some place that does four-handed massages and will make omelets at two in the morning at the ring of a silver bedside bell. I think about the tennis player who wore round glasses and rubbed his lips a lot when he was thinking and how we could've ordered four-minute eggs and caviar, how we could've traveled everywhere for fun if we'd only hit it off more. I hit the button again and ask the stewardess to bring me more magazines, more options. But I'm bad with decisions, really bad. If you choose one, you cannot have the others. I can't decide whether to read news or trash. The news will make me feel intelligent. A woman's or a home magazine will make me wistful for things I do not have. I can tell the stewardess is impatient, so I grab a home magazine and tell her thanks. She tries to smile. I notice that her lipstick is gone and realize I don't think I've ever seen a stewardess without lined lips.

* * *

Bob walks with me off the plane. He trips on the top flap of his sandal twice as we walk down the concourse. Bob's tall, really tall—six-four, six-five. And he's got a handlebar mustache I want to cut. I almost tell him he should get a shave as we pass the salon in the main section, but I figure I'm just tired, in a bad mood, maybe hypoglycemic or something.

"Bob, it's been great," I tell him. "Enlightening." He seems like the kind of guy who would take it as a compliment—remember it before he goes to bed and smile. We shake hands and he turns and walks toward the international concourse.

Bob's going to Bali to smell jasmine and find love with a weightlifter. I feel like I'm dreaming: where do these people come from? These people who are blithe, untroubled, immune to dark days and loneliness. He was probably the type of child who ate all the sugar cereals he wanted, all the cookies, ran around naked and barefoot. People like that make me sick. As if the more you put into a body, a person, the more sugar, the richer the food, the more uninhibited they are, the more they have a chance of being interesting, of being free, being unconstrained. It's like people are taking a gamble, stuffing themselves full of everything, doing anything, just hoping that the mixings somehow make genius. Not even huge genius, just little genius. Product: LIBERATION. Something a parent can be proud of, something they can think they had a part in.

My head starts to hurt, so I get in line to buy a drink at a pretzel stand near a window that looks out onto the runways and baggage belts. These men paid sixteen bucks an hour sling bags like dead bodies onto a ramp that carries them away. They seem to be happy about the tossing. It's got to be a great job. They can hurl anything they want as hard as they want. They probably go home, get bitched at for a jammed Disposall and a garage full of cobwebs, and then just wait for work when they can throw whomever they want on the belt. Wife, kids, boss, annoying strangers—over and over again on the belt.

I'm about to order a Diet Coke, but I change my mind. "Tea, please," I tell the boy behind the counter. "It doesn't have caffeine, right?" He tells me no.

"The lemon mint would be fine," I say. I take a sip, and it's terrible. I'm talking strong and manufactured terrible with the kind of aftertaste that is specific to food courts. I ask the kid where the condiments are and he points with a hooked pinky to a table around the corner. Who does that? Points with a pinky. It's unnatural. Where the hell did he pick up something like that?

I grab a packet of Sweet'N Low and rip it open. I realize I've ripped three packets stuck together, and for some reason—I don't know, call it my own small version of self-martyrdom—I dump all the bags in instead of throwing the extras away. It's my daily contribution to the environment, a little tick mark in my column for not being wasteful. Now the tea is sweet on top of food court. Revolting. Absolutely revolting. I go get my bag and catch a cab.

As we're driving away from the airport, me sipping this tea that I've decided tastes like it has coins dropped in it, I see this plane—this big jetliner in a glide slow and even. Then I see the fire, balls of it, coming out of one of the engines and some part of me can hear the screams of the passengers, these high-pitched banshee wails. I feel this welling, this flood of energy, this desire so strong and hot that makes me think that if I believed enough I could stop that plane. If for one second I had faith—a passionate intuition, to be Wordsworthian about it—that I believed I had the power, then I would. In my mind, I can even see the passengers hugging their knees. I would reach out a hand and pluck them from the sky if I could. And all I can say is "Oh my God." It nearly comes out like a sob. I'm so surprised that I suck in, suck some of that tea down the wrong way, the sugar ting bright in my throat. So, I'm coughing hard and my head slams the seat in front of me. The hacks come from down low like I've just sucked in a fly or I'm last-stage emphysema. I see this spray of spit on the back of the bench and while my coughs quiet I fish out a Kleenex and wipe it up. Deep breaths rake through me. The wet smears start to disappear. Then I notice—everything is paralyzed. And I mean everything. It's all one big pause. Like someone punched a button. The driver's head frozen in a turn. The cars all around me still.

I get out of the cab and stand in the middle of the highway. It's all quiet, except this butterfly starts to dance yellow across the road. And he makes it. From one side all the way to the other, across twelve lanes. When I look at it shaking on the other side, twittering off above the lawns of buildings, I think, "That was a miracle. It's alive now and it wouldn't have been before." I feel stupid standing out in the middle of the highway not a hundred paces past the on-ramp thinking miracles about butterflies, so I reach for my phone, but it's dead. I gather my things, slam the door with my bag, and start walking.

* * *

There's this BP station situated perfectly at the airport exit. You know the kind—the ones that suck up all the business because they're on the right side of the median. The kind where only the misers drive the extra tenth of a mile, make the left, and hook around to save five cents on ten dollars. I go to the BP too. You can only walk so far in stacked heels before your tiny toe goes numb. A lady in a scarf with Jackie O. sunglasses stands by a Beemer, this silver 525i, and she's frozen placing the gas nozzle back. I walk by the car and touch it and the CD player starts; I can hear the music through the car frame. It makes me jump. Forget a phone! I open the passenger door and sit inside. I listen to the music and then turn the key. The car starts, so I pop the trunk, and throw in my bags. I look at the lady who is still frozen and drive off.

The highway has cars all over it. I weave in and out going about twenty. Then I think, this is stupid, so I drive in the emergency lane. I turn towards home, to my small apartment with three bushy peace lilies, perfectly ordered file cabinets, a fully stocked wine case, and no fresh milk. I find only one radio station with a show and I assume it's been pre-recorded because all the others are static except for one other which just plays the same song over and over. So I listen to the pre-recorded show. This Reverend talks about how nobody prays anymore. The only time people pray, really pray, is when they're scared. Perhaps I should be scared—everything has stopped, has changed—perhaps I should want to go to church and kneel down and pray for things to be like they were. This could be it: the end. But I don't want to and, even if I did, I don't know where a good church is.

And finally, I am struck by the quiet, this imposed aloneness. Instead of all of the world sifting about making me feel like one lone grain of sand, everything becomes such a marvel. This is the feeling, I'm sure, that extremists have sought—the men hunkered in the ice crags of Abruzzi's Ridge on Mt. Qogori, the feeling Peary felt when consuming the vast horizons of the Arctic, or that Mike Fay felt at moments as he hacked his way through the forests of Africa on the megatransect. It is immaculate and unaffected calm. It makes all of humanity seem insignificant, not just the one trivial person, but all of it, every single one of us packed onto one grain of sand buried down four feet on a beach in the Asian Pacific. The men's search, maybe even every man's search, seems to me suddenly rather humble: to feel and comprehend that which is larger than self.

This isn't bad, driving on the shoulder of the road, the air whipping my hair around so it stands up like little snakes. And I think what Medusa would've done with a car and a full tank of gas. "We need to ask the Lord for forgiveness," the preacher says. "Lord, can you help me? Lord, can you help me to be the best person I can be?"

I exit and drive back into the hills by the coast. That's when I start to get a little shaky. There's this group of kids frozen in the act of piling off a school bus. It's picture still. This mother is in the process of leaning over to embrace her son, but an inch of space splits them. Seeing this almost-hug bothers me because that's how I feel. I know there are people who love me, my family, a friend or two, but they are separate from me. They are near, but they do not comfort. I slam the accelerator down and fly through a red light.

I check my watch and it's still ticking. The digital on a bank reads seventy-four degrees and flashes stock signs that all read zero. It dawns on me then: why am I going home? I can go anywhere! I backtrack a bit, cross the bridge, and park near my favorite jewelry store. I go in and start looking. Renaldo and Rene run it. They're two brothers with good eyes for design. Renaldo and Rene are such good businessmen they have a file in the back office, and as soon as a customer leaves they write down everything she's touched in the store. They know her birthday and her anniversary, if she has one. Problem is, my file's thick. I go in and lust after this one pair of diamond studs pretty often. That's what you have to do when you don't even have a retirement fund set up—lust.

The people here are paralyzed too. I realize I have to go when I start to think about stealing things; I'm looking at the standing mint tray and thinking the base of it could easily break the glass counter. I could take a pair of diamond studs. I cringe. I want to do it so badly. No one would know. As I'm walking out the door, I give one last look into the emerald case at the rings—I've always loved the limeness of a Colombian emerald—and I bump into a person who is frozen, this guy in a navy suit. He had been hunched over inspecting the tanzanite. When my body touches his, he moves. "Excuse me," he says, even though I bumped into him. "I'm so sorry."

"Oh," I say. "Oh. Oh." The rules have been expanded. He talks. He moves an arm.

"Are you okay?" he asks. "Are you okay?"

"Oh, I'm fine," I say, though I can feel the bruise starting on my shin.

He looks at me, holds my upper arms like he's about to shake me, except it's tender. He looks into my eyes with a genuine concern, the type of concern that nails you to a board—you feel pinned, chosen, loved. "You sure?" he asks.

"I'm sure. Just shocked me is all." I feel this almost overwhelming urge to kiss him, but he goes right on back to looking at the jewelry. It's got to be a birthday he's almost forgotten; he's got fervor. He has not looked up and noticed that the others are motionless. Part of me wants to stay around to see what happens when he realizes Renaldo isn't looking up from the gold hoop earrings on the suede pad and that Rene's like a statue with one of those little black magnifiers hooked on his finger, but the other part of me doesn't. I turn too quickly again and knock over this tall, skinny display case and it crashes to the floor.

"Whoa," the suit says. He rushes to help me, but I'm already picking things up and putting them on the counter. He helps, picks up some gold bangles and a pile of money clips. Then I see it—this gaudy little brooch. I can't take my eyes off it. There's this clouded emerald bust of a girl set in the middle of a gold, spade-like shape with two rows of chip rubies and diamonds around the outside. The girl's face is so peaceful; the hair lies full and somehow germinal on her shoulders. I feel like she's chosen me. Instantly I know I love it. I can't let it go. "Your day must be worse than my day," the suit says. I laugh and while I'm setting a sterling thimble and engraved locket on the counter, I drop the brooch into my pocket.

"I'm late for an appointment," I lie. Then I leave, my right arm stiff and holding the brooch inside my pocket to my leg because part of me would bet in a store like that that they have a camera. I'd just die if Renaldo and Rene knew it was me because I don't steal things.

I sit in the car and look at the green girl's profile, the smooth bridge of her nose, the rushing curve of shoulder, and think someone should have bought this for me. So I drive to Charlie's house, the man I went out with before the short tennis player who wore round glasses and rubbed his lips a lot when he was thinking. I was in love with Charlie. He's married now to this blonde-haired powerhouse of a woman who he says he loves, but really she's just good in bed. Actually, I think they love each other in a rather comfortable sort of way; they're just not in love—neither one has ever glowed around the other. They fight all the time and everyone says their marriage is one big make-up. I hate her. She changed him so that he doesn't do things that used to make him laugh, like playing his guitar or watching the city league's pee-wee soccer practice. That, and he hardly ever visits his family, which he was close to before he met her. He even talks differently now—so what if his grammar is better, he's stilted. He's ready to give a formal lecture and out of place in a bar. I know where he hides the house key, on a nail inside the far left cabinet door in the garage, and when I see that his wife's car is gone, I let myself in. She, no doubt, is off massaging a fat old businessman and, for once, the thought of her standing in a darkened room filled with soft music, her strong fingers slicked with oil, a body relaxing beneath her touch, does not make me the least bit jealous.

Their house smells of chlorine and basil. Dishes are piled in the sink and books are stacked on the kitchen table. Their black Lab bounds at me and smells my crotch. I scratch him for a minute and decide to go to the bedroom. Old loves sometimes make me heady. I just want to see the bedroom, to find out what's important enough to set on the dresser.

It startles me to see Charlie, his fixed body, towel wrapped around him with his face half-shaved, foam all fluffed on the other half. I stand there and stare at him for a minute. You know how it is—when you search a face that's changed for something you once knew. I don't see anything I know, which is why I start to take off my clothes. I think maybe if I'm naked too, just skin to skin, he'll be him and I'll be me. I take off my blazer and fold it on a chair, remove my tank, my sandals, my underwear with the stretch pulls and elastic showing through around the legs. So there we are and I touch him.

Charlie cuts himself when he sees me in the mirror and this line of red starts up, five beads in sized succession. "What are you doing here?" he says and turns around.

"I just stopped by," I tell him. "To say hello."

"What are you doing here?" he asks again.

For a second I don't have another answer. Then I say with my voice all low and sultry, "I don't know, it's your dream." Don't judge me on that, though.

"Not again," he says like he's been defeated. And part of me right there wants to call it off, but I don't. I'm a crashing plane. I spit on a piece of tissue and stick it to his neck.

"You're bleeding," I tell him. Then I finish shaving him. We kiss, fall into bed, and make hard love.

"Please," he says. "Please, please, please." And it's like that until I fall asleep curled up to his back, the night falling. I wake, hours later, to my own hot breath condensed and patched wet on his back. I wipe it off with the sheet, dress, fill the Lab's water bowl, and leave.

* * *

The night has a lick of cool in it and I'm thinking how I could use a stiff drink, a Black Russian with cubes of ice. Then I smell rain in the air—smell the chemical that the leaves release when their stomata open wide before a storm. I can hear the surf below crashing rocks. My hair is all snakes again because you can't drive a car like that and leave the windows up. I reach around for an umbrella in the pouch behind the front seat, to see how much of a Girl Scout the woman who owns the car is, and I touch something. Then there is singing. "So I wanna, wanna, wanna go. Wanna, wanna, wanna, wanna go." This sweet little child's voice, singing no real melody. "Hey, it got dark," the voice says. And right there, I feel sick.

"We're going to go get your mother right now," I tell it. "So don't worry. Why don't you come up here and sit beside me?"

"I can't," it says. "I'm not supposed to sit in front."

"Well, how about you just buckle up in back for me," I tell it. The kid worms into the seat behind me and fastens the buckle. "You were hiding," I say.

It giggles. "Where are we?" it asks. "Do you know the password?"

"No," I tell it. "I don't know the password. I just borrowed the car for a bit. You fell asleep. We're going to get your mommy right now."

"Okay," it says.

I don't know what to say to it, but I like the humming, its little jumps of half and whole steps. I look in the rearview mirror and I can see the kid drawing on the window with a finger, the grease leaving swirls that glisten like slug trails when the moonlight hits them. I keep forgetting that cars don't have their lights on and I almost hit three—swerve, brake, swerve.

"Whee," it says.

We get to the gas station and I touch the mother. She sucks in, looks at the dark sky all around, and then says, "What?"

"I didn't say anything," I tell her.

"Where's my car?" she asks. I don't answer her because she asked so rudely. "My car?" She's getting upset. "My child's in the car," she says.

I tell her it's okay and point at the curb where I parked it. "Your kid's in the back." She walks over at a fast clip, opens the door, and says something to her child. She gets in the front seat, starts to pull away, and I realize that I'm standing there holding my purse and that my suitcase and carry-on are in the trunk.

"Excuse me. Excuse me." I'm running alongside the car, knocking on the window. She looks scared at first—I admit I must look like a piece of work, sex-crumpled and a bit crazed—but she does stop. I try to explain it to her. She blankly stares at me, not registering anything I say.

Then finally she says, "Get in. The least I can do is give you a lift."

"I'll catch a cab at the airport if you drop me there," I tell her. "But watch out for the cars—they're all stopped." She looks at me like I'm crazy and nearly hits one in the process.

"Jesus Christ," she says.

"Dime," the child says.

"Everything is so damn dark," she says.

"What?" I ask and then notice she still has her sunglasses on.

"Dime," the child says again.

"I'm trying to stop cursing," the mother says. "Every time I say a bad word I have to pay a dime to the family jar. At the end of the year we give the money to charity."

"That sounds like hell," I tell her.

"Dime," it says.

She drops me off at the terminal and I stand there and watch her pull away, steer little quick turns. She's probably what everyone would call a nice lady. She was concerned, level-headed, well-mannered, all around nice. "But those sunglasses have got to go," I yell at the car just before it makes the bend.

* * *

The glass airport doors whish open and I walk in like a god, but not a big one—maybe Medea, Parvati, or a female version of

Ixtliton. Why I didn't have that woman drive me home, I'm not sure—I didn't even ask which way she was going. Things always become so obvious in retrospect—like one big, eternal pilgrimage where you realize over and over again you didn't have to go anywhere but only had to shift your perspective. So, I leave my bags stashed behind a dying palm tree in a big white pot. Terminal in the terminal. As I start to find my way to a cab stand, I cut a corner too close and brush arms with a woman who is frozen in the check-in line. She's wearing a flowy skirt and looks as if she could model for a gardening magazine. She bumps the guy in front of her, hits her face really hard against his back. She holds her nose and says, "Excuse me. I'm sorry." She sees me look back over my shoulder at her and she looks down. People get nervous like that; they do not want you to notice them in weak moments. There are another couple of seconds before she realizes everyone's frozen and things are quiet. "Hey. Hey," she calls to me. "Hey. What's going on? Why is everyone still?"

"I don't know," I say. And then I realize that the man didn't unfreeze, so I turn around. "Will you touch him again?" I ask and point to him. She touches the man.

"He's warm, but even his jacket won't move," she says. She tugs at his sleeve and then yanks on his whole arm, but it doesn't budge. The man stands there studying his ticket. He looks like an aging action star, the kind that only plays intellectual roles now though. His hair is the right color of salty brown and he has that brooding thing going. "You touch him," she says in a frightened voice.

So I move behind him and touch the hair on the back of his neck. He clears his throat, keeps on looking at his ticket, and leans down to get his bag. He just kind of looks to one side, then the other, looks down the line of counters, and then he takes his bag and nudges the man in front of him who doesn't move, of course. He nudges the guy in front of him again and looks side to side, again.

"Hey, you," the woman says.

He startles. "What? What's going on?" He swings around, then asks, "Who are you?"

"I'm Jane," she says. I just smile at him; I don't feel like telling him my name. It's somewhat amusing, the look on his face.

"Is this some sort of a prank?" he asks me with a hint of nastiness. "Like a TV thing?"

I shrug. "I'm going to go get something to eat," I tell them. "I'm hungry." I can feel them watch me walk away. Each person I pass who is in arm's reach, I touch. They come unfrozen—three businessmen, an old lady, two college girls, and a husband and wife. And the whole time all I want to know is what Jane and the Harrison Ford think of me. What kind of awe. What kind of fear. I turn around and say, kind of announcing to the whole lot of them, "This is a test. It is only a test. You have hated life for too long and you all need to think about your sins. You must repent or die." Jane stops smiling; she thought we were on the same team. Jane and one of the businessmen I just touched drop to their knees and start to pray. The man looks so desperate and frightened. Good, I think. And then I realize that I'm really, really hungry and that maybe I shouldn't have said that.

I hop over the counter to one of the fast-food places to get a Diet Coke and grab a handful of some of cold French fries and snatch a revolving pretzel. I walk down the concourse looking out the windows at the blue and red lights lining the runway; they're just bright enough that I can make out the nose of that jetliner I saw earlier with the frozen fire lit up behind it. It is beautiful, the fin of its tail stuck up and glowing, the fire bright and jagged.

I finish the pretzel and fries and turn to find a trash can for my cup when I see Bob sitting in a chair. I go sit next to him. He's still wearing the tight Wranglers and the turban. He looks like a Punjabi version of a cowboy, but somehow he looks exactly right. Sane. By contrast perhaps. Maybe it's because his glasses ride low on his nose and his index finger is mid-scratch on his moustache. I touch his knee.

"Jesus," he says and grabs his chest. "You scared me."

"Sorry," I tell him.

He straightens his back and says, "It's dark out."

"I know."

"What time is it?" He looks at his watch. "Is it really after three?"

"Yes," I tell him.

"It can't be."

"It is," I say.

"I can't believe I missed my flight," he says and leans over and opens his sack. "I don't know how I did that."

"Bob," I say. "Just look." I nod my head to the hall. He looks down the hall, then swivels around and looks behind him.

"Nobody's moving," he says. "What's going on?"

I pull him up and point at the plane above the runway.

"What do you make of that?" I ask.

He's quiet for a minute. "Well pinch my ass and call me a ninny," he says. He gives a loud *ha* and then I see the flicker in his eyes, the terror I've been looking for. He notices I'm studying him, so he says, "Whoo, my therapist is just going to love this one."

The plane hangs in the air, its defiance of gravity nearly incomprehensible. My eyes keep looking for a string shooting up to the heavens.

"How many people do you think are on the plane?" Bob asks.

"I don't know."

"Two hundred or more, I bet."

And the plane, its metal glinting, sure as when you're looking at the vase and suddenly see the two faces, becomes a casket.

"Bob, I think we have to get the people out of the plane."

"That plane?"

I nod.

"Of course," he says and waves a hand. We stand there and look out the window for a minute and Bob says, "How come we're not still?"

"Watch," I tell him and touch one of the stewardesses who's in the middle of the concourse. She walks away, heels hitting hard, and then she looks up at the lights, pauses for a second, and keeps on walking.

He goes up and touches another stewardess and nothing happens. "Does it work for everyone?" he asks.

"Yes."

"Do it again," he says.

"No."

"Just one more."

"I think we need to find ladders," I tell him. "Can you help me?"

"Touch just one more."

"No."

"Please," he says and touches me.

"Okay." So I tap this backpacker curled up on the floor sleeping. The packer breathes in, shifts, and keeps on sleeping. "Satisfied?"

"What we need," Bob says and slings up his backpack, "are firemen—lots of them."

"We don't need firemen," I tell him. "What we need to find is an airport crew." So I push open an emergency exit door and the alarm doesn't go off.

"Hey," Bob says. "They've suckered us."

We go out and I start touching people to find someone who can get the crash crew out. We finally talk to a guy name Mac who looks like he should be on a farm. Mac says, "Yes, the airport does have an emergency team with fire trucks and ladders, but not the extra tall ones. You might need some extra tall ladders to reach that there plane."

"All right," Bob says. "Tell us how we find them."

"Probably one of the big fire stations would be best," Mac says.

"You've got to be kidding me," I say to Mac. Then I look at Bob and say, "Aren't you just the lucky one."

I touch one of the big trucks so it will start and we all pile in, go to a fire station, and I unfreeze the firemen.

When we get back to the airport with everyone, we all end up in one big line looking at the plane as the sun crests the horizon. A welder hooks himself into a harness at the top of a ladder and starts to torch the side door of the plane; sparks fly. One of the firefighters comes up and stands at the fire chief's shoulder. "Well, Chief, how're we doing this one?"

The chief looks at me, "If you touch it—it goes down?"

"Presumably," I tell him.

He nods. "We're going to have to wrap you up," he says to me. "Boys, get over here. Take off your jackets," he says to the men. "Lay them down. We need some cord too. John, get some cord. We're just going to wrap you up and carry you in there," he says to me. "You touch them one at a time, and they leave down the ladder. In and out. Who's volunteering to carry her?" Four men raise their hands. "Good," he says.

The door crashes to the ground and some of the firemen clap; the welder salutes and waves.

"Boy, I wish I had my camera with me," Bob says. He watches one of the young fireman walk by. "I bet I could teach that one a thing or two," he says and tightens his headscarf.

The firemen bind me in their fire jackets, the cord tight around my legs and feet. My right arm is free though and I've got a hold on the cord. "You ready?" the chief asks.

"As ever," I tell him. The four men hoist me up under their arms and walk me over to the ladder where the climber, a husky looking redhead named Sisel, hooks me onto his harness; he's going to climb the ladder, dragging me behind him. We've decided there isn't time to find a crane. The Chief doesn't trust the physics of any of it and somehow he got it in his head that everything will unfreeze at noon—something about equinoxes and balancing eggs.

The four men climb ahead of him. "See you at the top," they say.

"Is someone going to spot me?" I ask.

"I am," the chief says.

The climber starts and I hear Bob yelling, "Good luck. Break a leg. Shake your fanny." The neon reflector strips on the jackets wrapped around me flash in the sun.

We reach the top of the ladder, about sixty feet up, and the men lift me into the plane so carefully I really do feel like a priceless mummy. "What are your names?" I ask them.

"I'm John. He's Jared. Joe and Jim." The men nod at me.

"We're doomed," I say. "Too many J's." They laugh even though it's not funny. I start to touch people one by one.

Sisel explains to each passenger to follow him, quietly, quickly, and carefully, then climb quietly, quickly, and carefully down the ladder. Those words seem to scare the passengers when they hear them, so not one of them says anything. They just file out. In Row 5, Jim loses his balance and I almost touch a seat.

"Watch it," John says.

"I am. I am."

"It's okay," I tell him and tap a ten-year-old girl on the head.

She looks at us and says, "You look funny."

"You said it, sister," I tell her and they back up and position me for Row 6. About an hour into this my arm starts to cramp and shake and I'm afraid it's going to drop down on its own. "Can't we go faster?" I ask.

"No, they're getting backed up on the ladder. Some people are afraid of heights," one of the J men says.

"Well just have Sisel kick their hands," I say, and John laughs. There's something darkly amusing about people who've just been saved from a crashing airplane falling to their deaths on the ground because they fell off the rescue ladder.

"It's not funny," another J says. Maybe it wasn't funny and

was just the stress, our minds groping for humor, but we laughed again anyway.

We finish and the last person I touch is one of the stewardesses strapped down in back. "She's writing something," John says before I touch her.

"What's it say?" I ask.

"I just wanted to say that I—" John reads.

"Hey now," a J says.

"I think I'm going to die and I wanted you to know that—"

"Hey now. I mean it. That's private," the J says.

"Private my ass. She'd be dead if it weren't for us," John barks. "Don't you want to see what's really in her heart?"

"Hey now, it's fine. We're fine," I tell them. And I touch her. She looks up at us and screams. The men tense so badly they almost drop me. They tell her that it's okay and where to go.

"Can we hurry? I'm sweating like a whore in church," I tell them.

When we get back to the runway people are listening to Bob who's standing on a block trying to run the show. "We just got more coffee right over here," he shouts and points to two firefighters lugging a container. Bob hands out yellow blankets and the people have started to file away to the terminal where groups huddle and shake. Bob sees me and comes over. "You were amazingly brave. Doesn't quite seem real, does it?" He hugs me and then looks at me hard. "Do you know that you have flecks of yellow in your eyes?"

"Do I?"

"You do," Bob says and hands me a coffee.

"You want to see something?" I ask.

"That depends," he says.

So I get out the brooch and say, "You like it?" He looks from her face to mine. I want to give it to him.

"Where'd you get it?"

"I stole it."

"Really?"

"Yes. I want you to have it."

"Oh, I couldn't," he says.

"I insist."

"I really can't take it."

"Why not?"

"It just kind of has a bad feeling around it. Like evil. You should get rid of it," he tells me matter-of-factly.

"Is that right," I say. For a minute, I'm so mad at him for not accepting this gift, this token of how connected I feel to him, that I run for the plane and throw it—hurl the brooch long and hard, the kind of throw you feel in your lats. The emerald girl arcs through the air, catches a gust of wind, flies up, and tinks the side of the jet. The jet's screaming body surges and falls to the ground. The heat from the fire singes my eyebrows, and I know I can't hear for at least ten seconds. I'm on the ground and I taste blood. People's mouths move, the fire chief waves his arms, and over his shoulder I can see one of those baggage trams snaking and people running to me. I look in the sky and the planes are moving and one of the guys with the orange batons starts to wave frantically; he's waving at this milling mass of blankets that have appeared in his space, streaming in a yellow line off the runway to the terminal.

"My God, are you all right? Don't move," Bob says to me, but then adds, "You're going to be fine." I nod. "Don't move," he says again. And then he brushes my cheek with the backside of his finger. "You're amazing," he says. "Absolutely extraordinary. Will this ever be a story for me."

* * *

I love to think that I'm some phantom in stories now, that even when I don't know it's happening, I am living through these people. I know that taxi driver has got to tell people how he drove a woman who disappeared into thin air right on the highway—*ella se esfumó sin dejar rastro*. Charlie, when he sees me at holiday parties or randomly in the video store, most definitely looks at me like I'm different somehow; I think it might even rift his marriage a bit. Who knows what Jackie O., Jane, and Harrison Ford think? Bob went to Bali. He sent me a postcard: "No one believes me," he wrote. I'm sure he told the weightlifter and everyone he smoked with how he saved a burning airplane, how this woman with some magic power chose him because she just sensed that he would be able to handle a crisis. Who *would* believe him? I doubt that any of the men in the fire squad mention it, but I'm sure a few will tell the story to their grandkids someday—how they wrapped a woman in fire jackets, carried her into a crashing plane held frozen in the sky by God himself, and held her while she touched two-hundred-and-seventy-three people back to life. Their kids will send them to a home for sure.

These days, I use sweetener every chance I get, in coffee, tea, sometimes even water depending on my mood. I might even have a few stray packs at the bottom of my purse. Little white granules get stuck in the stitching. Equal, Sweet'N Low, aspartame, saccharine, it doesn't matter—it's the sweetness that counts, the sugar of it, the extra skips of the heart, the heady rush, the quick suck of air, the simple fact that for a day I believed, I became, I mattered. I'd never read the packaging labels before: *0 Calorie Granulated Sugar Substitute. A blend of nutritive and non-nutritive sweeteners. Use of this product may be hazardous to your health. This product contains saccharin which has been determined to cause cancer in laboratory animals.* Sometimes I sit and think about the thousands of rats that died for it, grew tumors so that I could have .035 ounces of perfect sweetness. And in the end, the price seems so small.

Juan Franco, photograph

JoLee G. Passerini

Hospital Nursery

At work, my friend Charlotte wears flowered scrubs. She is
a rag doll, an angel, worn soft from many washings.
She pads softly through the room.

Surrounded by plastic and latex, metal rolling carts, stacks of linens,
diapers, cases of formula, IV stands garlanded with tubing,
she makes her way deftly through this jungle of non-human, non-person—

to calm another crying infant: *Baby, baby, baby*.
She nods into their startled faces—the world so much and all at once—
her thumb lightly across the forehead, hand cupped

over the pulsing fontanel. She whispers, *I know, I know, I know.*
Sweet boy. Sweet girl. (What happened to make her this way?
Such sweetness as hers grows with pain. It glows an oxygen-rich red.)

She changes the diapers. She pats. She talks about
security measures. She shows me the curled, inked feet.
She shows me the tiny one working hard: *breathe, breathe*.

It seems everyone is working with him, thinking about what alveoli do.
His puckered mouth flutters. Machines do their possible work . . . .
The swaddled babies sleep, wake, and protest. *Breathe, breathe*.

My friend moves silently among the bassinets ready to hold
these children that are hers, not hers, and hers again.

Kim Davis

Prayerstone

When she was ten and her father lay
pallid and curled in a bed
that buckled at the waist and knees
she went to her room
and hugging herself
set her will against his death
like two hands braced
on the boulder they'd seen
near Lake Placid.
Kidney-shaped, the great rock stood
in an open field
lichens slowly inscribing
blue-green and mustard circles
on its shoulders and face.
"An erratic," they said, explaining
nothing. Determined to budge it
she was determined, if only an inch.
An inch was all her father required
to free his life from the musty vault
under that granite slab
a fissure she would open
with the fervency of her mind.
No mere prayer was this.

After his death she felt
not that she had been too weak
but that her resolve had faltered
betrayed by thoughts
which could already imagine him gone.
How they tugged at her hands
like little children
peeling back her fingers
one by one. Then she remembered,
water had carried that stone
lifted it and carried it
all the way from Quebec
nestled in the body
of a frozen sea:
A miraculous voyage.

King Alfreds, First Light

The King Alfred daffodils lean into the light.
Pink! says the light, and Orange!
The sunlight opens like a speaker, with jokes.
The daffodils tolerate him. In an hour
he will shine them an earnest yellow.
And so they lean—how far I never noticed,
like fishing poles with yellow lures
or cups on sticks dipping for yellow in a well,
like bugles blowing after a yellow note.

Blowing for the forsythia, the crocus.
Early spring lets in a spill of blue, a dab of white,
squills, snowdrops—but only as counterpoint,
only to invent a purer yellow.
Yellow that aches with its lack of irony.
Yellow that is more a belief in color
than the color itself, fall's dying
muted golds purified and resurrected.
What endures after the winter is yellow.

Why can't my daffodils be more like the tulips?
Late-risers!—agnostics standing straight up,
pleased with any color so long as it can go to a party,
lipstick reds and cocktail-bar purples, tulips in green throats,
tulips sporting frilly petals, we're talking *tulips*.
People say the daffodils are happy. They're wrong.
Just look at how they crane their yellow selves,
straining on arched green stems, searching, wounded, soulful,
kings of trying to understand.

Unknown

Prickle and shim of nape
and skin; the feeling

enters
like an intruder

at the June wedding
of some limpid girl

or today packing
our footfalls bounding

room to empty room
unfastened with the furniture.

We aren't moving
only re-sanding the floors.

Still, in our seventh year
of marriage
there are moments

we shift nearer
our unknown selves

who we once were

or never will be again
in another's gaze.

They brush past us
lifting up the fine hairs.

Jim Tilley

Dog and Mulberry

She said it was a Japanese
maple shrub, the kind that seldom
grows tall, but I know
that it's really a mulberry bush, and those leaves
beneath it are ashes, fallen
from the tropical storm that washed away
all my sins but one.

I am my dog now, tethered
in the shadow of my house, hunting
for rabbits in the sun. They always scamper
beyond reach; my world
spirals slowly into mulberry. I stand my ground
on all fours among the ashes, having found
no way to unwind time.

Mika Yamamoto

Ice Cream

Hinako was thirty-five.

"Too young to already be alone!" They lamented around her. She had one daughter, Yumeko, who was three years old

"How unfair."

"How cruel God is."

Hinako did not say a word when she heard people talk about her life as if she were not there.

"Perhaps you will meet someone else," some said, as if this would be a solution.

Her mother, especially, was distraught. "You poor thing, you poor thing." She would come to Hinako's house on Saturday afternoons on her way back from flower-arranging class.

Hinako would continue to chop green onions. She would stand at the kitchen counter with her back to her mother. Ton, ton, ton, ton, ton. . . . Rhythmically, quickly, the green onions would be sliced in slivers to be eaten with tofu or miso soup for dinner. Hinako never once looked out the window in front of which she was standing.

Her neighbor would come over in the evening, when Hinako was washing the dishes.

"Did he leave you any money?" Her neighbor would ask. This was typical of Masako—to be so indiscreet. Hinako had been startled by Masako's crassness when she had first met her. Now, she was used to it. Hinako's mother said that the reason Masako was so meddlesome was because she was from the country. Hinako's mother tended to forget her own rural origin when it was convenient.

"Well, I hope he left her *something*." Masako would speak to no one in particular when Hinako wouldn't answer.

"*Nantoka*," Hinako would say. Directly translated this means, "Somehow." This is the proper way to answer someone in Japanese when you don't want to actually answer the question. The answer reassures the other party that the concern is appreciated at the same time that worry is unnecessary.

At night, Hinako slept next to her daughter. She heard that in America, children and parents sleep in different rooms even when the children are very little. She was glad to be living in Japan. Yumeko's warm, sleepy breath was slow and peaceful next to her. In contrast to the people who came to her home, the people at work never uttered a single word to her about her situation. She knew that they discussed it only when she was not present. Only once, when she had made an error in her work, did her boss say, "I know it's a difficult time for you, but you are going to have to be more careful."

It was fall when Satoru had, one day, simply, died. He had no good reason. He was 39 and in perfect health. That morning, he had gotten up early to go to the gym. He said that he would be late for dinner. Later that day, he went to inspect a factory several hours away in Chiba. Masa, his co-worker, was driving. There was a car accident. Masa had a broken arm. Satoru was killed on impact. The leaves were crimson and gold. Fall, the season of appetite, sports, study; the most intensely alive season in the year, and Satoru died.

There was the funeral.

There was Masa, coming day after day to the house. The first time he had come with his arm in a sling. She had opened the door, and he fell to the ground. He kneeled with his forehead touching the entranceway tile.

"*Gommennasai!*" His apology was more than an apology. It was a plea for forgiveness, knowing there was no forgiveness; knowing he would never forgive himself. It was a plea for a chance to make amends, knowing here was no way to make amends for a life that was lost. Hinako had stood dumb with his head at her feet. She understood his suffering. But her suffering was so much more. She knew it was not his fault. But she could not forgive him.

"Please, take yourself home," she finally said quietly. Knowing her wrath towards him, he finally left, walking backwards with his body still bent at the waist.

He came the next day, not even ringing the bell. He just knelt in front of the door with his forehead to the ground, crying out his apologies. She saw him from her bedroom window, but did not open the door.

This continued, day after day.

Finally, one day, she opened the door.

"Please take yourself home," she said to him, again, quietly. He understood. This time, she meant for him never to return. He did not return the next day.

She started to receive envelopes with money in them every month. It was quite a substantial amount of money. She did not know what to do. She knew trying to return it would be futile. He would deny it was he who sent it. She was angry, frustrated, and at a loss. Finally, she just found a drawer and deposited the envelopes there as they came, unopened. It was unsafe practice, she knew, but she did not even have the desire to take care of this money that came to her unasked and unwanted. Maybe she hoped secretly that it would be stolen. She was not touched by the gesture. She was not grateful. It only made her angrier.

Time passed, unbelievable as it seemed. The tree in front of her kitchen shed its leaves, bloomed again, and filled the window. But she did not notice any of this. Her daughter learned to tie her shoes, sang in the pre-school variety show, started to speak thoughts, but she did not notice this either. At work, the time to take inventory came, the auditors came, and she noticed this, but barely. At the greengrocer's sweet potatoes and sweet clementines were replaced with strawberries and bamboo shoots. She bought what was available, not aware of what it meant. Her mother talked of the hassle of changing wardrobe and futon-cleaning. Hinako didn't hear her. But time was passing, she knew, because she stopped turning around every time the sliding door opened, or feeling hope every time the phone rang. She stopped feeling as if she had to consult Satoru to make expensive household buys. She knew time was passing because others mentioned Satoru less and less. But at night, she still dreamed about him. The clothes in his closet still smelled of him.

"Get rid of his things. It's bad luck," her mother would scold.

"*Ne,*" Hinako would say. It was a one-word agreement; agreement to everything, commitment to nothing. The summer came, and it was hot and muggy, as all Tokyo summers are. The cicadas were deafening, even in the city. One could hear the drums practicing for the summer festivals and smell the firecrackers. Young people's voices floated through the streets as they stayed out late into the night. Mosquito repellent burned in spirals. Hinako could hear Satoru's voice inviting her to go eat shaven ice after dinner. He'd swing Yumeko onto his shoulders and the three of them would walk to the noodle shop around the corner.

"Cheaper than air-conditioning," he'd laugh. Remembering this, Hinako's chest would begin to ache.

Obon came. *Obon* is the Japanese holiday for homecoming. Once a year, during *Obon,* they say the spirits come home to visit. Hinako lit the incense, and put out the food that Satoru liked. It was Satoru's first *Obon*. The holiday had always been a ritual for Hinako. But this year was different. This year, there was a very real, very silent desire. She looked forward to it as children look forward to New Year's Day, or their birthdays. It was not that she expected anything supernatural or miraculous to happen. It was just that this holiday was the only one that had any meaning. She fervently wanted Satoru's spirit to come home. Just the hope that this holiday gave her was enough.

Of course, she dreamed of him more vividly during the holiday week. It was probably due to having him so strongly on her conscious mind. All these months, she was acutely aware that she should not think of him so much, should not focus on him. Her mother warned her that she would become delusional, slip into insanity.

But on *Obon,* she had permission to think about him. In fact, the holiday encouraged remembering the dead. So she remembered him—in the most exact details. She reminisced about the time she spent with him.

Masa came of course, one night during *Obon*.

"I was wondering if you would be so generous and allow me to light incense at his altar," he said, keeping his eyes low.

"Please come in," Hinako said.

Masa lit a stick of incense, rang the bell, and put his hands together in front of Satoru's altar. He bowed his head for a long time. The sound of the bell, though soft, lasted a very long time. Masa kept his head bowed twice that length of time. Hinako watched the back of his neck.

"I have been receiving your envelopes," she said when he finally turned around. She saw that he was getting ready to deny it.

"It's okay. I am not trying to return it." she quickly assured him. She opened the drawer stuffed with envelopes.

"I"m sorry. I have not been physically able to handle them until now." She pulled the envelopes one by one. She opened one and took out 30,000 yen.

"Satoru loved eel. Do you think you could go around the comer and buy him some? I want to entice him home tonight. And buy us some too. Don't forget Yumeko. She is little, but she loves eel, too. And maybe pick up some ice cream?" She put the bills in his hands. He tried to reject them.

"No. You must use this money," she said firmly. He understood and protested no more.

That evening, Yumeko, who was only a child, was happy because her home was festive for the first time in a long time. She clapped her hands with glee at the eel and chatted away at Masa. The adults laughed at her and responded to her questions as best they could. "Why do fireflies light up? What do rabbits on the moon eat?"

After dinner, they ate the ice cream that was refreshing in the heat.

"'Cheaper than air-conditioning,' Satoru always said," Hinako remarked lightly; then caught her breath. Masa faltered for a moment, and then it was too late. Only Yumeko chatted away obliviously, and made her ice cream disappear. The adults let theirs melt in silence. The cicadas continued to cry outside.

W.T. Pfefferle

Losing Clare

I prayed for a foggy morning,
one that would somehow shield me
from the inevitable.

A little plane can't leave this island in the fog.
Even a wind will change schedules.
It happens all the time.

I stood on the shore and watched clouds,
I made deals with God
and with the angels.

I could feel the water splash up against me,
surprises, little jolts of something nice and happy
and distant from the other world.

When the sun came up the next morning,
it was clear.
The water lapped lazily.

I talked about some bad movie and some bad seafood
and you ticked off in your head
all the reasons you were leaving.

Perfect sunny morning and you wore
tortoise shell sunglasses I had paid too much for
years and years before.

Later, on the beach,
I looked up and cursed the clouds
that arrived too late.

I watched children and mothers.
I drank white whiskey right out of the bottle,
and pretended you would be emerging soon

from a cabana behind me
whispering something funny
ready to lead me back to where we'd been.

Norm Levine

Coming Up for Air

My mother, the archetype,
saw beyond symptoms
when I was sick
into the theatre of opposing forces.

She could sniff out
how I got it, what to blame—
the three sweaters I didn't wear
or the dreaded draft
she recognized as miasma.
To do battle with that noxious fume
as it seeped under the window sill
she released the rubbing alcohol
or steamed the room with vapors
of benzoin and eucalyptus.
Germs had nothing to do with it,
just good air against the bad.

From my bed the wind was visible
in the trees and I wondered
if that was the foul breath of dragons
or a gust from an invisible knight
blowing in on his invisible horse.
It was my scene to choreograph,
which force would carry the day.
And when I was pronounced healthy
and banished to the great outdoors
it was to inspire me
with large draughts of oxygen
sufficient for the next scenario
and the next.

Olga Costopoulos

White Magpie

Work-morning, parking lot,
our first sighting of a new species—
a magpie in shape, but white, white as gull-breast,
pale gray wings stolen from a dove
and slightly darker tail. Not an albino.
The feathered anomaly moves a few magpie paces off,
a proverb in action, whose wings will remain
fluttering against the edges of the mind.

September 29th, my mother's birthday,
another dream of her—I'm carrying her—
she is almost weightless—
into a house for shelter,
or out of a house that's burning.
I always awake distraught, having to remind myself
she's been gone these eleven years
and I couldn't save her then, either.

She was small, bird-like toward the end.
With no more malice than manners,
a small boy once called her "an old crow"
despite her waves of pure white hair.
Her own granddaughter, nicknamed "Sugarplum,"
named her "Granny Sugarprune."

The bird steps closer again
looks at me with one gold, knowing eye
then, as in a dream, opens its beak
to explain itself, but I hear no sound
through the closed window.
The golden eye keeps watching me.
I keep hearing the gold claws
on the tiled floor of my dreams.
How like her quiet humor
to come as this ruffian fowl
but wearing the colors of a dove.

George Moore

Caduceus

> The nurses pass and pass, they are no trouble,
> They pass the way gulls pass inland in their white caps.
> Doing things with their hands, one just the same as another,
> So it is impossible to tell how many there are.
> —*Sylvia Plath, "Tulips"*

My father became invisible after the first injection.
It was to quiet him down. His heart had been racing
to get through the world, to reach the finish line,
perhaps to wake on the other side of an uncrossed road.

The nurse said he would be fine. Which meant
he was soon to die in any case, so whatever happened
was somehow in the natural order of things.
I said perhaps, but how natural is it to live to eighty-nine?

In the emergency room there were others of more importance.
Gunshot wounds, a man with his leg near severed,
a small girl who was barely breathing. My father
was a doctor himself. He would know there were no cures.

With the right tubes and ECGs, with the right electrical
surveillance, there's really no need to worry, and no need
for a constant professional presence. He was a doctor,
they said, so he would understand. I was the one worried

that he might live another day, and find this silence
in the machinery disturbing. The hospital was big
as a cathedral, and though he worked there, I myself
was always lost. It was not that the faces changed;

they were all one face, unchanging. What I once thought
was a snake from the head of Medusa turned out to be
the staff of Hermes, the alchemist, the conjuror. A symbol
of restraint, control. And if you strike down hard with it

they say a river of weeping will rise up out of the stone.

Laura D. Weeks

Beethoven's Ghosts

My bad hearing haunted me everywhere like a ghost and I fled—from mankind.
—From a letter to Wegeler, November, 1801

Even at midnight
It's breakfast in my ear.
Sausage sizzles in the tympanum
Releasing legions
Of unnatural noises.
A gnat's thin, high-pitched whine
Compounds the mélée in my brain.
Whole and quarter-tones war
With shades of now-stilled voices.

Everywhere they bedevil me!
Afternoons along the Landstrasse
In every promenading *mädchen* I see
Her dear dead face—
My sister—her childishly soft
Brown hair, blue eyes
Deep as heliotrope;
In every pram I see my other self—
My infant brother
Dead, and buried with my name.*

Evenings, in salons
Or in the concert hall,
They gather, grouping
And regrouping, laughing
As they shoot provoking looks
My way. Some raise a glass to me,
One proffers a child's slate
As if to summon me
By automatic writing.

Once, when my hands wandered
Lost among the forest
Of white birch keys,
A hand no bigger than a toddler's
Reached out and touched me
From behind.
So terrible, so slight
That touch, and clinging like warm wax.
I must have jumped a foot
Before I ran.

No, I have it all backwards!
They, they are the living, while I—
I am a freak, a phantom in a frock coat,
Born of a howl and a whimper,
And of my Father's ineluctable lust
For pure sound.
Never to be exorcised, I am
This stubborn ringing
In the celestial ear.

* Beethoven had both a brother and a sister who died in infancy. The presence of the dead brother, christened Ludwig Maria, gave rise to some rather spectacular mental gymnastics on Beethoven's part, including his own deliberate denial of his birthdate.

The Music Lesson

She is as fragile as faiënce
Sitting on my piano bench,
Hair—red as Basho's lantern,
Skin like fine rice paper.

A perfect miniature in porcelain
Down to the deft calligraphy
Around her crinkled eyes and nose
When she smiles.

Then, something shatters.
Behind thick chunks of glass, her eyes—
Like headlights—high beams straying
Into oncoming traffic.

Frantic to undo the damage,
Casting wildly about for a stone
To unlock her private language, I
Surround her with my voice.

"No. Again. Remember, for a pianist
The ring finger is number four, not three."
She uncoils a moist fist, stretches
Fingers that betray her.

"Here. Try this." I place
My long loose-jointed bamboo shoots
Over her slim white tubers,
Manipulate both hands together.

And as I thwack the keys, I sing.
She stares, all eyes, into my mouth,
Rounds her small plum blossom into a howl,
And music issues from her blasted mind.

Suzanne Heyd

The Woman in Baghdad

hanged   beautiful
curse for raising her

hand *if anger if anger*

It is hard to remember.

I keep a secret
soldier at the cave, facing in.

Her face.

Gash basket of bone
immersed bowl.

I save my own life.
Admit to feeling

(as if I were)
music: invisible and
arranged.

Flocked   birds
wheel through fathom
less   black
shadows
shadow
desire

Oh lovely, your cypress
body your silver breasts.

Mourning does not bear me
into her presence.

Knot bear me:

she she she

Time begins or is a result.
There has been ever since

speaking between
speaking, clutches of

the tongue. Still
more than I

hear. A ripped garment
a piece of paper.

Sound of the cup.

Reeds press one living
voice after
another into clay.

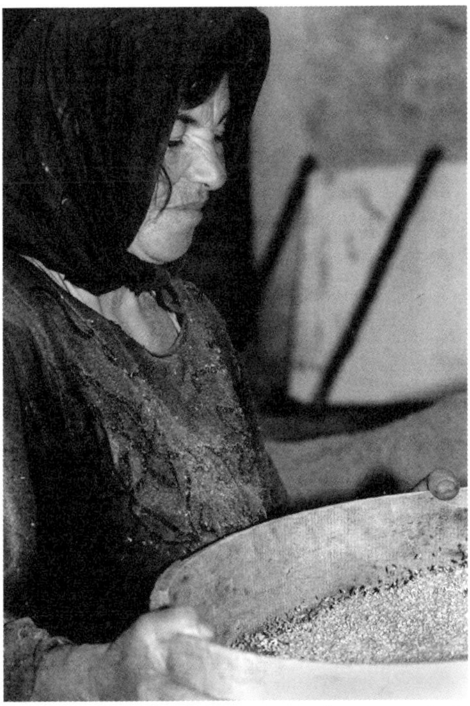

M. Teresa Valero, from *The Levant: Lebanon and Syria Through Western Eyes*, photograph

Rations

no grain
no fish
neither syrup nor wine
not rain
not grow

only one-half quart
only one-half quart

to account for
an outrage

who sleeps on the roof
perishes on the roof
who sleeps in the house
remains unburied even the earthworms

flailing themselves
at hunger

a layer of dirt
no trace

Field

hands trace the hardened print
here lies: a daughter a sun frozen
positions of the elusive I
once was years prior a gratitude
spare & nimbus a guarded
meshwork of tongues at the wrist
story told halfway in seasons
of swarm harvest locust plant
devoured in plural the hard print
voracious before the lilies
the body   parts   folded   a bow
ornate filigree unpronounced
like a thing before we name it alive
out of nowhere out of the changing

Manjula Rajan

Vacation

Naina leaned over the balcony and stared down at the courtyard twenty floors below. Her ankle-length printed dress flapped in the breeze coming from the other side of the hotel—the side that faced the ocean—and brought with it the sharp salty ocean air and a faint aroma of roasting peanuts. She stood for a few seconds like this, deep in thought.

If these bars gave way, I'd fall and die, she thought, patting the fat pink pimple on her nose. One second here and the next, splat, there I am on the ground. She idly imagined the ensuing funeral. Her parent's best friends, Soshamma Aunty and Mani Uncle, red-eyed and sniffly, would attempt to comfort her distraught parents.

"Oh why did I have to live to see this day?" Mum would weep noisily into the side of her sari.

"Only thirteen, but already so mature and thoughtful," Papa would say, rubbing a wet cheek with his neatly manicured hand.

Naina felt the sting of tears in her own eyes and blinked them away. A feeling of affection for her parents grew in her and a small smile came to her lips. She backed away from the balcony and entered the hotel room where Mani Uncle, Soshamma Aunty, and Mum and Papa were sitting around a metal fold-up table, playing cards. Their children had long ago coined a term for them—The Four.

The two families lived in the same neighborhood in the Bangalore suburbs, knew the same people, and attended the same small dinner parties weekend after weekend, usually starring the same set of friends. The Four were all doctors, but Mum had stopped working after Naina was born and never gone back.

Papa had just called Trump and there were the usual mutterings from Mani Uncle.

"Clubs again," said Uncle, "and me without a single one."

The other three usually didn't bother even to acknowledge this, because he always made this same claim.

"Your hair turns a brighter shade of white each time you do that," Papa said to Uncle.

"Do what?" asked Soshamma Aunty.

"Says he has no trumps when you know he's holding nothing but," said Papa.

"He's only forty-five and already such white hair," said Mum, shaking her head.

Naina had a feeling that she had heard that same exchange before. With The Four, it was always the same old banter, the gossip about the very same people, the same jokes, and the same Rummy game with a complicated set of rules that nobody but they seemed to recognize. She cast a baleful eye around the table, grabbed a book, and slouched into a chair beside them.

Vacations usually meant an overnight train ride in a freezing air-conditioned carriage from their house in the Bangalore suburbs to her grandparents in Kerala, where there was sure to be a gaggle of cousins also on holiday. But occasionally, one of The Four would find a bargain price for a hotel room. Now that Soshamma Aunty and Mani Uncle's two children were in college, it was just The Four and Naina on these trips.

Papa stared at his cards with a small, satisfied smile.

"A brief golden age, almost an age of justice," he said.

Soshamma Aunty smiled in appreciation at this and Papa beamed, like a small schoolboy who has just been given a pat on his head by his favorite teacher.

"Children to the Motherly, that they prosper, carts to good drivers, that they be driven well, the valley to the waterers, that it yield fruit," finished Soshamma Aunty.

Naina noted with renewed interest the change that Soshamma Aunty's presence induced in Papa. She had noticed it before but the extent of his transformation became suddenly clear. When Soshamma Aunty was around, there were frequent witticisms, quotes from writers they both admired, and a laid-back charm to his every action that was completely hidden otherwise. It was such a contrast to the occasional behind-the-paper grunt that made up the bulk of his conversation at home.

Mani Uncle raised one bushy white eyebrow, so incongruous in his otherwise boyish face.

"Show-offs," he said to Mum, who, in response, tinkled her shy, girlish laugh that crinkled the corners of her large, soft eyes. Unlike Papa, who was a neat and fussy dresser, she was in her usual state of disarray that morning—untamed curls stubbornly resisting her weak attempt at a bun, wrinkled blue sari paired with a dark green blouse, fluorescent pink rubber *chappals* on her feet and an unfashionably large black *bindi* not quite centered on her forehead.

"Soshamma adapted *The Caucasian Chalk Circle* to feudal eighteenth-century Kerala in college, remember?" gushed Papa.

"Of course," said Mani Uncle, "I played the drunken priest. A small part, but yet my name was given a particular mention in the college paper, if I remember correctly."

"He has that story clipping somewhere," said Soshamma Aunty, "and probably knows it by heart."

"I keep it as a souvenir of when I first fell in love with you, my dear, no other reason," replied her husband.

"Hah!" said Soshamma Aunty.

"What's the chalk circle?" asked Mum pleasantly. There was a second of eye contact between Soshamma Aunty and Papa before he replied.

"A play by Berthold Brecht," he said and, apparently anticipating the next question, added, "A German author and a fine Communist."

But Mum had already turned her attention back to her cards. She pulled one out from the fan in front of her and after some hesitation replaced it back in the same position.

Soshamma Aunty adjusted her red spectacles that perfectly matched her crisply starched sari.

"What would Marx have made of us Keralites, I wonder," she said, "a small Indian state by the ocean, the first people ever to elect a Communist party into power. A people so different in language and custom from any he'd ever known."

Mani Uncle pounced on the card that she had just discarded.

"Aha! Now we're getting somewhere," he said. "By the way, did you hear about Narayan's transfer to the Philippines? Bali, apparently, lucky dog."

Both Soshamma Aunty and Papa raised eyebrows.

"Unless Bali suddenly seceded, I think you mean Indonesia," said Soshamma Aunty.

Soshamma Aunty's sari slipped a little and to Naina's horror, she noticed that Papa was suddenly very intent on his cards, as if he was afraid to look up and find himself accidentally staring at her chest.

Naina flounced out of her chair, clapped shut the copy of Agatha Christie's *The Mysterious Affair at Styles* that she had borrowed from Mum and announced loudly to nobody in particular that she was going up to the hotel terrace to read. No one bothered to look up from their cards.

"Mmm. Okay," said Mum vaguely, "Right-o," said Papa, and Soshamma Aunty said, "Have fun." Mani Uncle said nothing at all.

Upstairs on the covered terrace, the Kerala sunshine was being tempered by a cool ocean wind that teased her short hair first to one side and then to another while white ceiling and floor fans stirred up their own airy froth. The hotel was one of those new skyscrapers that had been built right on the beach and Naina walked over to the railing and stared at the expanse of sparkling blue-green water. The busy wooden canoes of the fishermen mingled with placid large ships full of spices—nutmeg, cardamom, pepper, ginger, tea and coffee, all on their way to faraway places.

It is strange, thought Naina, that everything looks the same as yesterday, even though ships must be coming and going, canoes being filled and emptied, people taking photographs or walking along the beach and leaving—a hive of activity really, but looking down from here, nothing seems to have changed at all.

Her favorite corner table was empty so she hurried to claim it. It had the advantage of being somewhat secluded yet she could observe the rest of the terrace from here. The furniture on the terrace was white metal, with pink cushions and painted gold vines creeping up the legs and arms of the chairs and tables. Potted plants and tall, flowering bushes separated tables from each other. Black-and-white-suited waiters moved languidly about, holding wooden trays and calling to each other in a friendly manner.

Naina attended an all-girls convent school and her experiences with boys so far had been limited to cousins and family friends. The young waiters at the restaurant, with their good-natured smiles that flashed regularly from their faces, their slim, lithe bodies and graceful movements about the terrace, filled her with such self-conscious terror that she could barely stammer out her order each time. The recently arrived pimple on her nose added to her apprehension—each day it seemed to grow bigger and shinier. That morning she had looked in the mirror and had seen the pimple first, then the rest of her face looming up behind it.

She turned to Mum's book but reading about English villagers being picked off slowly by one of their own failed to keep her interest. She was tempted to skip to the final climactic scene where everything was revealed but realized that she'd better read slowly as there were still four more days at the hotel to go. Placing the open book on the table in front of her to give the appearance that she was reading, she settled back in her chair. It was time for dedicated people-watching.

One young Indian couple at the hotel absolutely fascinated Naina. They arrived at the terrace at the same time every morning and evening, she dressed in light chiffon saris and he in Madras shirts and khaki pants. They would spend the next few hours reading separate books. Sometimes the woman would pull out a little spiral notebook and energetically write in it.

What amazed Naina about this couple was that, as far as she could see, they did not speak to each other at all. They ordered their own drinks and sometimes had short conversations with the waiter. But they remained aggressively silent the entire time that they were alone together.

But as Naina watched this morning something very strange occurred. The woman had broken protocol and was apparently trying to make eye contact with her companion.

She stared intensely at him.

He concentrated diligently on his book.

Still staring, she removed a ring from her hand, her wedding ring perhaps? Naina wasn't sure, and with a flick of her wrist the woman threw it over the railing. The sunlight caught at the gold as it flew first upward towards the sky and then down towards the sea. The woman scraped her chair back slowly, adjusted the end of her silvery sari so that it covered both her shoulders like a shawl and left without a word. The man continued to read with a small unwavering smile. He poured himself some more tea and delicately raised the white porcelain cup to his lips.

Naina was strangely disturbed by this little show. In spite of their silence, their body language had suggested that there was a bond here, a deep connection between the two of them. It was in the way they looked at the other when they thought that nobody could see, how they sat, and in their every small gesture. But now the woman had gone and thrown a ring into the ocean and the man was pretending not to care.

The man continued to sit there, one leg crossed over the other, staring at the ocean. He lit a cigarette and Naina watched him as he smoked, tapping the ashes from the red-tipped smoldering end into a black ashtray and turning his head a little to the side to exhale. After he lit his second cigarette, she decided to head down to the hotel room and to find The Four.

Her parents had left a folded note on the coffee table. She was to meet them at the café downstairs or, if later, then at the terrace for an early dinner. There was a PS tacked on at the end—No hurry, it said, whenever you feel like joining us.

It was nice to experience an empty room. She shared the standard double with a so-called "courtyard" view (it overlooked the hotel parking lot with a concrete garbage dump in one comer) with her parents and it was a rare moment when she had it all to herself.

The scene on the terrace was still fresh on her mind. She struck a pose, holding her chin high. She pretended to take a ring off her finger and with a flick of her wrist released it. She adjusted a phantom sari around her shoulders and clicked-clacked haughtily to the balcony. Then she doubled over in laughter.

She wondered if the couple had noticed her at the corner table. She imagined the two of them walking up and saying, "You're a good little watcher, aren't you? I hope we're keeping you entertained?"

Naina cringed.

She lay on her bed and stared at a spot on the ceiling. Look hard enough at anything, she thought, and you will see a face looking back. As if everything in the world has a personality. Indeed, the spot on the ceiling seemed to grow a nose as she watched, then eyes, then a mouth that it twisted into a scowl.

Naina closed her eyes and was soon deep in a dream where she was sitting as usual in her spot on the terrace. Everything was gray, except for the ocean, which was white and over which small black ships steamed. The woman in the silver sari appeared beside her and stared as intensely into Naina's eyes as she had into the man's that afternoon. It seemed to Naina that she was being accused and she strained to understand the charge against her.

"I plan to kill myself," the woman said, "You can watch if you want."

The woman's face began to blur and she turned away from Naina. Walking over to the railing, the woman swung herself over it and stood for a moment on the other side, silhouetted against the setting sun. Then with a small wave back at Naina, she jumped.

When Naina rushed to the railing, she saw the woman's sari trailing like a river of silver in her wake. Meanwhile, she became aware that Papa and Soshamma Aunty were locked in a passionate embrace.

The slowly falling woman turned her face up towards the three of them.

She had Mum's face.

Naina opened her eyes with a small shout. Her mouth felt hot and dry, parched for water. She shook the sleep from her head and gulped the water straight from the pitcher by the bed. Being alone in the room no longer held any appeal and she decided to go looking for The Four.

They were no longer at the downstairs café but had moved to the terrace and were sitting at her favorite corner table. Papa was pointing out something in the menu to Soshamma Aunty and Mum was laughing at something Uncle was saying. In spite of the warmth of the day, Naina felt a chill ripple through her body.

"You look terrible, are you on your period?" asked Mum in a loud stage whisper. Naina shook her head.

"Poor thing—doesn't she look sickly?" Mum turned to the other three.

"Do you have a headache? I have some aspirin," said Soshamma Aunty.

"Food, she needs food," said Mani Uncle, patting his stomach.

"I hope you've been drinking only bottled water as per our discussion," said Papa.

Naina dragged a chair from another table and sat between Papa and Soshamma Aunty.

"I'm fine," she said, "what's for dinner?"

When Naina saw the couple walk onto the terrace a few minutes later, she felt her stomach tighten. The woman had thrown a cream-colored shawl over her shoulders but otherwise she looked as she had in Naina's dream. They sat down at their usual table and soon had their usual drinks, she the sweet limewater and he a pot of tea. They did not speak to each other.

As they tended to do, each of The Four was trying to influence the orders of the others because it was their habit to share all the dishes.

"I'm ordering the *biriyani* but the mango *pulisherri* looks delicious also," said Papa.

"Make sure you take a look at the Chinese food," said Mum, tapping at that portion of her menu with one finger.

"If I hadn't decided to order the Goan curry, I would definitely have picked the Avial," said Soshamma Aunty.

"Fried fish or fish curry?" wondered Mani Uncle.

Predictably, it was only her Papa who was influenced and, when the time came, ordered Soshamma Aunty's second choice. And Naina ordered the Chinese fried rice as her Mum had suggested.

Naina had heard that if you dream about a person that you know, however slightly, chances are high that you will make an appearance in their dreams as well. Some subliminal interaction has gone on, not yet registered by either consciousness. She tried to avoid people that she had recently dreamt about, afraid that it might show somehow, both that she had dreamt about them, and even worse, what she had dreamt—as if all a person had to do was to look into her eyes and there would be her dream, starring them, instantly replayed for their benefit. She didn't believe it completely, but avoided eye contact with the Four throughout dinner anyway.

They were still talking about their college days.

"Remember what that old master used to say to us?" began Papa. "A thing of beauty is a joy forever."

"He was looking straight at your wife when he said that, if I remember correctly," said Mani Uncle, "the poor man was afflicted with a classic case of schoolmaster's crush, and who could blame him?"

Mum giggled. "What rubbish—he was old enough to be my father," she said.

Naina noticed that they all looked slightly flushed. Apparently, it was not just tea that had been consumed in the café.

"Probably not much older than we are now," said Soshamma Aunty gaily. "We are just as young as we feel, I've always thought."

"I completely agree. Time itself is such a modern invention—such a contrived concept, really," said Papa.

Naina blew loudly into her soup.

"I think people should act their age," said Naina, "the way that some people act these days makes me sick."

The Four laughed as though she had made a joke.

"My daughter, the disciplinarian," said Mum.

There were more remarks along those lines but Naina tuned them out. She plunged her spoon into the soup and it rose in a mini tidal wave and splattered onto the table. She looked guiltily around to see if anybody else had seen the widening brown stain on the tablecloth and noticed with a jolt that the woman in the silver sari was now standing by the railing. She turned a little and it seemed to Naina that she had looked directly at her for a moment.

Just like she had in Naina's dream. It was the dream and it was really happening. Naina was suddenly as sure of this as she was of her name.

Everything happened in a rush after that.

Naina leapt to her feet, spilling the rest of the soup, and ran towards the railing.

"Please no!" she shouted. "Don't do it!"

The dinner buzz quieted a little as people craned their neck towards her to see what the noise was about.

Naina's heart knocked against her chest. She reached the woman, who turned to her with a startled expression.

"I'm sorry?" the woman said. Her companion had risen from his table and was quickly weaving his way through the tables towards them.

"Don't jump," said Naina.

"I'm sorry but I don't understand what you mean," said the woman. She brought together two thin eyebrows to a point just above her nose.

Naina tried to explain, "I dreamt that you jumped." To her astonishment, she realized that she was still shouting.

Comprehension dawned. "You thought I was going to kill myself?" asked the woman.

The man arrived and placed a protective hand on the woman's shoulder. He asked what the matter was.

"This girl thought I was going to kill myself by tossing myself from the building," said the woman. The corners of her mouth began to twitch and she suddenly opened her mouth and a single low-pitched laugh escaped.

The man looked at her and then at Naina. He smiled to hide his confusion.

"Why in heaven's name would she think something like that?"

"A dream," said the woman. His hand moved down from her shoulder and she placed hers in it.

Naina's stomach lurched and her knees trembled. Her only desire now was to get away. Mumbling an apology, she turned and walked stiffly back to The Four who were wearing open-mouthed expressions of horror.

"What did you think you were doing?" asked Mum.

"Are you sure that you are feeling all right?" asked Soshamma Aunty.

"How rude, how terribly rude," said Papa.

"Check please," called Mani Uncle.

Naina blinked hard to keep the tears at bay.

What a fool she was, what a complete idiot. She had really thought the woman was going to kill herself. But in her dream it had been Mum, and not that other woman who had fallen.

"I did it for Mum," Naina said.

This silenced The Four for several moments.

Mum arched her eyebrows and said, "What do you mean, for me?"

Then Mum's annoyance appeared to get the upper hand.

"Sometimes," she said to the other three, "I just don't understand what goes through the mind of this girl."

"I know," Papa weighed in, "exactly what you mean."

They moved closer to each other and peered at Naina.

The injustice of it all brought a renewed threat of tears to Naina's eyes. But before she could succumb to that final embarrassment, she walked away.

"I'm going down to the room," she said, and rushed off before anyone could say anything.

Downstairs, Naina locked herself in the bathroom, knowing that The Four would soon be down. She couldn't remember a time when she had felt more like being alone. She remembered how the man had put his arm around the woman and how they had held hands just then. Perhaps her little outburst had done some good after all.

When The Four filed into the room a little later, she was sitting on her bed with a book. Her parents had a kind of pinched look on their faces and Aunty and Uncle hovered protectively around them.

"Want to go for a walk on the beach with us?" asked Mani Uncle in a falsey-cheery voice.

"No."

"Okay, fine. If the girl wants to be stubborn and just sit around being rude and feeling sorry for herself there's nothing we can do to . . ." began Mum.

"She's just feeling a little tired," interrupted Soshamma Aunty. "Why don't you three go on ahead and I'll catch up with you?"

"Oh no, Soshamma Aunty, absolutely no, I'll be fine here by myself, I just have a small headache, that's all," said Naina.

"And a headache was why you made that galata upstairs?" asked Papa, "I ree-ally don't think so."

"Look," said Naina hotly, "I'm just having a little rest here, okay? Sheesh!"

"We went to say sorry to those people, poor things," said Mum, "they were very confused about what happened. But such a nice young couple. You told them you had a dream or something like that?"

"I'm sure I don't want to talk about it," said Naina.

"You dreamt that that woman killed herself or something like that?" continued Mum. "I mean, do you even know her? And why did you say it was my fault?"

"She never said it was your fault," said Papa.

"Oh yes, I heard her say it. She blames me for everything, even her bad dreams now," said Mum.

"Oh don't start all that again," said Papa.

Naina straightened up on the bed and swung her feet into her slippers.

"You don't start," said Mum, pointing at her husband. "All your family is a little *kirki*—and it looks like our poor Naina has taken after them."

"Oh!" cried Papa, "O-oh! My family is *kirki*? And whose great uncle had to be put in a sanatorium?"

"If you're talking about my poor Shankaran Maman, he was a mathematics genius before he had that breakdown," Mum replied hotly. "Geniuses go like that sometimes, that's the price they pay."

Papa looked ready with a comeback but then Mani Uncle raised his voice a bit.

"Maybe you're having trouble sleeping, Naina? I can prescribe something for you if that is the problem."

"No, no, I'm fine," said Naina, "but I'm going to the terrace to read."

"Oh no, you don't," said Papa, "not till we have a little explanation here."

Naina set her lips into a straight line. She spoke slowly.

"Okay. I had this dream that the woman fell from the top of the building. Because the four of you pushed her off. And then the police came and arrested you all and I became an orphan."

Then she walked out and slammed the door behind her.

On the terrace, she hurried to an unoccupied table. When the waiter with the dimple on his chin came by, she managed to squeak out her order of lime juice. But before he returned with it, two shadows lengthened over her table.

"Do you mind if we join you?"

It was the couple. Naina felt her face grow hot with embarrassment. She scraped her chair back and stood up.

"I'm so sorry about this afternoon, I don't know what happened . . ." she began.

"Oh please, don't be silly," said the woman, "We just wanted to make sure you were feeling okay."

The man pulled out the woman's chair.

"Thank you, chweetie," she said to him with a big smile.

He pulled his chair next to hers.

"You're welcome, chweetness," he said, pinching her nose. They held hands then and giggled at each other.

Naina sat down, stunned. These were the same two people who hadn't said a word to each other for days. The woman pulled her hands away and there on the ring finger was a little turquoise ring set in silver—Naina recognized it from the gift store downstairs.

"He's just being silly, just shee-lee," said the woman to Naina, while she pulled at the man's ear lobe. She introduced herself as Mala and the man as her husband, Giri.

"Giri as in Grrr," Mala said, barring her small teeth and holding one hand out as if it were a claw. But underneath the jollity, Naina caught a momentary glimpse of the same tension that she had witnessed earlier. It was gone so quickly that she wondered if she hadn't been wrong about them all along.

"And you're Naina, we know," Mala said. "We already met your parents and their friends earlier today. Your mother is so pretty, like that fifties movie star whose name I can't remember."

"My . . . my Mum? Oh thank you," said Naina because she couldn't think of anything else to say.

"Speaking of whom, look," said the man pointing.

The Four were on the terrace, squinting into the sunset as they walked towards them. The couple greeted The Four like old friends and Naina moved her chair to make room for everybody at the table.

She sat there for several minutes observing. Mani Uncle and Mala were having an animated discussion, apparently about islands—"No, I completely agree with you actually, islands are the most romantic places in the world." Giri and Mum were sitting slightly leaning towards each other and talking about the latest Bollywood blockbuster—"a really sweet story but the ending was a bit much, didn't you think?" Soshamma Aunty and Papa were pointing out birds to each other—"look, there's a jacana, a juvenile by the plumage, quite rare in these parts, I believe."

They were all flirting. There was no doubt about it.

And when she realized that, Naina decided that the world of men and women and the complicated nature of their relationships was something that she would never, ever understand, however long she might live.

She got up, unobserved, and walked over to the railing to catch the end of the sunset.

The sun sets the same way every day, she thought, yet there must be a difference because the Earth is in a different position along its orbit. But the change is so small, or we're so small compared to it, that we see no difference.

She looked over her shoulder at the table that she had just left. Take my parents, she thought. They change every day, probably every second. But they look in the mirror each morning and see the same person each time although it must be that they've changed since they last looked. A line has begun to form on the forehead perhaps, or an eye looks just a little sadder or a mouth just a little more satisfied. And the changes keep adding and adding and in the end, as if by magic, they'll look at our photo album one day and say—look how we've changed, look how young we used to be. Astounding, she thought, it's all just so incredibly bizarre when you go to think about it.

The sun had almost disappeared behind the water and a small knot of people joined her at the railing.

"Magical, isn't it?" said a passing waiter.

Indigo clouds floated serenely through the peach and tangerine sky. The blood-red sun unfurled a golden beam onto the cerulean water. Birds, exhilarated by the overwhelming sense of transformation, flew in ecstasy over the quivering ocean. They opened their beaks and filled the air with their raucous cries, bidding the dying sun a safe journey down, to the other side of the world.

Warren Woessner

Our Hawk

It was the summer the hawk hung around.
I might not have noticed if I didn't watch
birds a lot, but this one was hard to miss—
soaring and cree-ing, then dropping below
the canopy of big cottonwood trees along the creek.

I started seeing it perched, sitting still,
everywhere—in the dead elm, on the power line,
then even on the railing, half-way up
the front steps. Not scared, not moving
until I got out of the car.

It was the summer friends fell, left
and right, old and too young.
Sharon and Tony's cancer came back.
Karen and Barb's T-cells turned
on them. I stayed on hold
with Mayo, MGI and NeoRx
searching for new drugs,
clinical trials, for anything at all.

And all summer, hawk kept watch.
I knew it was just learning to hunt—
trying to catch the next rat or vole
over and over again.
Still hawk taught, "Pay attention!"
Every day, it drew sharp lines
in the air around the territory

we shared, defended it.
Kept us safe by killing
all the dirty little creatures
crawling toward us, one
after another, that we could never
spot or stop in time.

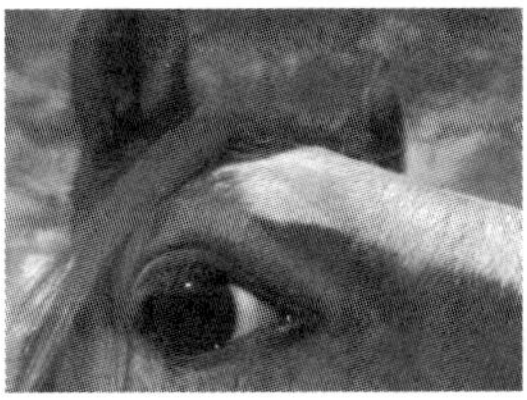

AMY E. PAYNE

Hard Bargain

Emma'd thought the seal was dead at first. It floated fifty yards out, one flipper extended from the sea. Unusual. For the hour she'd walked the shell- and garbage-studded beach she'd kept an eye on it, until its flipper moved, a casual flap against the soft blue water, and she realized the seal was alive, intentional, happy. Her walk drew to an end when the dunes leveled off to reveal aging condos and the low sea wall fronting them. Three small figures sat on the steps carved into the wall and one, her father—she could always recognize her father—began to wave his arms above his big straw hat. Something to show her. Must be the seal, she thought, one dark flipper above a flat sea. Her father waved in a dramatic sweeping motion that called her in; she lifted an arm in acknowledgment. He'd always liked to show her things. Even now, this seal. Over a tiny crest in the sand, just before she'd leave the water's edge for the condos, she came upon a scattering of her kids' possessions. *Lazy thing,* she thought at the flipper, *where is your family?*

Emma waved again to her father then gestured at the stuff scattered across the sand. If she didn't collect it now she'd have to trek across the beach to collect it later. She began to pick up—chair, buckets, shovels, towels—hanging things from various parts of her body so she could make it in one trip.

In the strong heat of the day's end, the salt bit into her pores. The chair in the crook of her elbow pinched the loose skin of her arm. Finally, loaded like a packhorse, everything hurting, scratching or scraping, she turned to look up the long stretch of beach to the small group on the seawall.

Emma smiled. One of the group was her nephew. Her father sat between him and a small dark-skinned man she didn't recognize. He flung his hand high overhead as though he'd been impatient for her to look again. "Mary and Joseph," Emma muttered, "hold your horses."

She looked once more to the flipper. Hours, hours the seal had lain there, so undemanded it could hold a random body part out of the water for no reason other than joy. She'd been like that once. Sweat rolled between her glasses and her eye but she had no

* Chico Seay, photograph

free hand to wipe it. She began to cross, her family's load dragging her feet through the hot sand. As she trudged toward the little group her father waved again, urgent, excited. It wasn't like him, this relentlessness. It disturbed her. She wanted to yell at him she couldn't do any better, but this was only partly true. Because the closer she got, the more her feet churned the sand, the more she wanted to turn and walk the other way.

* * *

Emma drew close enough to identify the small dark man as the one who sold carved ironwood figures on the beach. He sat next to her father as though they had a relationship, which she supposed they did after yesterday when the men in her family bought enough to support the man for the next six years. The ironwood man watched her through squinched eyes as she struggled through the sand. "Thought you guys were cut off," she called out, but no one laughed. It was then she understood, from the way their bodies leaned toward her, the intensity of the ironwood seller's stare, how her father pressed his hands flat against his swollen bloodshot knees, that they were not waiting for her because of the seal. She was too close to swear. She looked at her nephew and he grinned and shrugged. She loved this nephew, his lovely height, the way he played with her children, the contradiction of his clean-cut ghetto clothes. Now seventeen, he was the closest thing she'd met to her first love, kind and gentle and only partly formed. Maybe it was just his slender height or the silent way he tucked his chin when he was amused. No matter, he had a way of bringing her past to life in a way that threatened no one, not even her, and periodically she was surprised and thankful for the fresh breeze of reminiscence in the middle of so much present.

She stopped at the base of the wide concrete stairs and let things fall from her body. Her father began to talk before the chair hit the sand.

"Look," he said, and gestured to a row of ironwood carvings lining the seawall's flat surface. "Look."

Two marlins. A ray. An Indian dancer. A large horse, one front leg raised in a high step. And a dolphin. Ever since yesterday Emma had been thinking about buying a dolphin, trying to imagine a place for it in her tiny California home, what it would look like inside, amidst toys and books, away from the open ocean, the desert colors of sand and flat dunes and stark sharp red cliffs. Clearly her father wanted her to buy something and she decided, yes, she could get a dolphin. So cheap! Emma laughed and something shifted in the bodies of the men, a relaxing. She felt it too, the muscles in her shoulders eased, she could make everyone happy and still have time to shower before her mother began to round them up for dinner.

Her father scootched closer to the figures, an act slow and lumbering and painful now that the cancer was roaring back, but as she watched his excited face there was no hint of the pain. "Look at this, Emma," he said and ran his thick hand along the back of the horse.

* * *

Two days earlier Emma had taken a long walk down the beach. As she reached the inlet to a freshwater bay, one where hundreds of birds gathered when the tide flowed just right, she spotted three dolphins swimming a little offshore. They surfaced and dove, close enough for her to hear their bursts of breath. They were feeding. Or playing. The water slid across Emma's toes as she watched them from the edge of the beach. She'd always dreamed of swimming with dolphins, grabbing onto a fin and flying through the water, being pulled deep into its darkness. Once she'd lain across the bow of a boat, hanging her head over the side to watch the cut of the water, when a school of dolphins had joined them, playing along the crest of the boat's wave. One had stayed even with her, just under the water, swimming sideways so they looked into each other's eyes.

Emma decided to approach them. Shuffling her feet to ward off rays, she waded out chest deep and called gently, patting the warm water lightly with her hands. It was murky; she could see nothing below her waist. Her chest tightened. Scanning the water, she breathed to calm herself. Finally the dolphins resurfaced, then closer, three times she heard a puff of air twenty, fifteen, ten feet behind her. So close. It was going to happen, this moment with a dolphin. Then, all at once, there was a strong, horrifying rush of water behind her knees that practically knocked her off her feet, and Emma screamed, the sound echoing off the empty beach. She'd imagined a scene from the movies, not this, not something giant and strong coming at her where she couldn't see it. Frozen to the spot, unwilling to lift her feet to swim to shore—one might swim right under her—unwilling to turn her eyes from the ocean, she shuffled backward toward the beach. But the dolphins didn't approach again and, as her heart found its rhythm, they swam off, surfacing and resurfacing. Oh no, Emma thought. Come back, she whispered once, and whistled low as though they were her dogs back home. The air cool against her wet skin, she believed again it would be amazing, beyond her imagining, and this time she would be ready. This time she wouldn't be afraid. But when they reached the place where the water turned dark, she lost sight of them.

* * *

Nothing about the carved horse fit her experience with Mexico. It was heavy and dark and formal. Although she knew there were horses in Mexico she had never seen one. Not one. She smiled at her father but it was hard to muster; she was tired, as though she still had every sandy accoutrement of her family hanging from her body.

"*This* carving is different," her father said and the small, ironwood-colored vendor nodded. "He's from an Indian tribe up north and it took his people a year to make it."

"How much is it?" she asked the man.

The vendor shrugged almost imperceptibly.

"It's not like a dolphin," her father said, his voice deepening and picking up the slight formal accent she associated with times he wore a tie and smoothed his thick hair down over his head. "This is a work of art."

She had not taken her eyes from the man. "How much?"

"Two hundred dollars," the man said and shifted his gaze to the horse.

She opened her mouth but no sound came out. Her nephew was no longer grinning. He gazed off somewhere over the ocean, but she could tell he was listening. Earlier the two of them had been discussing the Salinger story he'd read for school, about a boy who is in his final spiritual life on earth. Besides the floating seal, the ideas in that story were what she had used the silence of her walk to think about. The amazing love and acceptance that came through lack of attachment. Being safely past the process of letting go.

"Dad," she said, "that is way too much money."

"Emma," he said, "this is a collector's item."

"Two hundred dollars, Dad," she said and her voice was tight, " is a lot of money."

The small hard man watched back and forth. He must have been the age of her father but everything about him, sun-darkened and wrinkled as it was, breathed health. Things in his body still flowed one into the other, not like her father's where each place leaked signs of the beginning of the end.

"My people," he said, "work long time. Almost one year. They find wood and cure long time." He held up four fingers. "Four months. Then they carve. Solamente one piece, see?" He ran his hand along the horse's back, rested a finger significantly against one small ear. "No smooth," he said, tracing the rough ripple of the horse's flank, "because horse no smooth." He paused for a minute to consider the carving. "Look," he said, turning the horse's side into the lowering sun, "look."

His people! She didn't even know if his people existed. She didn't know why he had to be a part of her drama. She wanted him gone. "I have to think about it," she said.

"He doesn't come here every day," her father said.

"I no come back," the man said.

Of course he would. For two hundred bucks this man would come home with them and sort the thousands of medicines, support her dad as he made his way across the room grabbing one chair after another as though fording a river. But he couldn't help with the pain, this little man whose very skin seemed alive, he knew nothing about pain.

"I have to think about it," she said. She looked at her father, into his eyes to find him wherever he had gone missing, to make him hear her. "It's a lot of money, Dad."

He looked at his knees. "No more than one of your dinners out."

She didn't cry out, though she felt as if she'd been hit. Her father didn't hit her. Her father had never hit her. All three men looked beyond her to the ocean. To the water so warm, so big on your skin. Who are you? she wanted to say. What have you done with my dad? She took a deep breath.

"It's a lot more than one of my dinners, Dad," she said.

* * *

"Do you remember the cast-iron horse I got in China?" her father asked and in his voice she could hear a shade of return, a half-step of retreat.

Emma breathed deep the salty air, nodded. She loved that horse.

"I carried it all the way home, on all those flights, in my lap," he said. "I look at it every day."

Before her Dad got sick her sister used to joke about putting yellow stickies on everything of their folks' that she wanted when they died. With him sick the yellow sticky jokes had stopped; but, back when it had still been funny, the horse was the only thing she'd imagined bearing one of her own. ***Emma.***

"Sometimes," he said "I just put my hand on it."

The wind had come up; behind them she could hear the growing slop of waves against the sand. She lifted the horse, it was so heavy, there was no way she could manage this horse, a three-year-old, a five-year-old, their carry-on luggage, aboard a plane. It couldn't be checked either. First toss onto the baggage belt she'd have a jagged pile of broken ironwood. She rotated it to see its other side. Parts of the carving were beautiful, the depth of the wood like the shivering flank of an overheated horse. But some of it was too stiff, as if the horse had been frozen before it had been fully set free. One eye was bigger than the other.

She didn't want it.

* * *

"You always loved horses when you were little," her dad said.

All those years, every holiday, plastic horses, cloth horses, stuffed horses, horse books, each year she would wait for the real thing. It was the biggest thing she'd ever asked for. Something that never fit in the yard of a small house. Emma turned to the ironwood seller who'd known she was beaten before her first bucket hit the sand at his feet.

"One hundred," she said.

All three men sucked in their breath. There was an edge, it settled in the curve of her palm where she grazed it across the horse.

"Oh, Señora," the ironwood seller shook his head. "So many hours."

* * *

Her nephew began to sway slightly from foot to foot, his body riveted on the action, his eyes blankly directed at the water behind her. The seal must be gone by now. Her mother, freshly washed and dressed for dinner, came out of the condo forty feet away and waved happily in their direction. Her mother loved this place, with all of them there, where she could drop a little of her husband and his unknown, known, future onto everyone else's shoulders and just breathe in the ocean and warm air. Emma watched as she lifted both arms over her head, fluttered her fingers in the early evening air. "Dinner," she called.

"Emma." Her father's wistfulness made his voice soft. "This is not an ordinary thing," he said. "It's something you'll have forever."

She looked at him, at the thick wave of gray hair above his ear. When the pain hit, his hair thinned out and took on a light greasy sheen. She wanted to touch his hair now, in this moment, feel its vitality; this was all she wanted to do. The ironwood man nodded. Her dad put his hand on the horse's back. "Always," he said.

His eyes were gray blue. The color the ocean took on when the sun sank below the horizon. And though Emma was not yet ready to reach out, to take it into her life, her fingers began to uncurl.

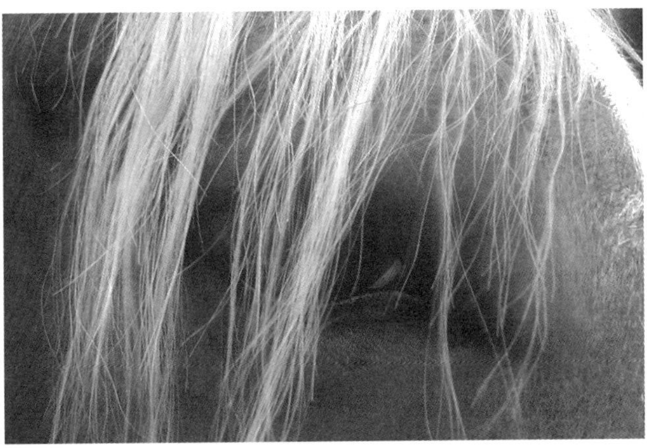

Chico Seay, photograph

Allan Douglass Coleman

Avram, no. 298773, on his 65th birthday

So now here is the time when I must earn my breath by saying something wise. And all I feel is stupid, but alive. What comes to me is this, just this: We did not eat each other. That's what they wanted, understand, the ultimate logic of the plan: consume ourselves in work, walk to the ovens on our grandparents' headstones, melt into soap to wash ourselves away, turn cannibal. They mostly had their wish; still, we did not fall to feasting when we could.

These things I cannot tell: The dreadful endless stink of it. The horror of goodbye. How it feels when you feel yourself break. Why I can never again step aboard a train. What it was like, the morning after freedom, to walk into a room filled with food I had forgotten how to eat.

Have I said I am proud of you for surviving me? Do not imagine I don't know the price you pay. I have learned to push away the plate when I am full, but Reuben, you who never missed a meal but fed on my tales of hunger, you leave no scrap, not one, your plate each time wiped clean with a last bite of bread. And Sarah, your wife, who sewed the salvaged scrap of my Rebecca's scarf into her wedding garb, knows that you eat to feed me, not yourself, and measures out your meals by spoonfuls to keep you fit and trim. I watch. I see.

These are your gifts to me. They matter. Now I share one with you. Your Sophie, so beautiful and wise, just eighteen and the future of the world, came to me after her classes weeks ago. "Grandpa," she said, "my friends all have tattoos. It's an experiment. They call it 'body art' today." I've seen, of course; I'm no recluse, I walk in the street, I watch the news: rings in their eyebrows, noses, other places too I hear. And why not? They are young, the world seems theirs. I can remember that, as in a different life.

"So?" I ask her. "What's to do with me? You're old enough, and raised to think free. I always tell you not to follow multitudes. Make up your own mind, then do as you wish. But tell me, why do you want this? You're not one for fads." She thinks a minute, then explains, "It's to possess yourself, to claim your body as your own."

And, across all these years between us, I know exactly what she means.

"Still," I say, "why are you here? Do you need my blessing for this?" She nods, surprising me. "Why?" "Because I thought about it a long time," she replies—you know she did, because she always does—"and there's only one design I want." "Which is?" I ask. Her answer: "Yours."

You know she's not a child. You know this was no joke, no casual idea. I looked deep into her eyes—and I have learned to search the face of the world—and found she spoke a truth, from some place in her soul she had discovered and explored. I did not insult her by asking if she understood what she'd said; the saying of it spoke for itself. I thought for a while, and when I saw the path of it I told her, "Here's the deal. We must always improve on the past. You must surround it with beauty, with life." She made her eyes like saucers, all startled innocence in that knowing way of hers, and replied, "But, Grandpa—then it would not match your own."

She had me there. And for a bit it was a puzzle, I admit. But we sat down with coffee to talk it through, for several afternoons, then went down to the tattoo parlor Tuesday to resolve it. She paid, from her savings—her birthday gift to me. Now we roll up our sleeves to show you: my Treblinka memento, on her forearm and mine, abloom in a field of wildflowers.

Don't look so shocked. Be proud of her. Be proud of us both. Be proud of us all.

* * *

And now we cut the cake and pour the wine.

John Glowney

Good Cloth

My surgeon said
he liked to work on younger men; in the older ones
the flesh splinters, falls apart too easily
to hold the stitching.

Afterwards,
when he had finished his rough splice
with his needle,

he sent me home, patchwork,
piecework, the body

balm, succor, suture
onto itself.

✻

My grandmother, her aging body
like a silken robe
draped in a chair,
her hands still strong enough to pull thread
and twine and knot,
made rugs
from left-over rags, quilts,
mended shirts, overalls. Let her lay hands
on me now.

✻

For weeks my body is a bed.
I can only lie quietly and finger the incision's
new embroidery.

✻

Hospitals are where you go
to die,
            and so I am more grateful
than you could know
for the patch of freckles floating near your eyes,
cloudy and vulnerable as sky,
                        and if possible
I am even more grateful
for the times now when we lay hands
on each other,
fumbling with the skin's byzantine codes,
its padlocks,
                        these moments
when we begin to leave our bodies,

when our skeletons reach out to embrace,
                        bone to bone, awkward, tender,

like prisoners set free,
rising up shuddering in the moiled flesh.

Leslie McGrath

When We Last Made Applesauce

When we last made applesauce, we made our last love.
For what other reason do blade and apple meet than separation?

So I used the knife and you doused the apples with brandy
and we took turns stirring them over a low flame

until they bloomed again, heaving and sighing
as they eased from their tight red jackets.

And though we set them aside to cool
while I walked the dog, while you must have napped,

the slurry in the bowl I steadied in my hands
as you worked the food mill was still warm,

flushed like skin in the moments of coupling.
Once we would have caught each other's glance

and stopped, smiling at what we had made,
but we'd already risen and dispersed like steam

through the windows we'd opened in the other,
leaving only applesauce, bowl, and blade.

The Red Stone

Give me molasses, honey,
the soft galumph of batter into bowl,
sweet yeast dough rising like a sigh
in the kitchen's warmest corner. Give me
an artichoke's extravagant demands and small pleasures;
a lobster clack-clacking her mottled tail like castanets.
Give me a jimmie pulled from a Chesapeake trap, playing
Taps in crab Morse code. Unload a bushel of peaches
on the old green table on the screen porch
this late August afternoon when their perfume's louder
than even the locusts. Give me time to teach you
how to twist a peach free from its red stone,
like a lid from a jar of something precious.

Mark Lewis, from *Painted Notes: The Tall Grass Prairie,* oil on paper

Green

Verde, que te quiero verde.
—*Lorca*

In the beginning of the end
of depression, color returned

like a promise
I'd forgotten

I saw green
for the first time in years—

it blinked from hickories,
hummed an obligato
under the wind's melody;
it smelled like horses,
new love, and opening.

It tasted like health.

I was not ashamed
to stuff it in my mouth
and let it stain my words.

Jen Collins

Who hasn't heard her story?

For many years she was my heroine. Thrown
away by Hamlet she threw herself in.
Held her breath, counted to ten. Little
did she think there would be paintings, velvet
gothicities, subtly lit in hushed British
museums. Nor could she imagine the
bourgeois beauty of her hard-flung heart.
Maybe she gagged as frogs dangled over-
head. Maybe she damned the dragonflies
who nervously hummed above. What words slipped
out and surfaced, to settle among the
reedy debris? Don't listen for medieval
whispers as you root among the muck. Fill
my ears with silt and sand to stop them up.

Juan Franco, photograph

Katy Didden

When the house fell

the bees
broke loose

from the walls

then floated
in a loose confusion
like a hatch of gnats.

I thought of you
and felt

I'd stepped out
    of my head

to watch
  the waggle and dart
of thoughts

try to make of air

a hive—
   a place to live.

The bee cloud
   held its shape
by the way
  bees

  charged the center
  (which was air),
circled out,
   charged again,

now and then
  colliding
   as though this

were a way back in.

Marjorie Stelmach

Camber

Robert Lowell writes in a letter of a worker "who comes with the noisiest machine known to man—he may come at 4AM or 6PM, he quits at will, he is usually waiting contemplatively for a machine he forgets, to be brought by someone who also forgets."

A plump blur off to my left,
erratic and stubborn at once,
for no discernible reason coheres
into *bee-behavior,*
                    and *buzz* lifts
from a background clutter of lawn mower,
birdsong, wind—an aural field
into which it falls again
in almost no time.
                    Sunlight hurts,
and my work here's stalled
until my optometrist proves
as *there* as his word.
                    Three days running
the plastic hands of the *Back-At* clock
are set for an hour he's sure to be gone.
The next, his note reads:
back in a flash.
                    He's not.
Maybe he's discontent with his life
of half-blind patients,
longs for a lab, for optical research—
philosophy even.
                    Maybe he yearns
to be a writer
of notes, a leaver just once
of an accurate message.
                    More likely,
He's fishing.
I wander down to the overpass

to watch the Express
take the long crescent curve
                    to New Orleans
and back to New York—each day, same track—
and to contemplate how *work* must feel
to the men who cut the kudzu back.

*

Late, down in the library
researching *Optics*,
I stumble onto the blurred
unfamiliar word *camber*,
                    its letters suggestive
of *candor* and *camphor*,
of alchemy's *ambers* and *umbers*,
of wheels of *Camembert* cheese,
their mushroomy skins and earthy interiors
                    thick with light. But
Webster claims *camber*'s an arc,
"a specified cut of ellipse or circle."
Ten times and it's yours:
                              in my dream
          a camber of waning moon falls
          to the curve of his cheekbone,
          the shadowed camber of his palm rises
          to cup my face,
                              and the camber of earth
          moves out and down toward the Gulf,
          bearing the endlessly parallel tracks, above which
          the kudzu's camber of hunger
          leans into space,
                              its suspended reach.

I wake awash in an aural field of ceiling fans
and distant trains, trying again
to account or forgive,
when I know. . .
                    better.
I know. But I'd hoped for more, hoped

for *balm,*
for a smoke of cream on the tongue,
for the muted gold an artist might spread
on a canvas the shade
of Camembert,
for the hover of meaning abuzz in the moment
before I opted for definition.
And I know, too,
that a dream's no more—
or less—than a single cast
of the self, a test of the life to be had
in another stream:

the line, released,
ascends until
too much, too far, *and the lure*
drops
to anchor a simple arc
which may linger aloft
for a moment impossibly long before
it sinks at the pinnacle, turned
to its equally elegant inverse—
a cup
that may hold
an instant beyond its time,
but will in the end succumb to fall,
become a seam
on the lake's still surface,
entering into the complex optics
of glint, refraction, and shimmer.
Briefly, the line lies lost
in the light.
Then back in a flash,
recovered,
recast.

The heart's
the loudest machine known, and it's true
you can always *quit at will,*
hang out your promise and go.

But mostly we stay,
awaiting the inexplicably late
arrival of that essential piece
we've forgotten, the one
we tell ourselves we must have *this moment*
just to go on.

John Milisenda, *My Mother*, photograph

Voices

Insomnia again, and
yes, it's back, that in-
comprehensible in-
ternal voice, tinny and
spinning on and on
to a periodic tonal lift
and pause—*expectant*
pause.

Well, apparently
you've missed your cue,
muffed your answer,
and it's off again,
but it's multiple now,
a vocal centipedal crawl,
a choir of whine,
multi-querulous.

You're pretty sure
you're the only one here.
So, *Who wants to know?*
you want to know!
No answer.
Angels, you venture,
though they sound
more like Munchkins.

Lilliputian.
And damned impolite,
seeming to promise you
revelations—but only on
a need-to-know basis.
At just what point,
you ask yourself,
will they suggest
that you sell your soul?

Could there be truth
in the myth of a cosmic
talk show filtered
through dental fillings?
Sinister whispers
host and guest
exchanging conspiracy theories?

By now, you're down
on your knees, face buried
in bedclothes begging.
But they're undiminished
in volume and need,
insisting you learn
their language—
but what tongue is that?

No single word
emerges from
the uniform wash.
An ur-language, rhythmic,
murmurous? or
a sad imitation,
deep in the deeper,
more solitary dark
of the lost heart
of the lost mother?

But listen: has
the urgency lessened?
Has understanding
been reached among you,
something to let you
sleep inside
the susurrus of
the inner Others?

If you simply assent
to *whatever*,
agree to curl up and
join the chorus,
become a plurality intent
on tormenting
some *other* Other,
will it buy you
some sleep? Well?
What do *you* think?

I await your answer.

Ivy Dempsey

Reading My Grandmother

I.
She's small, this grandmother,
Delicate bones — bird-like airiness.
Soft gray eyes, gaze fixed in a
permanent naiveté, from the far
place where she tries to find her way,
stunned out of time.

II.
Those final days in Kansas, no rightness
there: only emptiness, the old rhythm lost —
morning chores, promise in the new light,
that bright return — stepping out to feed
the laying hens, squawk and flurry for
the scattered grain. The garden over there . . .
maybe a bit of weeding. All: gone. *Gone.*

> *Not one radish to pierce the iron-hard*
> *ground, no single onion set! There*
> *must be, oh soon — another garden.*
> *Rescue! This ruin, each day only fire,*
> *the long drought beating, beating, brutal —*
> *an iron hammer. There must be rescue —*
> *our wide fields, sere, bleak tangle of straw,*
> *dust, constant shroud . . . oh, prayers pouring*
> *from the heart, the deep blood pleading. Please!*
> *All the promises: sun strong, no fury of fire,*
> *and rains to nurse the young wheat, our*
> *crops, our year, come right again. Yes. All*
> *made right. For the promises. And the black*
> *horror gone away. This pain. Please.*

III.
At home with us, far from her north,
she is never at home. Her pain swirls —

insidious mist over the respectability
in the house. It hovers at night, swathes
our well-fed bodies stretched along
fresh-laundered sheets. We fend it,
strain to dispel it in the nothingness

we make of her—blustery disembodiment
of her name, her wavering gentle gaze . . .
those tangles of puzzled non-words—
floated by a nightmare power, ceaseless
flood, tumbling as her raveled speech—
mumbled questions, untamable despairs.
Fearsome, these are, for us to name. Belong to.

Sundays, always church-going, and coming
home: the solemn traditional blessing (*God's*
own language) over roast beef—even then,
the fear. So: unstilled, children make sly
mockery of this "other"—as bullies on a
school playground—desperate weapon, here,
for *undoing* the work, the sounds, of pain in-
expressible in our common tongue; for *undoing*
that alien vocabulary—from her far place, the
gentle mumblings, discordant stutterings—
even as she lifts her fork. (She knows how
to sit at table . . . *where is she?* To feed herself.)

IV.
After time, it is tonight; I lift the book of poems
in lamplight, find her dwelling here, at home
among these weighted words—whipped by the
poet on to heavy largeness, sounding then some
vast unclever strangeness, as a temple gong: "*. . .giver*
of breath and bread;/... Thou hast bound bones and veins
in me, fastened me flesh,/ And after it almost unmade,
what with dread,/ Thy doing...."* Humbling, this
strangeness: as when we stand, near breathless,
solemn, looking up at mystery: the desert stars.

V.
Yes, *"what with dread," "almost unmade"*
she had become. Yet innocent, her drowning
on the Kansas plains in pain : so she is lifted
up, with all the innocents, a fearsome gift.

We keep our poems, harsh records of our
agonies, *"the strife of human hearts,"*** made
into song. Which we are born to love—for
reason far beyond all reason we can claim . . .
the hidden stars, our desert lives.

Inside the poem, my wandering grandmother
comes home—her garden's greening fruitfulness,
the morning glory all in bloom, a tangle on the
trellis by her door. Blue wilderness of light.

*Gerard Manley Hopkins, "The Wreck of the Deutschland."

**John Keats, "Of Sleep and Poetry."

Sonja Livingston

Nauset

When we're done, you lie belly-up and barefaced while I take in
the white of your beard,
Follow the ridges of your foul-weather brow, and though you've
no pipe,
I imagine one for you, cherry-carved and smooth-grained—
Its mouthpiece well-touched and worn, lying on a bedside table
Bare, but for an apple-green bowl made twenty years before by a
blue-eyed boy
Bare, but for the bowl, and the fluttering hand of your ladder-
backed wife.
My mind paints the pipe red as a newly fired brick burning in the
cool of that room,
Vulgar as a late summer rose twining itself into dove-gray and
white wainscot walls.

I land a finger on the bridge of your nose and know there can be
nothing but pale for you,
All ash and pine, but for the flicker of color in your face, which
pays no mind to strictures
And rises like the blood of the Nauset when you open your eyes
and look my way,
Uncertain of whether to touch or to run. Touch, you decide, and I
whisper don't worry,
Only I can see. To all else, you are brine and blue, true son of New
England,
Remnant of pilgrim and fisherman—these things I say till the
sounds of the Cape rattle like
Clamshells in your breath, which touches down like warm fog
behind my ear.

Later, we share a square of brown bread and you spoon thick soup
into my mouth,
And if there's one thing you must tell me, before I leave, it's that
you were there
Before the crowds ever came, were a good provider for your boy,
take mostly after your father.

And this is what I say, with my body, before I pack it up and head
west, I say that
Next to you, I am more silk than stone, that after all these years,
my wanting should be done
And over by now, and though I'm not nearly so long-lived as you, I
find it odd such hunger should linger.

J. Whiteford, *Low Tide*, hand-colored etching

Nancy White

Other Girl

When she cast her hook, she pulled out a fish,
nice-sized. She killed it with the butt of her knife,
slit the belly, and with the sound of tearing emptied it

of complication. Entrails she dropped in the current
and forgot, forever. At home, someone
fried the fish and she ate it all with pepper and salt.

The skin, the cheeks, the eyes. She went out
in a jacket too thin, did not allow
the blue hearts of tulips staring back

to disturb her. Did not play dolls, excel
in school, or cry. Didn't hate anyone or ask
why. You wanted to climb into her body

and hide, would bump against her as you
walked. She'd look sideways,
then step to place one girl-space in between.

Kathleen Spencer

Nurse's Nightmare

I dream I am the nurse assigned to care
for Osama bin Laden, treat his burned,
oozing face, blackened backfire of terror.
He draws each breath through charred nostrils, his turn
to taste rotting flesh ten times per minute.
Unless, he holds his breath, lungs aching,
hurtling him to death by pneumonia
with hellish fevers, chills, suffocation.

I pinch my mask to my nose, consider
giving a triple morphine dose, or no
dose at all. Perhaps the cream I slather
on his burns is partly saliva. Now

midnight monsters don't hide under beds
they wear my badge, my uniform, swirl in my head.

Phyllis K. Collier

Such Good Feng Shui

The wet autumn day she arrives

I sit in the window of the North Star.
Her worktables tower against
My ashen roots. In a cell

Big enough for one, balloons and streamers.
She is Athena and Lolita combined,
My once wished-for self. It is months
Before I face that fountain.
We dance to our separate hard drives until
We lay out the map.
It is I who learn,

And I alone again—
Something about the algorithms

Of her blood.
She can no longer stand to work,
The doctor decrees.
Our two peninsulas frame a lagoon,
I give her the Big Dipper, the pine tree.
One day without consulting the I Ching
They move us again.
In a windless cave, we wait

Before the blue lantern, willing the color
Back into her cells. Her stalactites
Gather all the green of Ireland.
The loose ends of us tangle across the floor.
In the last days we have it almost right.
I leave it for her
To rearrange first her shadow,
Then mine, to fill her space
With enough dance for the two of us.

Ellen Sullins

Apprenticeship

Hazelnut, walnut, maple, oak

I'm seven, trying to catch up with Mother
meandering through woods on our farm
in the sobering crispness of early fall

Sycamore, sumac, cedar

She names each one as she strokes the trunks,
sweeps low-slung leaves with the palm of her hand,
nods as if checking things off a list

She murmurs to herself, moving on, as I scramble
through briars that snag my rolled-cuff jeans,
her words drifting out of the air I enter

Dogwood, poplar, hickory, elm

I focus on pairing names with textures of bark,
patterns of leaves, proud to receive this ancient
code, worried I'll lose her, frightened

of the unknown thing that fuels her need
to call by name these earthly gods, her invocation
a warding off, a subliminal teaching of protection

Hazelnut, walnut, maple, oak

Carolyn Miller

Indian Summer

The high, beautiful days are here at last,
the endless blue skies we've waited for
while the world falls apart around us. The tomatoes
have finally taken on their sugar, and sweet corn
is still in the market. But the stone fruits
are almost over, and the apple harvest
is coming in. And we are thinking about
the infinite sky, and how everything we love
can be taken from us in the illusional world,
this realm of enduring sorrow and perfect rapture.

Alison Moore

Oklahoma Ground Zero

Tomorrow is the 10th anniversary of the Oklahoma City bombing. A strong west wind rolls over the Great Plains bending the trees as I drive east on I-40 from Arkansas. An enormous cloud formation emerges from the undifferentiated mass of purple and gold sunset. Soon, the setting sun becomes the head of a huge bird, wings outstretched, tailfeathers fanned. A few minutes later I know better. It's a phoenix, the mythological, improbable bird of transformation. The ashes from which it rises may be gone, a memorial erected, but the bird still has a long way to go.

The memorial isn't hard to find; the state has erected a brown National Monument sign along I-235 to mark the Harrison Street exit. I have been here before to research a novel I am writing, but I have never arrived just before an anniversary of the bombing. And I have never seen the memorial like *this*: six two-story scaffoldings rising above the street, each one labeled: NBC, CBS, Fox, ABC. Below these territories that have sprung up within the province of the memorial, 168 chairs stand in rows facing the reflecting pool, one for each victim. Each chair rests on a glass platform etched with the name of the victim, and each glass platform is lit from within, a humble flame compared to the spotlights that, just an hour earlier, shone on the luminaries presenting live evening news.

A lone anchorman remains on one flatbed truck on the local news side. A young man in a suit sits in a black deckchair watching two of his crew practice wide shots with a long camera boom. Behind him, sound off, a television, tuned to some reality TV show, flickers in the dark. Nobody watches. I hope the program isn't *Survivor* because that word means a lot in this town. It's the title that separates the living from the dead, not who gets to be on next week's episode.

Further downtown, in the lobby of the Bank One tower, a major media event is in full swing by the time I arrive. Brian Williams, anchor and managing editor of NBC's *Nightly News*, gives a keynote address on the impact of terrorism over the last ten years to a crowd of at least two hundred. Survivors, families of victims, rescue workers, local politicians, and several firemen from the

City of New York sit in white wooden folding chairs while waiters stand guard over the steaming buffet. When questions are invited from the audience, a woman in the front row raises her hand to speak and a microphone is quickly passed to her. She doesn't have a question. *She has a lot of gratitude she wants to share*. She lost her husband in the building and wants to go on record thanking the people who gave so much to the rescue effort. Brian Williams, though he doesn't move a muscle, becomes backdrop, reduced in size. The real story is not the media's retrospective assessment, but this real-time reminder of loss and how one woman can now, ten years later, say, "I lost my husband," without completely breaking down. And there's something else, too, in her story, a reason for Oklahoma to remind the nation once again: what we now call terror in many ways started here.

Oklahoma Ground Zero at Robinson and 5th is green these days and made beautiful by a memorial where even the families of the victims say they feel at peace, but there is still a hole in the heart of the country, its pulse forever quickened by the shock that Oklahoma City was singled out. If Timothy McVeigh can be commended for anything it's his genius in picking the heart of the country to leave a hole in. He left his message: terror can happen anywhere.

* * *

I return to the memorial after the NBC *Nightly News* event at Bank One, to walk through before it's filled tomorrow morning with cameras and microphones and crowds of people. As I walk in the candle-like glow from the chairs I can make out an enormous teddy bear on the small chair of Miss Baylee Almon, a one-year-old girl made famous by the photograph of the fireman carrying her lifeless, bloodied and plaster-powdered body from the wreckage.

She's referred to as "Miss" here, maybe because she was more visible in death than the other 18 children who died that morning. Maybe because as a symbol of the tragedy for the nation she should have some title. As I stand looking at Baylee's bear, a woman walks past me carrying a wreath of flowers and several bags full of clanking vases. I watch her kneel before a chair two rows down, place the flowers on the seatback, arrange a few vases at the base. I have a strong feeling about who she's honoring and I have to ask her when she's done.

"Your friend?"

"Oh, God, yes. My best friend in the world."

She cries and I put my hand on her shoulder. She tells me the story, or tries to, and it's too much, ten years later, to say it straight, without tears. Her friend Jill Diane Randolph had been in a meeting on the 3rd floor Federal Employees Credit Union office. At 9:02, her boss was blown back by the blast, and every other person in the meeting dropped through a shattered floor. It took over a week, she says, to find her. I stand there, my hand on her shoulder while she cries. It's what I can do: listen. Let it happen, whatever she needs to say or not say. When she stops crying I wait awhile and ask her what her favorite memory of her friend is.

"Oh," she says, smiling and wiping her eyes. "When I was pregnant and worn out she called me up one day and said she was going to take me to have my ears pierced. She said I was the last person on earth not to have pierced ears and she was going to rectify that."

I laugh with her, but it's the kind of laughter that can't last long. It's a semicolon between twin sentences of grief and memory, a small space to draw a breath in. Before she leaves, she hugs me. Oklahomans are like this, in my experience, and I feel grateful for the brief contact with her. And a little stunned. In my novel, my main character survives the blast while her best friend does not. Sometimes there is not a lot of difference between truth and fiction. It's just that I'm not here putting flowers on the chair, though in my narrative mind, forged by my own losses, I know the feel of that seat, the smell of the crushed grass before it, the weight of carrying on.

As I leave, a duck flies in from left field, skidding on the half-inch-deep pool which is more a wet mirror than a body of water. The duck rights itself quickly, shaking its feathers. Drops of water rain around it, absorbed instantly into the glassy surface. The reflection of 168 chairs comes into sharp focus again.

* * *

A typical Oklahoma spring day, now as it was then. Partly cloudy, windy. Where the famous yellow Ryder truck rolled up in front of the Murrah building, the reflecting pool now stretches between the gates of time, the two fifty-foot high bronze bookends of the memorial. Between 9:01 on the east gate and 9:03 on the west, the world changed.

It looks different in daylight, more hopeful somehow. We all sit in rows below the Survivor Tree on the north side. This tree is now extravagant with leaves after being blasted naked and nearly leafless ten years ago. It's the unofficial altar, a living reminder of life not only going on but thriving, and seedlings have been planted in communities outside the city who lost people in the bombing. The tree is the symbol of hope, and hope is the unabashed theme of this anniversary, a point driven home in all the printed publicity as well as the subject of the essay contest for school children across the state. In its recovery Oklahoma has set the bar for all other places affected by terrorism, at least in America. I'm sure the planners of this event thought hard about its focus. Is ten years long enough to be talking about hope? Will those still grieving feel prematurely pushed to move on? In New York, feelings are still raw. The controversy over their memorial makes it clear how difficult it is to take so many needs into consideration. Oklahomans, characteristic of their no-nonsense pioneer roots, got on with their memorial. They picked one democratically from many submitted designs, broke ground and built it, incorporated it into the character of this city in five years' time. Ask anybody here; they're shocked that something is being built on Ground Zero in New York. They take it for granted that one should be able to touch the earth where so much was lost. To claim the place for prayer rather than profit.

Across the reflecting pool, a few family members place last-minute flowers or teddy bears on the chairs of loved ones. The bells of several churches ring out the hour and the hundred-and-sixty-eight seconds of silence begin.

Strains of someone singing *The Star Spangled Banner* come through a speaker somewhere and everyone gets to their feet, turning to the stadium-sized American flag hanging from the side of the museum. On the rooftop, a SWAT team scrutinizes us through binoculars as some of us try to sing along.

Anthem over, we realize that the service is being held in First Church on Robinson, just across the street from the 9:01 gate. We make our way up the stairs, through the gate, and sit on a curb to listen to an hour or more of speeches by Bill Clinton, Dick Cheney, and various mayors, governors and congressmen. But first and foremost, there's the reading of the mission statement of the memorial, by children who survived the bombing. Several voices in unison. They were babies then and ten years has given them an odd maturity as they read the words inscribed on the gates:

We come here to remember those who were killed, those who survived and those changed forever. May all who leave here know the impact of violence. May this memorial offer comfort, strength, peace, hope and serenity.

You can hear it through the speakers, the silence when they finish. Outside, hardly anybody moves. Then *America the Beautiful* by the United States Air Force Band of Mid-America breaks through. Breathing resumes.

The speeches of the dignitaries are well-written, heartfelt, àpropos, and find a way not to minimize the scope of the tragedy while still getting the word hope in as often as possible. Clinton, to his great credit, focuses on something specific: the Survivor Tree. He talks about not forgetting our roots, how deep they go, while stretching our branches toward the future. He commends Oklahomans for not letting their hearts be "paralyzed by pain or hardened by hatred." Nobody mentions the word "peace." Hope is so much more neutral. So much more do-able.

Rescue workers walk their dogs back and forth in front of the church. Everyone wants to pet the dogs, these other, four-footed survivors. A renegade camera crew from Wing TV dressed entirely in black hands out leaflets. Their T-shirts say: Ten Years Later Still Looking for the Truth. The leaflets invite you to log onto their website to find out about the Oklahoma City Bombing Cover Up and to read about what the government doesn't want you to know. To many, McVeigh and Nichols were too easy, the case too quickly closed; further questions must be asked. To them and many others, it's over, but far from being finished.

The final part of the program is reserved for the reading of the names of the 168 who perished. Children who lost parents in the bombing take turns reading the names, their clear voices not faltering even as they say the words "my father." Or, "my mother." But the last girl to read breaks down completely when she gets to the name that's so painful to say out loud. She struggles through the final set of names, barely able to finish.

Finally, the band takes over with *Battle Hymn of the Republic*. I can't help but wish Woody Guthrie, a native Oklahoman, was here with some simple ballad to mark that day in 1995, a song about what happened in verse and chorus, like his famous ballad of the 1913 Massacre. But Woody died of Huntington's in '64 and he's still seen as controversial and too left-leaning for many, despite the fact that Woody was more interested in singing than joining political parties.

The doors of the church open wide. A lone bagpipe player, an elderly man in full Scots regalia from the Highlanders of Oklahoma Pipes and Drums, emerges, the bagpipe wheezing toward a note. He will lead the families and survivors and rescue workers out of the church to the memorial. He steps decisively into the sunlight.

On the second step he falls. The bagpipes go flying and several people rush to his aid. It's a horrible moment, this toppled human marring the fragile perfection. The cameras are rolling. He gets to his feet and reaches for his bagpipes, deflated now, on the step beside him. He puts the bag under his arm, the pipe in his mouth, and breathes into it. The bag fills, the pipes groan into melody. He continues down the steps, carefully now, not missing the steps but missing a few of the high notes. Maybe the pipes were damaged. Or his breath is short from the anxiety of falling in so public a place, under such enormous pressure to lead the procession. With great dignity he makes his way down the sidewalk, across the street, through the gates of time, a stream of people following after.

I stop one woman and ask her where the families had waited after the bombing, where that church was in relation to the bomb site. It's a detail I need to verify for the novel and I feel a little strange asking. I don't have a microphone and a camera. I'm just a woman with a question but this woman in front of me is happy to answer, or to try to find me someone who can. She brings another woman in her group over who tells me she never went to the Family Center, that she waited for news at her sister's. She hugs me and says, "I'm sorry. God bless you."

She becomes my pied piper. I follow her and her family into the memorial to the chair of LaKesha Richardson Levy. I can barely read her name hidden by so many flowers. At least thirty people circle the chair, three deep. The woman who hugged me and said "God bless you" is singing to some tape-recorded music now. Everyone is crying. A man in front of me hands a boot to the man next to him. I lean closer. The man says to his relation, "She wants to see. Let her see." They hand the boot carefully, reverently, to me. LaKesha's boot. The left one. With the sock still in it, the laces dangling from the crushed leather. Something sharp penetrated the leather completely, leaving holes behind. "You can see the devastation in this boot," the man says to me. And I do.

Holding LaKesha's boot, I try to imagine the force of something that could blow it off her foot. I remember that inside the museum there's an entire display case full of recovered shoes of all sizes and styles. Somehow the force of an explosion tends to blow the shoes right off people and the shoes are a poignant reminder of the power of that blast. This boot in my hand was identified by someone in her family among all the remainders gathered from the rubble: watches, I.D. badges, pieces of clothing. And now this boot is here, passed from hand to hand, an offering, a reminder. I didn't know LaKesha but I can see the love in her family. It's a powerful thing. At least as powerful as the force of devastation. The woman keeps on singing the song over and over as if to stop would be shameful. Her voice rises over the din, beautiful and solitary, but deeply personal. This is for LaKesha, not the evening news.

Around some other chairs I see no one gathered. Firemen walk down the rows putting a small bouquet on each so that no one is forgotten. The media move in, looking for stories. They're everywhere, the media and the stories. People kneel by the chairs, place a hand on the seat and pray. It's captured on camera. A blond two-year-old sits on one of the chairs quite happily, kicking her legs, her Mary Jane shoes into the air. She looks a little bewildered by the solemn adults around her. A generation removed, she could become the next symbol. Of hope—which is what they're looking for. I expect to see her face on the evening news on each and every channel.

The people of Oklahoma City open themselves to all this publicity and attention. Many haven't dressed up for TV. They arrive in jeans, work uniforms. One man has wrapped himself in a faded American flag, and says he is a survivor. Maybe so. Maybe no. Disasters draw all kinds. But this man is undoubtedly a survivor of something, even if it wasn't this, even if no one asks his story.

The media start packing up. The anchors are off to the airport in rental cars. The crew dismantles the scaffolding, the plywood platforms. A line a block long forms outside the museum.

Clouds move in from the west, pressing closer. The sky is darkening and thunderstorms are predicted for late afternoon. I walk through the 9:03 gate, past The Fence studded with stuffed animals, license plates, hair clips, keyrings—whatever people who visit can leave behind to say they were here. There are a few plastic-covered photos, faded now, of some of the victims. To many, this is the true memorial. Anyone can leave something here.

The people of Oklahoma City will no doubt be glad when this week is over. All of this is mostly for the rest of the country—a reminder. The people here have never forgotten. Before 9-11 there was Oklahoma City and McVeigh waited on death row and was gone a few months before the towers went down. While The Pile in Manhattan was slowly being pulled apart, grass began to grow between the chairs in this memorial. The lens of the country turned to New York and stayed there until this week when no one could believe ten whole years had gone by since that Ryder truck came to town. Those trucks are not even yellow any more, testament to the power of memory in marketing. The media will probably return in fifteen years but it won't be the same. Ten is a powerful number. When feelings are not too raw but can still be revealed. To the camera. To strangers like me. Some of the most visible wounds may have healed, but in this city, if not here in this very crowd leaving the memorial this morning, there is one man whose wife survived the blast only to commit suicide a year and a half later. I met him the last time I was here and I thought I saw him today, though when I turned again, he was gone. There is another here who will not ever be able to be around wailing children because that's the last sound she heard before she lost consciousness. The screams of the children in what was left of America's Kids Daycare echo always.

It's easy to lose consciousness. The body wants to, when in unbearable pain. The country needs to, when confronted with unfathomable terror. To come to Oklahoma City today is to be conscious, at least for a day. Grief, more than anything, holds us to humanity in spite of divisive acts of political and religious violence. The theme of hope is not impossible to come by. Who can dispute the need for it? But I can't help turning to read once more the last words engraved in the gates of time:

. . . may this memorial offer comfort,
strength, peace, hope and serenity.

What about peace? Do we even think it's still possible? Memorials are little museums of peace. Outside, drivers cut each other off and curse, suicide bombers detonate their bodies in public places. Somewhere, in a deserted farmhouse, some angry young man constructs a bomb from fertilizer left over from last year's planting. But inside this little memorial here, this enclave, you can get a glimpse of peace. It's an endangered species looking back at you, wide-eyed from its sheltered habitat. It's dangerous to feed it and it doesn't breed well in captivity. Look while you have the chance.

In Oklahoma, this sheltered place is open-ended, never closed, never locked. If peace is here, it can come and go freely. Peace can spread out and take root like the seedlings planted from the Survivor Tree. Peace is right in front of us like the man wrapped in the faded flag. A survivor we see but are not quite sure we can believe.

G. Jill Evans, *Chairs Facing St. Joseph,* photograph

About the Authors

Judith Arcana's poetry and prose have appeared recently or are forthcoming in *Poetica, BuffaloCarp,* and *Bridges,* and in two collections, *Women's Lives* and *Fresh Water.* She is the author of *Grace Paley's Life Stories, a Literary Biography*; her most recent book is a collection of poems and monologues called *What if your mother.*

Gay Baines is co-founder and poetry editor of July Literary Press in Buffalo, NY. Her poetry has appeared in *Rattapallax, Cimarron Review, Slipstream,* and other journals. In 2002 she published her first novel, *Dear M.K.*

Tony Barnstone, who won Honorable Mention for the 2004 *Nimrod*/ Hardman Pablo Neruda Poetry Prize, has had his manuscript accepted for publication by the Sheep Meadow Press. His forthcoming book is entitled *He Murders His Darlings: A Marriage and Divorce in Ten Chapters.*

Richard M. Berlin is an Associate Professor of Psychiatry at the University of Massachusetts Medical School, where he has established the Gerald F. Berlin Creative Writing Prize for medical student writers. His first collection of poems, *How JFK Killed My Father,* won the Pearl Poetry Prize; he also writes poetry for a monthly column in the *Psychiatric Times.* He practices psychiatry in a small town in the Berkshire hills of western Massachusetts.

Eleanor Berry's work appears in *Crab Orchard Review, Hawai'i Pacific Review,* and *Antioch Review,* as well as in the 2004 edition of *The Anthology of New England Writers* and *Herspace: Women, Writing, and Solitude.* A book of her poems, *Green November,* is forthcoming in 2006.

Michelle Bitting's work has appeared or is forthcoming in *Prairie Schooner, Glimmer Train, Swink, Chiron Review,* and elsewhere. Her work has been recognized with a number of prizes, including the 2005 Rock & Sling Virginia Brendemuehl Award and the 2004 Poets on Parnassus Award, as well as first place in the 2003 *Glimmer Train* Poetry Open.

Terry Blackhawk's book *Escape Artist*—including the poem "Mediterranean Crossing," which first appeared in *Nimrod*—received the 2003 John Ciardi Poetry Prize. Other publications include two chapbooks and an earlier volume of poems, *Body & Field.* Terry is founding director of Detroit's InsideOut Literary Arts Project, a poets-in-the-schools program that serves over 2200 children a year.

Daniel C. Bryant is a retired internist whose previous publications include poetry in literary and medical magazines, essays on literature and medicine, and crossword puzzles in the Los Angeles and New York *Times*. His long interest in the physician as writer led him to create a website, now maintained by NYU Medical School, devoted to the subject: <http://library.med.nyu.edu/library/eresources/featuredcollections/bryant/index.ntml>

Rafael Campo is on the faculty at Harvard Medical School and the Beth Israel Deaconess Medical Center in Boston, where he hopes to launch a medical humanities program to bring literature and art into the hospital wards. His first collection of poetry, *The Other Man Was Me,* was selected for the National Poetry Series Award; his second, *What the Body Told,* won a Lambda Literary Award, as did his book of essays.

Allan Douglass Coleman writes poetry, fiction and creative nonfiction, makes music, photographs, and produces various other forms of visual art. His poetry and fiction have appeared or are forthcoming in *Black Water Review*, *Medicinal Purposes*, *Hazmat Review*, and elsewhere. Under the pen name A. D. Coleman, he is an internationally published critic of photography, art, and mass media.

Phyllis K. Collier's poems have appeared in many literary magazines, including *Nimrod*. Her first book of poems, *Cain's Daughters,* was published in 2005.

Jen Collins is currently working on her PhD in creative writing at the University of Wisconsin—Milwaukee and is Poetry Co-Editor of *The Cream City Review*. She has won several writing contests in fiction and poetry; her short story "Bowers" was a finalist in *Glimmer Train*'s 2002-3 Winter Fiction Open.

Nina Corwin is a social worker whose work with trauma has taken her across the country and to Vietnam; most recently she provided stress debriefing for relief workers with Hurricane Katrina. Her poems appear or are forthcoming in *Atlanta*, *Poetry East*, *Spoon River* and elsewhere; she has published a collection, *Conversations with Friendly Demons and Tainted Saints*.

Olga Costopoulos lives in Edmonton, Alberta, where she writes, teaches creative writing at the University of Alberta, and, when the ground thaws, gardens. Her second collection of poems, *The Tiger Side of Night*, is due out in the spring of 2006.

Jack Coulehan, who teaches and practices medicine in Stony Brook, NY, is the author of four collections of poems, most recently *Medicine*

Stone. His poems and stories appear frequently in literary magazines and medical journals and are widely anthologized. He won the 1997 American College of Physicians award for best poem and was the 1999 Merck Fellow at Yaddo. His latest book is *Chekhov's Doctors* (2003).

BARBARA CROOKER, the winner of many awards, including Word Press First Book Award, 2005, and W. B. Yeats Society of New York Poetry Prize, 2004, was a finalist for a 1997 Spoken Word Grammy Award. Her poems have appeared widely, in anthologies and in such journals as *River City*, *The Beloit Poetry Journal*, and *Poetry International*. She has published more than 10 chapbooks and one collection, *Radiance*.

KIM DAVIS has published poetry and fiction in *The Iowa Review*, *Literal Latte*, and *The Beacon Street Review*. After practicing law for several years, she now teaches creative writing at the Cambridge Center in Cambridge, MA, and at the Duxbury Art Complex in Duxbury, MA.

IVY DEMPSEY, associate poetry editor for *Nimrod*, has taught writing at California State University, LA, and the University of California, LA, and conducted poetry workshops in California, New Mexico, and Oklahoma. Her poems have appeared in *Southern Poetry Review*, *Chariton Review*, *Calyx*, and elsewhere. Her book *The Scent of Water* won the 2002 Oklahoma Book Award.

KATY DIDDEN grew up in Washington, D.C., and completed an MFA at the University of Maryland. She now lives in Chicago and teaches at Loyola University. Her poems appear in the *DC Poets Against the War Anthology* and in *6x5*, the Tense Forms journal.

MARGUERITE KEIL FLANDERS, a poet and musician, has published poems in *Boston Review*, *Comstock Review*, and *Yankee Magazine*. She is an environmental activist working in the field of urban and community forestry.

M. FROST, when not working as a veterinarian, writes poetry, which has been published recently in *Barrow Street*, *The Healing Muse*, *Philadelphia Poets*, and elsewhere.

AMINA LOLITA GAUTIER's fiction has appeared in the *North American Review*, *Shenandoah*, and *Storyquarterly*, among others. A Waiter at Breadloaf, she is also the winner of the William Richey Award, the Jack Dyer Award, and a Pennsylvania Council on the Arts Award. She is the fiction editor of *Storyquarterly* and Assistant Professor of Creative Writing at St. Joseph's University.

REBECCA GIVENS lives in Brooklyn and has poems forthcoming in *The Hollins Critic, Seattle Review, Southeast Poems*, and *32 Poems*.

JANE ELLEN GLASSER's poetry has appeared in such journals as *Hudson Review, Southern Review*, and *Georgia Review*. Her first collection of poetry, *Naming the Darkness*, carries an introduction by W. D. Snodgrass; her second, *Light Persists*, won the *Tampa Review* Prize for Poetry 2005 and was published by Tampa University Press. She co-founded the nonprofit arts organization and journal *New Virginia Review*.

JOHN GLOWNEY has poems in recent or forthcoming issues *Alaska Quarterly Review, Mid-American Review*, and *Pontoon 8*. His poems have been nominated for a Pushcart Prize and have won the 1999 Richard Hugo Prize and the 2002 Robert Winner Memorial Award from the Poetry Society of America.

J. I. GOODMAN is a poet and performance artist with academic degrees in English, Fine Arts, Drawing, and Rhetoric and Poetics. An article from her dissertation is forthcoming in the journal *New Writing*. She hopes to complete a chapbook of her poems, *Late Blooms*, for publication this spring.

ALEX GRANT is a native Scot now living in North Carolina. His work has appeared or is forthcoming in *Connecticut Review, North American Review*, and *Midwest Quarterly*, among others. In 2005, he was a finalist for Discovery/*The Nation* and the Writers at Work Fellowship and received an honorable mention in *Nimrod*'s Pablo Neruda Prize for Poetry.

JONATHAN GREENHAUSE's work has recently appeared or is forthcoming in *Blind Man's Rainbow, Edgz*, and *Medicinal Purposes Literary Review*, among other journals. "During the week," he says, "I interpret back and forth between the Spanish and English languages; on the weekends, I can be found walking in circles and squares."

ANDREY GRITSMAN, a native of Moscow who emigrated to the U.S. in 1981, is a physician, poet, and essayist. He runs the Intercultural Poetry Series at the Cornelia Street Café in New York City. He has published five volumes of poetry in Russian; his work in English has been published in *Apalachee Review, Eclipse, Poet Lore*, and many other journals.

HEDY HABRA, born in Egypt of Lebanese origin, received her MFA from Western Michigan University, where she now teaches Spanish. Her critical work has appeared in such journals as *Hispanófila* and *Revista de Estudios Hispánicos*, while her poetry and fiction have been published in *Negative Capability, Sulphur River Review*, and *Puerto del Sol*.

GERTRUDE HALSTEAD was born in Germany in 1916 and fled from the Nazi regime to France, where during the war she was interned in Camp Gurs. After working as a volunteer interpreter, she was freed and left Europe from Portugal on the last ship for the U.S. Her work has appeared in *Sahara*, *Surroundings East*, and *Columbia Poetry Review*, and her first book will be published in 2006 by Adastra Press.

SUZANNE HEYD's recent work appears in *Beloit Poetry Journal*, *The Spoon River Poetry Review*, and other journals, as well as *The Anthology of New England Writers 2002*. She was a recipient of the NEH summer seminar award, runner-up for the Robert Penn Warren Award, and finalist for the James Fellowship for Novel in Progress.

ROY JACOBSTEIN's latest book, *A Form of Optimism*, won the 2006 Samuel French Morse Prize; his previous book, *Ripe*, won the 2002 Felix Pollak Prize. His new work appears in *The Gettysburg Review*, *The Iowa Review*, and *TriQuarterly*. A public health physician, he works in Africa and Asia on women's reproductive health programs, and lives in Chapel Hill, North Carolina.

EVE JONES has published poetry in *AGNI*, *Hotel Amerika*, *Poet Lore*, and other journals.

FADY JOUDAH, a Palestinian-American physician and field member of Doctors without Borders, has translated Mahmoud Darwish's poetry into English (forthcoming in 2006 from Copper Canyon Press), has poems appearing or forthcoming in *Kenyon Review*, *Prairie Schooner*, and elsewhere, and a manuscript recognized as a finalist in the Yale Series.

LOREN KLEINMAN, the recipient of the Spire Press Poetry prize and a Pushcart Prize nominee (2000, 2003), has published her work in the *Journal of New Jersey Poets*, *Resurgence* (UK), and elsewhere. Now a contributing editor for several publications, ranging from *Luxury Travel Advisor* to *Aesthetica: A Journal of the Arts* (UK), she was the assistant reviews editor for *Sidereality*.

CAROLYN KREITER-FORONDA's poems have been nominated for three Pushcart Prizes and appear in such journals as *The Ledge*, *Hispanic Culture Review*, and *Antioch Review*. She has published four books of poetry, *Contrary Visions*, *Gathering Light*, *Death Comes Riding*, and *Greatest Hits*, and has co-edited an anthology of poems, *In a Certain Place*.

MICHAEL KRIESEL, who lives in central Wisconsin, won the 2004 Lorine Niedecker Award sponsored by the Council for Wisconsin Writers. He is a reviewer for *Library Journal* and *Small Press Review* and a member of the Wisconsin Poet Laureate Commission. His poems have appeared in *Rosebud, Bitter Oleander,* and *The Progressive.*

CHRISTINE LECHE taught literature and creative writing for the University of Maryland's European Division from 1996 to 2005, work that took her to U.S. military bases and camps in Bosnia, Honduras, Italy, Spain, and Germany. She has won the American Academy of Poets Award, among other honors, and her work has been published in such journals as the *Mississippi Valley Review* and *Louisiana Literature.*

KENNETH LEE is a pathologist in Boston who has been writing poems as a hobby for 20 years or so and has recently begun attending the workshop of Barbara Helfgott-Hyett in Brookline, Massachusetts, and submitting his work for publication.

NORM LEVINE's work has appeared in many poetry magazines, most recently in *Janus Head, Mid-America Review,* and *Poetry New Zealand.* He has published three volumes of his poetry, the most recent, *At a Theatre Near You,* in 2003. He lives in California, where, he says, he practices pharmacy for a living and writes poetry for his life.

SONJA LIVINGSTON's writing has been honored with a 2005 Fellowship from the New York Foundation for the Arts, an Iowa Award, and an AWP Intro Award. Her work appears in such journals as *Fugue, The Iowa Review, The Seattle Review,* and others. She received an MFA from the University of New Orleans and now teaches at UCLA Extension Center.

CHARLOTTE MANDEL teaches a poetry workshop at Barnard College Center for Research on Women. She edited the Barnes Award anthology, *Saturday's Women*; her most recent collection of poems is *Sight Lines.* Two of her poems appeared in *Nimrod*'s issue on aging, *Clap Hands and Sing.*

DIANE K. MARTIN's work has appeared in *Crazyhorse, New England Review,* and *Zyzzvya,* among others. She won second place in the *Nimrod*/Hardman Pablo Neruda Prize for Poetry in 2004; her work was selected for inclusion in *Best New Poems 2005.* She lives in San Francisco.

COLLEEN J. MCELROY's work has been published in many journals, including *Hayden's Ferry, ZYZZYVA,* and *Crab Creek Review,* as well as such anthologies as *Blues Poems* and *Best American Poetry 2001.* Her most recent books are the travel memoirs *A Long Way from St. Louie,* the poems and the fieldnotes and translations of Malagasy writing *Over the Lip of the World: Among the Storytellers of Madagascar.* She has been awarded two NEA Fellowships, two Fulbright Fellowships, and a Dupont Visiting Scholar Fellowship. She is currently editor-in-chief of the *Seattle Review.*

LESLIE MCGRATH has worked as a psychotherapist, an options trader, and an artist's model. The winner of the 2004 *Nimrod*/Hardman Pablo Neruda Prize for Poetry and a Pushcart Prize nominee, she received her MFA in literature and poetry from the Bennington Writing Seminars. Her work has appeared in *The Formalist*, *The Connecticut Review*, *Black Warrior Review*, and elsewhere.

LISA MECKEL's work has been published in small press journals, local art magazines and on the Community of Voices Website. She won First Prize for Poetry at the Santa Barbara Writers' Conference; in addition she was awarded the Poetry Prize from the Santa Barbara summer Poetry Workshop.

JUDY ROWE MICHAELS is poet-in-residence at Princeton Day School and a poet-in-the-schools for the Geraldine R. Dodge Foundation in New Jersey. The University Press of Florida published her first poetry collection, *The Forest of Wild Hands*. The National Council of Teachers of English published her two books on reading and writing poetry with high school students, *Risking Intensity* and *Dancing with Words*.

CAROLYN MILLER's publication credits include *The Southern Review*, *The Georgia Review*, and *The Sewanee Review*. Her books include *This Is Mine*, a limited-edition chapbook, and *After Cocteau*, a standard-edition collection.

LESLIE ADRIENNE MILLER's collections include *Eat Quite Everything You See*, *Yesterday Had a Man in It*, *Ungodliness*, *Staying up for Love*, as well as *The Resurrection Trade*, forthcoming in 2007. A professor of English at the University of St. Thomas, she is working on a series of poems involving medical images of female anatomy; in addition to her work in this issue of *Nimrod*, poems from this series are forthcoming in *Kenyon Review*, *Antioch Review*, and *Prairie Schooner*, among others.

ANDREW MALAN MILWARD has studied fiction writing at the University of Arizona and the University of Missouri, where he taught writing and was the senior fiction editor at the literary journal *Center*. His fiction has appeared in *Crazyhorse*, *The Literary Review*, and *Confrontation*.

ALISON MOORE was the winner of the *Nimrod*/Hardman Katherine Anne Porter Prize for Fiction in 2004. She has published a book of short stories, *Small Spaces Between Emergencies*, and a novel, *Synonym for Love*. She is involved in many public outreach programs, including ArtsReach, a Native American literacy program in Arizona, and the Orphan Train Heritage Society of America, Inc.

BERWYN MOORE, a former respiratory therapist, teaches at Gannon University, where she offers a course in medical humanities called Literature and the Healing Arts. Her work has won awards from the Chester A. Jones Foundation and Negative Capability Press. Her publications include a book, *Dissolution of Ghosts*, and poems in such journals as *The Southern Review*, *Poetry Northwest*, and the *Journal of the American Medical Association*.

GEORGE MOORE's poems have appeared in *The Atlantic*, *North American Review*, *Orion*, and other journals. He has published the poetry collections *The Long Way Around*, *The Petroglyphs at Wedding Rocks and Other Poems*, and *Headhunting*, as well as the critical study *Gertrude Stein's* The Making of Americans*: Repetition and the Emergence of Modernism*.

MARTINA NICHOLSON grew up in California, where she now lives with her husband and two children. After several years as a health educator for the Peace Corps, she became a doctor and now practices obstetrics and gynecology.

JOHN NOLAND has published in *Chicago Review*, *Georgetown Review*, *Seattle Review*, and other journals. His chapbook, *This Dark Land Where I Live*, was published by Kulupi Press after winning the press's Poems of Place Chapbook Contest. He lives on the edge of the sea in Coos Bay, Oregon.

JENNY NOLLER's work has been published in *Cimarron Review*. She has an MA in fiction from Hollins College and an MFA from the University of North Carolina—Greensboro.

GABRIELLE PARENT has published poetry in *Victoria's Write* magazine; fiction in Vancouver's *Bleach Mag*; and a translation of Aimé Césaire's *La Tragedie du Roi Christophe* in the University of British Columbia's *Educational Insights Journal*. She is currently finishing her first novel, *The Heroes in the Seaweed*, for which she received an emerging Métis writer grant from the Canada Council for the Arts.

JOLEE G. PASSERINI has published poems in *Spoon River Poetry Review*, *The Hampden-Sydney Review*, *The Alembic*, and elsewhere. She teaches world literature, global and environmental studies, and interdisciplinary humanities courses in New College and the English Department of the University of Alabama.

AMY E. PAYNE's fiction has appeared or will appear in *The San Francisco Chronicle's Sunday Magazine*, *Puerto del Sol*, and *Amelia*. One of the 2005 winners of the AWP Intro Journals Award, she lives in the Bay Area and, like much of the world, is working on a novel.

JENNIFER PERRINE received the 2005 *Bellingham Review* 49th Parallel Poetry Award, the 2004 *The Ledge* Poetry Award, and the 2004 Writers at Work Poetry Fellowship. Her poems have appeared recently in *The Cream City Review, Paterson Literary Review, Quarterly West,* and elsewhere. She serves as poetry editor of *The Southeast Review.*

W. T. PFEFFERLE is the author of *Poets on Place,* a travel memoir and interview anthology of his yearlong trip around the country interviewing 62 American poets. His work has been published in *North American Review, Carolina Quarterly, New Orleans Review,* and elsewhere. He is the poetry editor at *Georgetown Review.*

MANJULA RAJAN has had one of her stories nominated for inclusion in the 2006 *Best New American Voices* anthology.

MARJORIE ROBERTS is a psychotherapist in Los Angeles, specializing in counseling cancer and AIDS patients. Awarded honorable mention in the Montalvo Biennial Poetry Competition, her work has been published or is forthcoming in *The Cape Rock, Confluence, Controlled Burn,* and other journals, as well as the *Meridian Anthology of Contemporary Poetry.*

GERI ROSENZWEIG's work has appeared in *Hotel Amerika* and *Wildlife Magazine,* and is forthcoming in *Poetry International* and *The Poetry of Nursing.* She has published three books: *Under the Jasmine Moon, Half the Story,* and *God Is Not Talking.*

SARAH ROSSITER's publications include a novel, *The Human Season,* and a short story collection, *Beyond this Bitter Air.* Her poetry has been published in a variety of journals, including *The Southern Review, The Sewanee Review,* and *First Things.*

MARGARET ROZGA has published poems recently in *Out of Line* and in the anthology *Red, White and Blues: Poets on the Promise of America.* The poems in this issue of *Nimrod* were written from her experience as the mother of an Army Reservist injured in Iraq.

RICHARD SCHAAF is the editor of Azul Editions, a small independent literary press he founded in 1986. He has published a volume of his poetry, *Revolutionary at Home,* and translations or co-translations from Spanish of more than 20 books, including work by Pablo Neruda, Cesar Vallejo, Alicia Partnoy, and others.

JEAN-MARK SENS, Collection Development Librarian at Nicholls State University, teaches at the John Folse Culinary Institute. Born in France and educated in Paris, he has lived in the American South for nearly 15 years. He has published poems in *International Poetry Review*, *Painted Bride*, and *North American Review*, among other journals; his first collection, *Appetite*, was published in 2004.

PURVI SHAH, born in India, lives in New York City and serves as the Executive Director at Sakhi for South Asian Women. Her poems have appeared in *Borderlands: Texas Poetry Review*, *Brooklyn Review*, *Descant*, and other journals, as well as in *Contours of the Heart: South Asians Map North America*, which won an American Book Award in 1997.

LEE SHARKEY is the author of *To A Vanished World*, a poem sequence in response to Roman Vishniac's photographs of Eastern European Jewry in the years preceding the Nazi Holocaust. She is the editor of the *Beloit Poetry Journal*.

JEFF D. SIMPSON is pursuing a master's degree in creative writing from Oklahoma State University. His poems have recently appeared or are forthcoming in *Oklahoma Today*, *Poet Lore*, and *Pebble Lake Review*. The former poetry editor for *The Oklahoma Review*, he is now an assistant editor for *Cimarron Review*.

CAROLE SINENI has published her work in such journals as *Pleiades*, *Bitterroot*, and *The Pittsburgh Quarterly*. She is the editor of the e-zine www.hotmetalpoets.com.

REBECCA A. SPEARS has published poems in such journals as *Concho River Review*, *Minnesota Review*, and *Calyx*. She has taught writing for the University of Gevale in Sweden; Inkberry, Houston's High School for the Performing Arts; and the Honors College of the University of Houston.

KATHLEEN SPENCER, editor-in-chief of *Plastic Surgical Nursing Journal*, practices as a post-anesthesia care nurse. Her poems have appeared in *Rosebud*, *Red Rock Review*, *Clackamas Literary Review*, and other journals, as well as in the collection *Intensive Care: More Poetry and Prose by Nurses*, and a chapter in the upcoming *The Poetry of Nurses: Work and Commentary by Major Nurse Poets*.

MARJORIE STELMACH'S first book of poems, *Night Drawings*, was selected by David Ignatow to receive the Marianne Moore prize; a second book, *A History of Disappearance*, is forthcoming. Her poems have appeared in *The Kenyon Review*, *Prairie Schooner*, *River Styx*, and other magazines. Her work has been honored twice with the *Malahat Review* Long Poem Prize and groups of her poems received the first Chelsea Award.

ELLEN SULLINS has a master's degree in counseling and a Ph.D. in social psychology. A retired university professor and researcher, she is now a practicing psychotherapist. Her work has appeared in *Byline Magazine*, *laughing dog: strictly poetry*, and *The Moon*.

JOHN SUROWIECKI has published one collection of his poems, *Watching Cartoons before Attending a Funeral*, and four chapbooks; the first of these, *Caliban Poems* (2001), contains poems that originally appeared in *Nimrod*. Recent acceptances or publications of his work include *Poetry*, *Alaska Quarterly Review*, and *Wisconsin Review*, among other journals.

MARIANNE TAYLOR teaches literature and creative writing at Kirkwood Community College. Her work has been published in *Paterson Literary Review*, *Chiron Review*, and *North American Review* and is forthcoming in the anthology *Family Matters*.

SUE ELLEN THOMPSON, winner of the 2003 *Nimrod*/Hardman Pablo Neruda Prize for Poetry, is the author of three books. Her newest book, *The Golden Hour*, is forthcoming in 2006. She recently edited *The Autumn House Anthology of Contemporary American Poetry*.

JIM TILLEY retired in 2001 after a 25-year career in insurance and investment banking. His recent poems have been or will be published in *New Delta Review*, *Sycamore Review*, and *Rattle*.

ALISON TOWNSEND has published work in such journals as *Crazyhorse*, *Fourth Genre*, and *Michigan Quarterly Review*, as well as in many anthologies. She won the 2003 Lois Cranston Poetry Prize from *Calyx* and first place in *Diner*'s 2004 poetry competition. Her book of poetry and prose poems, *The Blue Dress*, was selected for the Marie Alexander prose poem series and received an Outstanding Achievement award from the Wisconsin Library Association.

SUSAN VARNOT's work has appeared in *Beloit Poetry Journal* and *American Poetry Journal*. A previous contributor to *Nimrod*, she holds an MFA from Arizona State University and teaches at Northern New Mexico College.

DOROTHY WALL has taught poetry and fiction writing in California colleges and is co-author of *Finding Your Writer's Voice: A Guide to Creative Fiction*. Her essays and poems have appeared or will appear in *Witness*, *Sonora Review*, *Prairie Schooner*, *Cimarron Review*, and elsewhere. Her creative nonfiction book *Encounters with the Invisible: Unseen Illness, Controversy, and Chronic Fatigue Syndrome* was published in 2005.

LAURA D. WEEKS's literary translations have appeared in *Russian Literature Triquarterly, The Literary Review*, and elsewhere; her poetry has been published in *The Chaffin Journal* and *Branches Quarterly*, as well as in her chapbook, *The Mad Woman*.

PAULA WELD-CARY's poems have been published or are forthcoming in *Poetry Motel, Blueline*, and *Hawai'i Pacific Review*. She also writes fiction and has just completed her second novel manuscript.

JACKSON WHEELER is the author of two collections, *Swimming Past Iceland* and *A Near Country: Poems of Loss*, with Glenna Luschei and David Oliveira. For 10 years he co-edited *SOLO: A Journal of Poetry*; his work has appeared in *Shenandoah, Poetry International*, and *Carolina Quarterly*.

NANCY WHITE's work has appeared in *Ploughshares, New England Review*, and *Virginia Quarterly Review*, among other journals. Her book *Sun, Moon, Salt* won the 1992 Washington Prize for poetry.

DEBRA WIERENGA's poems and essays on love and work and family are published in print and online. She holds a BA in English Literature from Kalamazoo College and an MFA from the Writing Seminars at Bennington College.

WARREN WOESSNER is the senior editor of *Abraxas*. His recent chapbooks include *Iris Rising* (UM-KC Press) and *Chemistry* (Pudding House Press).

MIKA YAMAMOTO was born in the U.S. and moved to Japan at the age of 15. She now lives in Skokie, Illinois, where she spent much of her childhood. A single mother and a substitute teacher as well as a writer, she has work forthcoming in *Karamu* and *Palo Alto Review*.

About the Artists

Judy Baker, artist and book designer, has exhibited her paintings in Tulsa, Oklahoma City, and Taos, New Mexico. Her sketches appeared previously in *Nimrod* 30, Spring/Summer 1987.

G. Jill Evans is a photographer of the Oklahoma City National Memorial.

Juan Franco, photographer, is a native of Colombia. He has explored and photographed all over the world, especially South America. He sees his work as providing a cross-cultural platform for discussion, interaction, increased understanding, and awareness, as well as offering a permanent record of people and places.

Manly Johnson, poet, collagist, and photographer, is a widely published writer and artist. His books include *Anecdotes of a Time and People*, *All Morning in Her Eyes*, *Present and Accounted For*, and *Every Other One* (with Francine Ringold-Johnson).

Mark Lewis, who teaches painting and drawing at The University of Tulsa, received a BFA in painting from the Kansas City Art Institute and an MFA in painting from Yale University. In 2002, Mark was a visiting artist at the New York Studio School; he had his first and second solo New York exhibitions of paintings in 2002 and 2005 at the Tatistcheff Gallery. He has three solo exhibitions scheduled for 2006, at Living Arts of Tulsa, Georgetown University, and Northwestern Missouri State University.

John Milisenda's photography has appeared in over 125 shows and in publications including *Smithsonian* and the *New York Times*. His work is in the permanent collections of New Orleans Museum of Art, the Museum of Modern Art, and the Bibliothèque Nationale. He is currently working on a photography book of his family.

Chico Seay has been an art photographer in Oklahoma since 1992. His work has been shown in numerous group and one- and two-man shows across the country and internationally. His work is represented in galleries in Dallas and Portland. He lives in Mannford, Oklahoma.

James S. Seebass, physician and photographer, is a public health physician with the Tulsa City-County Health Department and Professor Emeritus and former Chairman of the Department of Internal Medicine at Oklahoma State University Health Science Center.

JAMES ANDREW SMITH attended the Kansas City Art Institute. He worked for ten years as a designer before formally beginning his art career in 2001. His work is exhibited in Tulsa through Joseph Gierek Gallery, and in galleries in Oklahoma City, Fort Worth, and Naples, Florida.

M. TERESA VALERO, Director of The University of Tulsa's School of Art, is the co-founder and creative director of Third-Floor Designs, a student-run design studio. In addition to teaching, she is an award-winning photographer and graphic designer. Her photographs have been exhibited throughout the U.S., as well as in Venezuela, Lebanon, Syria, Spain, and Canada.

MARK WEISS is an ophthalmologist in Tulsa and an award-winning photographer.

J. WHITEFORD is an artist living in Cornwall, England.